Constitutional Peril

Constitutional Peril

The Life and Death Struggle for Our Constitution and Democracy

Bruce Fein

First published in 2008 by PALGRAVE MACMILLAN® in the US—a division of St. Martin's Press LLC, 175 Fifth Avenue, New York, NY 10010.

Where this book is distributed in the UK, Europe and the rest of the world, this is by Palgrave Macmillan, a division of Macmillan Publishers Limited, registered in England, company number 785998, of Houndmills, Basingstoke, Hampshire RG21 6XS.

Palgrave Macmillan is the global academic imprint of the above companies and has companies and representatives throughout the world.

Palgrave® and Macmillan® are registered trademarks in the United States, the United Kingdom, Europe and other countries.

ISBN-13: 978-0-230-60288-5
ISBN-10: 0-230-60288-6

Library of Congress Cataloging-in-Publication Data is available from the Library of Congress.

A catalogue record of the book is available from the British Library.

Design by Scribe

First edition: September 2008

10 9 8 7 6 5 4 3 2 1

Printed in the United States of America.

This book is dedicated to my wife, Mattie,
whose ethereal beauty charmed each page.

I would like to acknowledge the tireless and meticulous efforts of Corrie Sirkin and James Miller in preparing the footnotes.

Contents

PREFACE

Who Cares?.. ix

ONE

Impeachment or Executive Despotism 1

TWO

What Have Bush and Cheney Done? 29

THREE

Looking Backward 53

FOUR

Setting the Stage..87

FIVE

The Foreign Intelligence Surveillance Act.........................99

SIX

Demonstrating President Bush's FISA Crimes.................131

SEVEN

Secret Government 151

EIGHT

State Secrets—Extraordinary Rendition 181

NINE

Military Commissions—
Tyranny for the Sake of Tyranny 189

TEN

Coda 199

Conclusion 203

Notes 205

Index 231

Who Cares?

Most everything in life is trivial—sound and fury signifying nothing. As was said in Ecclesiastes, "Vanity, vanity, all is vanity."[1] Professional sports, video games, movies, bacchanalian revelries, designer clothes, palatial homes, race cars, American Idol, and fabulous wealth contribute nothing to civilization or to an immortal epitaph. Very few subjects are worth writing about except to evoke laughter or to distract ennui with entertainment.

Constitutional Peril addresses one of the few subjects that rise above the jejune: the dignity and thrill derived from self-government to secure unalienable rights to life, liberty, and the pursuit of happiness. In his *Essay on Man*, Alexander Pope errantly insists, "For forms of government let fools contend; whate'er is best administered is best."[2] Pope's insistence anticipated adulation of Mussolini for making the trains punctual despite his fascist rule. Government forms are decisive in elevating life above vassalage or serfdom. Government of the people, for the people, by the people crowns citizens with dignity by entrusting them with the power to be their own governors. Government errors will be their errors. Government triumphs will be their triumphs.

They will be the captains of their fates and masters of their souls both in their personal and public domains. Their lives will be enriched by struggling to fashion enlightened government and by actively participating in decisions that shape their polities. Rule by Platonic guardians might usher in peace, prosperity, and domestic tranquility. But citizens under their sovereignty would be reduced to bovine adolescents. Shakespeare sermonized in *Hamlet*, "What is a man, If the chief good and market of his time be but to sleep and feed? A beast, no more. Surely he that made us with such large discourse, looking before and after, gave us not that capability and godlike reason, To fust in us unused."[3]

The ongoing life and death struggle over the Constitution explored in *Constitutional Peril* is not confined to President George W. Bush's and Vice President Richard B. Cheney's vandalizing of the nation's birth certificate. Even if the U.S. Constitution were destroyed, individual freedoms and protection of political minorities might still endure. Great Britain, which features parliamentary supremacy in lieu of a constitution, celebrates freedom vastly more than does Russia or China, both of which have written basic charters.

Constitutional Peril thus also examines the alarming degeneration of America's political culture, which is sapping the Constitution of its strength: pervasive and staggering ignorance, widespread apathy, a subordination of statesmanship to small-minded partisan advantage, wholesale evasions of responsibility, a preoccupation with creature comforts, a disdain for excellence and exaltation of mediocrity, a craving for simple answers to complex questions, and a fierce resistance to the truth that enlightened politics is more chiaroscuro and matters of degree than prime colors or integers. If the American people neglect to understand and venerate the Constitution's philosophy, the text will not save the day. As St. Paul sermonized, the letter killeth, but the spirit giveth life.[4]

The political effeteness and decadence in the United States is no historical novelty. Centuries ago, Edward Gibbon observed,

"In the end, more than they wanted freedom, they wanted security. They wanted a comfortable life, and they lost it all—security, comfort, and freedom. When . . . the freedom they wished for was freedom from responsibility, then Athens ceased to be free." Eternal vigilance is the minimum price of liberty.

Readers will be intrigued by this book only if they believe that life is devoid of elevated meaning without struggling to secure, maintain, or strengthen the institutions of self-government and repudiating paternalism. Persons who do not share that conviction will naturally be indifferent to whether the Constitution bows to executive despotism so long as their fleshly pleasures remain undiminished, like the Romans who reveled in the bread and circuses of successive emperors. They have sold their political birthright for a mess of pottage.[5]

The probability that the current tides daily eroding the Constitution can be reversed is slim. Human nature inclines more toward kings and despots than toward democrats and checks and balances. Thus, both elders and the Jewish people generally clamored in the Old Testament for a king over Samuel's strong warnings of the exorbitant costs and prospects for oppression or abuses.[6] Not a single trajectory in the prevailing political culture points toward regaining the Constitution in all its moods and tenses: the rule of law, transparency, statesmanship, education, wisdom, Aristotelian balance, or the rebuke of partisanship when the Constitution hangs in the balance.

Alexis de Tocqueville declared in *Democracy in America*, "What I most reproach in democratic government, as it has been organized in the United States is not, as many people in Europe claim, its weakness, but on the contrary, its irresistible force. And what is most repugnant to me in America is not extreme freedom that reigns there; it is the lack of a guarantee against tyranny."[7] But a guarantee is illusory. No government form or constitution is sufficient to the task. The check against tyranny lies in the hearts and souls of the American people. No constitutional limits will arrest government oppression unless the people will retaliate politically and legally for transgressions. What Judge Learned Hand sermonized about liberty applies equally to the entire constitutional order:

> What do we mean when we say that first of all we seek liberty? I often wonder whether we do not rest our hopes too much upon constitutions, upon laws and upon courts. These are false hopes; believe me, these are false hopes. Liberty lies in the hearts and minds of men and women; when it dies there, no constitution, no law, no court can save it; no constitution, no law, no court can even do much to help it. . . . [8]

Caesar Augustus transformed the Roman Republic into a dictatorship because Romans came to prefer comfort to the stern responsibilities and multiple vexations of popular government.[9]

A few pages of history corroborate the vertical plunge in the nation's political culture:

In 1831, William Lloyd Garrison commenced publication of his antislavery newspaper, the *Liberator*, without the votes to end slavery. He suffered ostracism, beatings, ridicule, and worse. But he persisted for more than three decades and in 1865 he was there to celebrate the ratification of the Thirteenth Amendment to end slavery.[10]

In 1848, the women's suffrage movement was launched at Seneca Falls, New York. Its advocates did not then have the votes. Susan B. Anthony was prosecuted for illegal voting in 1872. Elizabeth Cady Stanton died in 1902 with the Women's Suffrage Amendment still unattained. But Seneca Falls was ultimately crowned with success by the ratification of the Nineteenth Amendment in 1920.[11]

In 1868, Republican Senator Edmund G. Ross (KS) bolted from his party to cast the deciding vote to acquit President Andrew Johnson of concocted impeachable offense by the Radical Republican House of Representatives.[12] The vote predictably occasioned his political ruination. But Senator Ross later explained:

In a large sense, the independence of the executive branch of government was on trial.... If ... the President must step down ... a disgraced man and a political outcast ... upon insufficient proofs and partisan considerations, the office of the President would be degraded, cease to be a coordinate branch of government and ever-after be subordinated to the legislative will. It would practically have revolutionized our splendid political fabric into a partisan Congressional autocracy.[13]

In *Profiles in Courage*, then-Senator John F. Kennedy assessed Senator Ross's contribution to the nation's constitutional dispensation:

In a lonely grave, forgotten and unknown, lies "the man who saved a President" and who as a result may well have preserved for ourselves and posterity Constitutional government in the United States—a man who performed in 1868 what one historian has called "the most heroic act in American history, incomparably more difficult than any deed of valor on the field of battle"—but a United States Senator whose name no one recalls: Edmund G. Ross of Kansas.[14]

Now fast forward to November 2006. Democrats have captured control of Congress. President Bush has reduced Congress to an ink blot through unlimited war powers, deceit, secrecy, signing statements, and outright defiance of the law. He even refuses to permit former presidential advisers to appear before Congress to answer questions. House Speaker–designate Nancy Pelosi—confronting the greatest threat to the Constitution's checks and balances since President Andrew Johnson's impeachment trial—flinches. She nixes the idea of an impeachment inquiry by the House Judiciary Committee. Speaker Pelosi bemoans that votes for impeachment are not there. Of course, that observation could also have been made at the outset of the

Senate Watergate Committee's inquiry into President Richard M. Nixon's multiple abuses. She also discerns no benefit to the Democratic Party from an impeachment of President Bush. She thus categorically declared at a news conference on November 7, 2006, "I have said it before and I will say it again—impeachment is off the table."[15]

Her fellow Democrats largely followed like sheep. Her reassurance emboldened President Bush and Vice President Cheney to ever-greater usurpations. And the American people watched like disinterested spectators preoccupied with "more important" matters than rescuing the Constitution—for example, the price of gasoline. The more things have changed since ancient Athens, the more they have stayed the same.

Impeachment or Executive Despotism

The worst crimes were dared by few, willed by more, and toler-ated by all.

—Tacitus, Roman Historian

As the Roman Republic degenerated into dictatorship, the Roman Senate passed a law conferring upon the emperor "the right and power . . . to transact and do whatever things divine, human, public, or private he deems to serve the advantage and overriding interest of the state."

In the days after 9/11, Congress gave President George W. Bush, with public acclaim, similar power by enacting the Authorization for Use of Military Force (AUMF): "[T]he President is authorized to use all necessary and appropriate force against those nations, organizations or persons he determines planned, authorized, committed, or aided the terrorist attacks that occurred on September 11, 2001, or harbored such organizations or persons, in order to prevent any future acts of international terrorism against the United States by such nations, organizations or persons."[1] This means that, among other things, the AUMF empowers President Bush to use the American military to kill any individuals in the United States whom he declares were complicit in the terrorist acts committed on 9/11—on his say-so alone. In other words, the president is not required to supply evidence to a neutral or detached magistrate establishing reasonable cause for his belief that the target of the planned killing is a terrorist before employing lethal force. For example, if the president suspects that a dozen "high value" Al Qaeda adherents are living in a suburban Los Angeles home, the AUMF authorizes him to order an aerial bombardment of the residence to kill its occupants. If the president's suspicions are later proved wrong—as they were regarding the stockpiling of weapons of mass destruction in Iraq before the U.S. invasion in March 2003; the numerous erroneous detentions at Guantanamo Bay, verified by the Defense Department's voluntary release of hundreds of suspected unlawful enemy combatant detainees since September 11, 2001; and a June 23, 2008, federal appeals court decision nullifying an unlawful enemy combatant finding—the homicides would still be considered legal. The laws of war allow the killing of innocent civilians mistakenly believed to be lawful or unlawful enemy combatants.[2] Moreover, if the house bombing kills bystanders or neighbors, their deaths will be dismissed as unfortunate collateral damage. Just ask the relatives of the hundreds of civilians who have been killed by the U.S. military in Iraq and Afghanistan.

On July 17, 2007, President Bush issued a draconian Executive Order entitled "Blocking Property of Certain Persons Who Threaten Stabilization Efforts in Iraq."[3] Without notice or an opportunity to be heard, a person's assets can be frozen if President Bush believes the individual "poses a significant risk of committing an act or act of violence" whose effect might weaken the stability of the government of Iraq. The order enables the president to impose financial death sentences on detractors of the Iraqi government based solely on his uncorroborated gut instincts, as the following example demonstrates: A critic verbally assails the Iraqi prime minister for permitting illegal private militias, sectarian police and military forces, and massive corruption in the oil and gas ministries. The president can decree that his gut tells him that this person poses a significant risk of committing such violent acts as flag burning in order to dramatize his or her concerns and attract media attention and is therefore a threat to the stability of the Iraqi government because the criticisms are incontestably true. Under the executive order, the critic's assets can be frozen, and it will then be illegal for any person to provide goods or services to the critic—for example, food to prevent starvation, medication to prevent a heart attack, or legal services to prevent a wrongful conviction!

The AUMF and executive order highlight why I believe that the nation confronts a choice between the impeachments of President George W. Bush and Vice President Richard Cheney or a degeneration of the U.S. Constitution into executive despotism. James Madison admonished in Federalist No. 48: "An elective despotism was not the government we fought for; but one in which the powers of government should be so divided and balanced among the several bodies of magistracy as that no one could transcend their legal limits without being effectually checked and restrained by the others."[4]

Those who do not support impeachment might counter that President Bush has not yet exerted his military power to bomb residences or to freeze the assets of Iraqi war opponents; these evils remain hypothetical. There will be time enough to respond after the president acts contrary to the law or the Constitution. Impeachment should not be like preemptive war—striking a blow against the executive branch before concrete and demonstrable harm to society has been inflicted by the president and vice president. Detractors also say that the impeachments of Bush and Cheney would be too prolonged, politically convulsive, and detract from attention to more important domestic or foreign policy issues.

Both defenses of impeachment inaction are unconvincing. With regard to the latter argument, impeachment can be a strong force for healing and unifying—the opposite of being convulsive. After President Richard M. Nixon was forced to resign in the face of an imminent and assured conviction for impeachable offenses, his successor, President Gerald R. Ford, in his August 9, 1974, inaugural statement, declared: "My fellow Americans, our long national nightmare is over." If President William Jefferson Clinton had been convicted in the Senate of impeachable offenses, the transition to an Al Gore presidency would not have been politically jarring. In contrast, removing both Bush and Cheney from office for impeachable offenses would leave the White House in the hands of Democratic House Speaker Nancy Pelosi. That change in party control would begin tension with popular government because voters in 2004 supported a Republican in the presidency. Moreover, impeachment proceedings would confront Pelosi with a conflict of interest and place a cloud over her impartiality. She would be the beneficiary of successful impeachment initiatives against Bush and Cheney. That appearance of bias, however, could be resolved by Pelosi promising to yield the speakership to a Republican if Bush and Cheney were ousted. Impeachment proceedings against the duumvirate could also be swift. Evidence of their impeachable offenses is open and notorious: detentions of U.S. citizens indefinitely without accusation or trial; executive orders; imperial assertions of executive privilege; suspension of habeas corpus; presidential signing statements; military commissions; violations of the criminal provisions of the Foreign Intelligence Surveillance Act of 1978 (FISA)[5]; abductions, imprisonments, and torture abroad, and so on.[6] Nothing akin to a protracted archaeological expedition to unearth incriminating facts would be required of the House Judiciary Committee. All that would be needed would be a vote on whether the Bush–Cheney constitutional usurpations and abuses satisfy the impeachment benchmark of "high crimes and misdemeanors." And as to the idea that impeachment detracts from presidential or congressional attention to more urgent issues, experience points to the contrary.

The impeachment ordeals of Presidents Nixon and Clinton did not prevent the enactment of domestic legislation or paralyze national security decisions. Central Intelligence Agency Director George Tenet was definitive in his book *At the Center of the Storm*: "I never saw any evidence that Clinton's personal problems [with Monica Lewinsky] distracted him from focusing on his official duties."[7]

The impeachment of presidents or vice presidents is not commonplace in the United States. Many instinctively shun the idea because it seems novel or irregular. Either of these feelings customarily evokes magnified anxieties or apprehension that reason should quiet. Impeachment of the president or vice president would not be like the assassination of Julius Caesar or the beheading of England's Charles I, presaging political upheaval or a political revolution. It would not be like a criminal prosecution threatening imprisonment. The most it entails for the accused is removal from office and ineligibility to serve in the government of the United States. Article I, Section 3 of the Constitution provides, "Judgment in Cases of Impeachment shall not extend further than to removal from Office, and disqualification to hold and enjoy any Office of honor, Trust or Profit under the United States."[8] Impeachment is not the type of sanction that provokes a president's supporters to armed resistance. There is life after impeachment—even political life.

In 1868, President Andrew Johnson was impeached by the Radical Reconstruction Congress, but was acquitted in the Senate. After his term expired, he served as a U.S. senator representing Tennessee in 1875.

President Nixon was forced to resign on August 9, 1974, after three articles of impeachment were voted by the House Judiciary Committee, and a Supreme Court decision exposed his own words on tape recordings demonstrating his complicity in the Watergate cover-up. But Nixon came to serve the role of elder statesman—even though the vast majority of Americans believed him guilty of felonies, for which President Ford pardoned him.

He was occasionally consulted by later presidents. He wrote books—for example, *RN: The Memoirs of Richard Nixon* and *Beyond Peace*—and spoke to prestigious gatherings. He established the Nixon Center in Washington, DC, a respected think tank headed by Dimitri K. Simes. Nixon was not ostracized. His funeral was attended by all of the living former presidents, dignitaries from 88 countries, and the glitterati. He was eulogized by both former national security adviser Henry Kissinger and then-President William Jefferson Clinton.

President Clinton was impeached by the House and acquitted by the Senate in 1999. His impeachment ordeal, like Nixon's, has proven no impediment to his postpresidential financial success and political clout. He has amassed a substantial fortune through staggering speaking, consulting, and lobbying fees. On February 23, 2007, the *Washington Post* reported that the former president had amassed $40 million in speaking fees over the last six years, including $9–$10 million in 2006 and $475,000 in a single day for two speeches in Canada. Huge sums have been donated for the $165 million Clinton Library in Little Rock, Arkansas. In addition, President Clinton has raised enormous contributions for the Democratic Party, and he was a major campaign figure in his wife Senator Hillary Clinton's failed bid for the Democratic presidential nomination. He eventually became a campaign liability, not because he had been impeached for perjury and obstruction of justice by the House of Representatives, but because of his racist insinuations about Senator Clinton's rival, Illinois Senator Barack Obama.

In sum, history teaches that impeaching a president does not threaten political or social upheaval or even the president's political death. However, that does not mean that impeachments should be undertaken cavalierly. Removing the president or vice president from office disturbs the results of a free and fair election, which ordinarily should be honored. But the Constitution makes exceptions, not only via the power of impeachment, but through the authority of the House and Senate to expel members for misbehavior. Nevertheless, an undemanding impeachment yardstick could intimidate presidents from robust assertions of executive powers and reduce them to congressional vassals. One hundred and forty years ago that was a real danger in the impeachment of President Andrew Johnson. His alleged "high crime and misdemeanor," in the eyes of the Radical Reconstruction Congress, was insisting on his Article II right to appoint or dismiss his cabinet, an authority expressly upheld by the U.S. Supreme Court in *Myers v. United States* (1926).[9] In contrast, the problem that has beset checks and balances for the past 75 years has not been congressional eagerness but reluctance to impeach the president or vice president for crimes against the Constitution. To paraphrase British philosopher Samuel Johnson, a president's knowledge that he will be impeached in a fortnight for usurpations and abuses will concentrate his mind wonderfully on staying within constitutional bounds.[10]

The defense of impeachment inaction because presidential claims of dictatorial powers have no victims is also unpersuasive. Dictatorial claims inflict immediate harm. They hang like the sword of Damocles over any citizen who might contemplate criticizing the Bush administration. They are silenced by the fear of retaliation: They could be detained as unlawful enemy combatants. Their assets could be frozen. Their conversations could be seized and disseminated without judicial warrants. Their homes could be burglarized to gather foreign intelligence. They could be "inadvertent" collateral damage if President Bush should choose to unleash the military in the United States against suspected international terrorists. Bush's assertion of monarch-like powers induces an inert, docile, frightened citizenry—the death knell for democracy.

In any event, some of the Bush–Cheney crimes against the Constitution do feature actual victims—for example, the American citizens who are targeted by the National Security Agency for electronic surveillance in contravention of the FISA, or detained indefinitely without charge or trial as unlawful enemy combatants.

Moreover, the president could fatally cripple the Constitution at any time through the imposition of military law. President Bush might announce that his gut instincts have convinced him that thousands of Al Qaeda members are nesting in our midst, and can be detected and apprehended only if civilian law is suspended and the military can search, arrest, and detain at will.

The Founding Fathers understood the folly of waiting to respond until after tyrannical powers have been exerted. The British parliament passed the Stamp Act of 1765,[11] which imposed a tax on every piece of printed paper: ships' papers, legal documents, newspapers, playing cards, and so on. The Founding Fathers successfully protested this taxation without representation. The same day that Parliament repealed the Stamp Act, it passed the Declaratory Act of 1766,[12] which asserted that Parliament "had, hath, and of right ought to have, full power and authority to make laws and statutes of sufficient force and validity to bind the colonies and people of America, subjects of the crown of Great Britain, in all cases whatsoever."[13] In response, Thomas Jefferson commented, "By one Act they have suspended the powers of one American legislature, & by another they have declared they may legislate for us themselves in all cases whatsoever. These two acts alone form the basis broad enough whereon to erect a despotism of unlimited extent."[14] The Declaratory Act was predictably followed by the Townsend Acts of 1767,[15] by which Parliament reimposed taxes on the colonies. The colonists soon came to recognize the odiousness of the Declaratory Act's theory of parliamentary power. In the 1775 Declaration of the Causes and Necessity for Taking Up Arms,[16] Congress proclaimed, "By one statute it is declared that parliament can 'of right make laws to bind us in all cases whatsoever.' What is to defend us against so enormous, so unlimited a power? . . . They boast of their privileges and civilization, and yet proffer no milder conditions than servitude or death."[17]

President Bush's theory of a unitary executive (which I will explore further at another point) and claims of tyrannical powers are no less dangerous to Americans and no less deserving of rebuke than was the Declaratory Act of 1766. We should learn from our Founding Fathers' example—waiting for the tyrannical axe to drop is foolhardy.

There would be nothing novel about employing impeachment to remove a president from office for making unexercised dictatorial claims. The law is both forward- and backward-looking; it punishes both threatened harms and accomplished harms. The knowledge that dictatorship is an option for the president justifies impeachment because of the clear and present danger to constitutional government.

The law of criminal conspiracy penalizes simple agreements to commit a wrongful act without proof of actual harm. Suppose two businessmen agree to fix the retail price of gasoline at $5.00 per gallon, but they take no steps to implement the agreement. Their conspiracy has no effect on gasoline prices, yet they are guilty of a felony under the Sherman Antitrust Act.[18] The danger to society of a conspiracy is considered sufficiently great to justify legal action against the conspirators before harm is inflicted. The same goes for conspiracies to provide material assistance to a foreign terrorist organization. The United States has prosecuted and convicted persons like José Padilla for conspiring to train in a foreign terrorist camp without proof of harm to a single American.[19]

The Bush–Cheney claims of unlimited and unchecked presidential powers have emerged from a twisted understanding of a unitary executive. Their claims undo centuries of Anglo-American democratic evolution stemming back to the 1215 Magna Carta and its celebration of habeas corpus—that is, the obligation of the executive to demonstrate before an impartial magistrate the factual and legal foundation for executive detentions.

The unitary executive theory of presidential power is indistinguishable from executive despotism. The Founding Fathers debated the wisdom of a unitary, as opposed to a plural, executive during the Constitutional Convention of 1787.[20] A unitary executive was chosen primarily to promote political and legal accountability, and to create incentives to do good and avoid evil. Alexander Hamilton elaborated in Federalist No. 70:

> But one of the weightiest objections to a plurality in the executive, and which lies as much against the last as the first plan is that it tends to conceal faults and destroy responsibility. Responsibility is of two kinds—to censure and to punishment. The first is the most important of the two, especially in an elective office. Men in public trust will much oftener act in such a manner as to render them unworthy of being any longer trusted, than in such a manner as to make [them] obnoxious to legal punishment. But the multiplication of the executive adds to the difficulty of detection in either case. It often becomes impossible, amidst mutual accusations, to determine on whom the blame or the punishment of a pernicious measure, or series of pernicious measures, ought really to fall. It is shifted from one to another with so much dexterity, and under such plausible appearances, that the public opinion is left in suspense about the real author. The circumstances which may have led to any national miscarriage or misfortune are sometimes so complicated that where there are a number of actors who may have had different degrees and kinds of agency, though we may clearly see upon the whole that there has been mismanagement, yet it may be impracticable to pronounce to whose account the evil which may have been incurred is truly chargeable.
>
> "I was overruled by my council. The council were so divided in their opinions that it was impossible to obtain any better resolution on the point." These and similar pretexts are constantly at hand, whether true or false. And who is there that will either take the trouble or incur the odium of a strict scrutiny into the secret springs of the transaction? Should there be found a citizen zealous enough to undertake the unpromising task, if there happened to be a collusion between the parties

concerned, how easy is it to cloth[e] the circumstances with so much ambiguity as to render it uncertain what was the precise conduct of any of those parties?

In the single instance in which the governor of this state is coupled with a council—that is, in the appointment to offices, we have seen the mischiefs of it in the view now under consideration. Scandalous appointments to important offices have been made. Some cases indeed have been so flagrant that ALL PARTIES have agreed in the impropriety of the thing. When inquiry has been made, the blame has been laid by the governor on the members of the council; who on their part have charged it upon his nomination; while the people remain altogether at a loss to determine by whose influence their interests have been committed to hands so unqualified and so manifestly improper. In tenderness to individuals, I forbear to descend to particulars.

It is evident from these considerations that the plurality of the executive tends to deprive the people of the two greatest securities they can have for the faithful exercise of any delegated power[:] *first*, the restraints of public opinion, which lose their efficacy as well on account of the division of the censure attendant on bad measures among a number as on account of the uncertainty on whom it ought to fall; and, *second*, the opportunity of discovering with facility and clearness the misconduct of the persons they trust, in order either to their removal from office or to their actual punishment in cases which admit of it.[21]

If the president is to be held accountable for the conduct of his administration, then he must enjoy the power to discharge any officer of the United States who exercises significant executive power. Otherwise, the executive branch could be at war with itself and executive action could be paralyzed. Thus, in the First Congress, then-Congressman James Madison insisted that the president must enjoy the power to discharge the secretary of state for any cause whatsoever to enable the nation to speak with one voice abroad. Think of the embarrassments to the foreign policy of the United States if the president and secretary held opposite views and policies about Iran, Iraq, Russia, or nuclear proliferation.

The unitary executive as conceived by the Founding Fathers has been twisted by the Bush–Cheney presidency to mean that if a power can be classified as "executive," then neither the legislative nor judicial branch may regulate, oversee, or check the president's actions. The power to wage war is an executive power. According to Bush's unitary executive theory, Congress is impotent to limit or regulate his commander-in-chief discretion over what war strategy or tactics to adopt. That imperial view contradicts Hamilton's observation in Federalist No. 69 that the commander-in-chief power is vastly inferior to that of a British king:

> The President is to be the "commander-in-chief" of the army and navy of the United States, and of the militia of the several States, when called into the actual service of the United States. . . . In most of these particulars, the power of the President will resemble equally that of the king of Great Britain and of the governor of New York. The most material points of difference are these: —*First*. The President will have only the occasional command of such part of the militia of the nation as by legislative provision may be called into the actual service of the Union. The king of Great Britain and the governor of New York have at all times the entire command of all the militia within their several jurisdictions. In this article, therefore, the power of the President would be inferior to that of either the monarch or the governor. *Second*. The President is to be commander-in-chief of the army and navy of the United States. In this respect[,] his authority would be nominally the same with that of the king of Great Britain, but in substance much inferior to it. It would amount to nothing more than the supreme command and direction of the military and naval

forces, as first General and admiral of the Confederacy; while that of the British king extends to the *declaring* of war and to the *raising* and *regulating* of fleets and armies—all which, by the Constitution under consideration, would appertain to the legislature.[22]

Moreover, Hamilton added in Federalist No. 75 that the president was too vulnerable to treason, bribery, or other corruption to trust to make treaties unilaterally:

However proper or safe it may be in governments where the executive magistrate is an hereditary monarch, to commit to him the entire power of making treaties, it would be utterly unsafe and improper to [e]ntrust that power to an elective magistrate of four years' duration. It has been remarked, upon another occasion, and the remark is unquestionably just, that an hereditary monarch, though often the oppressor of his people, has personally too much stake in the government to be in any material danger of being corrupted by foreign powers. But a man raised from the station of a private citizen to the rank of chief magistrate, possessed of a moderate or slender fortune, and looking forward to a period not very remote when he may probably be returned to the station from which he was taken, might sometimes be under temptations to sacrifice his duty to his interest, which it would require superlative virtue to withstand. An avaricious man might be tempted to betray the interests of the state to the acquisition of wealth. An ambitious man might make his own aggrandizement, by the aid of a foreign power, the price of his treachery to his constituents. The history of human conduct does not warrant that exalted opinion of human virtue which would make it wise in a nation to commit interests of so delicate and momentous a kind, as those which concern its intercourse with the rest of the world, to the sole disposal of a magistrate created and circumstanced as would be a President of the United States.[23]

In sum, the Founding Fathers never intended to crown the president with unchecked imperial powers on the naïve assumption that the White House would be uniformly occupied by the likes of George Washington. They viewed President Washington as a fluke prodigy who would appear less frequently than Halley's Comet. Accordingly, they made proper deductions for the ordinary depravity of human nature by subjecting the president to legislative and judicial constraints in the exercise of executive powers or otherwise.

Bush's unitary executive theory also stumbles on the false assumption that identifying powers as "executive," "legislative," or "judicial" is an exact science, like the Linnaean system of classifying plants and animals. James Madison explained in Federalist No. 37, "Experience has instructed us that no skill in the science of government has yet been able to discriminate and define, with sufficient certainty, its three great provinces[:] the legislative, executive, and judiciary. Questions daily occur in the course of practice, which proves the obscurity which reigns in these subjects, and which puzzles the greatest adepts in political science."[24] Madison wrote a similar message to Thomas Jefferson: "Even the boundaries between the Executive, Legislative & Judiciary Powers, though in general so strongly marked in themselves, consist in many instances of mere shades of difference."[25]

Hamilton amplified the difficulty of classifying the treaty power in Federalist No. 75:

> I venture to add, that the particular nature of the power of making treaties indicates a peculiar propriety in that union [of legislative and executive branches]. Though several writers on the subject of government place that power in the class of executive authorities, yet this is evidently an arbitrary disposition; for if we attend carefully to its operation, it will be found to partake more of the legislative than of the executive character, though it does not seem strictly to fall within

the definition of either of them. The essence of the legislative authority is to enact laws, or, in other words, to prescribe rules for the regulation of the society; while the execution of the laws, and the employment of the common strength, either for this purpose or for the common defense, seem to comprise all the functions of the executive magistrate. The power of making treaties is, plainly, neither the one nor the other. It relates neither to the execution of the subsisting laws, nor to the enaction of new ones; and still less to an exertion of the common strength. Its objects are CONTRACTS with foreign nations, which have the force of law, but derive it from the obligations of good faith. They are not rules prescribed by the sovereign to the subject, but agreements between sovereign and sovereign. The power in question seems therefore to form a distinct department, and to belong, properly, neither to the legislative nor to the executive. The qualities elsewhere detailed as indispensable in the management of foreign negotiations, point out the Executive as the most fit agent in those transactions; while the vast importance of the trust, and the operation of treaties as laws, plead strongly for the participation of the whole or a portion of the legislative body in the office of making them.[26]

The dispersal of legislative, executive, and judicial power is one of the Constitution's hallmarks. The president participates in legislation by either signing or vetoing bills passed by Congress. As a practical matter, moreover, the president issues more legislative decrees in the form of administrative regulations than does Congress under the delegation doctrine ratified by the U.S. Supreme Court. The doctrine authorizes Congress to delegate legislative power to the executive branch if it provides a reasonable standard to guide its exercise. The reasonableness limit on delegations is toothless because the Supreme Court has sustained such amorphous congressional standards as "the public interest," which can mean many different things to different people. Administrative agencies in the executive branch—for example, the Environmental Protection Agency, the Social Security Administration, or the Department of Homeland Security— issue thousands of regulations annually, a vastly greater number than the new laws enacted by Congress.

The legislative power exercised by the president through the delegation doctrine is additionally augmented by the Supreme Court's so-called Chevron rule, named after *Chevron USA Inc. v. NRDC* (1984).[27] It instructs the judiciary to sustain an agency's reasonable interpretation of an ambiguous congressional statute. And congressional opaqueness is the rule, not the exception. The president also exercises legislative power through executive orders. Presidents John F. Kennedy and Lyndon B. Johnson fashioned a virtual civil rights act for government contractors through executive orders requiring affirmative action hiring before Congress enacted the landmark Civil Rights Act of 1964.[28] The U.S. Court of Appeals for the Third Circuit upheld the executive orders in *Contractors Association of Eastern Pennsylvania v. Secretary of Labor* (1969).[29] Even today, executive orders govern the employment practices of government contractors as supplements to federal nondiscrimination statutes passed by Congress.

The U.S. Supreme Court exercises legislative power in issuing rules governing federal court procedures under delegated authority provided by Congress. These rules carry enormous practical implications for the enforcement of substantive rights, yet the Court had no difficulty in sustaining their constitutionality in *Sibbach v. Wilson & Co.* (1941).[30]

Executive power under the Constitution is as fragmented as is legislative power. The power to make treaties is shared with the Senate. Under Article II, Section 2, Clause 2 of the Constitution, the power to appoint officers of the United States is divided between the president and the Senate by the requirement of confirmation. Further, Congress may entrust the appointment of inferior officers to "the President alone, in the Courts of Law, or in the Heads of Departments." In *Morrison v. Olson* (1988),[31] the Supreme Court upheld the power of Congress to entrust to the federal judiciary power to appoint independent counsels to investigate and prosecute the president and his executive branch subordinates for suspected crimes. The president is authorized to issue pardons for offenses against the United States, but Congress can also legislate amnesties for groups, as has routinely been done after great wars.

The president is entrusted with the power to ensure that the laws be faithfully executed. But Congress may constitutionally entrust the enforcement of federal laws to independent agencies or to persons appointed by the federal courts outside the control of the president. That is the lesson of the Supreme Court's decisions in *Morrison v. Olson* (1988) and *Humphrey's Executor v. United States* (1935).[32] Congress has entrusted independent agencies like the Federal Communications Commission (FCC), the Securities and Exchange Commission (SEC), the Federal Trade Commission (FTC), the Consumer Product Safety Commission, and the Federal Reserve Board with sweeping powers to enforce economic regulatory statutes. The House of Representatives also acts as an executive branch prosecutor in the trial of impeachments before the Senate.

The federal judicial power is also splintered among the three branches. The Senate exercises adjudicative power in impeachment cases prosecuted by the House. Both the House and the Senate exercise judicial power in adjudicating election disputes involving its own members. Article I, Section 5, Clause 1 provides, "Each House shall be the Judge of the Elections, Returns, and Qualifications of its own Members."[33] Congress has also delegated to administrative agencies adjudicative powers to resolve disputes between individuals or private business and the government. The FTC adjudicates whether certain practices or mergers violate the antitrust laws. The SEC decides whether certain practices violate the federal securities laws. The FCC rules on whether certain words are "indecent" and thus cannot be broadcast at times when children are likely listeners or viewers.

Section 554 of the Administrative Procedures Act elaborates extensive procedures to be followed in agency adjudications to be made on the record after a hearing.[34]

This brief constitutional survey discredits the core assumption behind the Bush–Cheney unitary executive theory—namely, that the Founding Fathers were enamored of the idea that the exercise of legislative, executive, and judicial power (putting aside the difficulties of classification)—should each be monopolized by a single branch. To the contrary, the Constitution's makers were not infatuated with intellectual tidiness. Their North Star was the prevention of tyranny. They championed a constitutional architecture that was designed to achieve that end. A building block assumption was that unchecked power would invariably be abused, and thus all powers required some degree of sharing, checking, or vetting.

The Bush–Cheney unitary executive theory carries alarming implications. President Bush argues that he may flout any law or treaty that he believes impairs his power to achieve victory over terrorism—for example, laws prohibiting torture, breaking and entering homes, kidnapping, detentions without accusation or trial, or the use of military force in the United States to kill American citizens suspected of affiliation with Al Qaeda.

Suppose Congress prohibited the expenditure of monies to carry the war against international terrorism into Iran. The Bush–Cheney theory claims that the limitation could be ignored if the president believed an invasion of Iran could assist in international terrorism's defeat. Suppose Congress passed a law reducing the number of active-duty soldiers by one hundred thousand, pursuant to its express constitutional power to "raise and support armies."[35] The Bush–Cheney theory teaches that the limitation could be disregarded, that President Bush could recruit and field whatever size military he believed was appropriate to safeguard the national security. The power to gather foreign intelligence is an executive power. According to Bush's unitary theory of the executive, neither Congress nor the Supreme

Court can place limits on the methods he employs to collect foreign intelligence, including torture; the targets he chooses; or the creation or maintenance of massive foreign intelligence files on U.S. citizens based on constitutionally protected freedom of speech or association.

Bush's unitary executive theory is indistinguishable from the idea that the president is the law whenever he declares a national security objective, no matter how concocted it may be—for example, President Nixon's phony claim that investigating Watergate would expose Central Intelligence Agency assets in Mexico.[36] It represents a philosophical attack on the Constitution that is every bit as dangerous as Soviet communism was during the height of the cold war. Would you have trusted Soviet leader Nikita Khruschev to have respected the U.S. Constitution's checks and balances if he had been president of the United States? Contrary to President Bush, the Constitution intended some blending of judicial, executive, and legislative power in each branch to frustrate tyranny.

Suppose President Bush aped Napoleon's self-coronation and pronounced himself emperor of the United States. Suppose Bush promised that he would resist exercising the powers of an emperor but for "rare" occasions when the national security was threatened by international terrorists. Would not Bush's self-coronation, even with its explanatory gloss, justify his impeachment, conviction, and removal from office? Should the nation have to wait until a constitutional vivisection had been completed? And truthfully, how is President Bush's unitary executive theory different from self-coronation?

My conviction that President Bush and Vice President Cheney have committed impeachable high crimes and misdemeanors is not motivated by any partisan opposition or a disdain for conservative philosophy. I voted for President Bush and Vice President Cheney twice. (Although I would not have voted for the duumvirate in 2004 if I had known then of the magnitude of their constitutional wrongdoings that would later be revealed.)

I applauded President Bush's appointments of Chief Justice John Roberts and Associate Justice Samuel Alito. (I did, however, denounce his nomination of Harriet Miers as insulting to the Supreme Court and the Constitution.) I urged President Bush to create the Supreme Court in the image of defeated nominee Judge Robert H. Bork. I testified before the U.S. Senate in favor of Chief Justice William H. Rehnquist and Associate Justice Antonin Scalia. I deplored Senate filibusters of President Bush's judicial nominees. I championed the impeachment of President William Jefferson Clinton and, with greater enthusiasm, the impeachment of President Richard M. Nixon. I served as associate deputy attorney general and general counsel of the Federal Communications Commission under President Ronald Reagan. I served as Research Director to then-Congressman Dick Cheney on the Joint Congressional Committee on Covert Arms Sales to Iran. I served as Visiting Fellow for Constitutional Studies at The Heritage Foundation. If there are any domestic or foreign policy planks of the Democratic Party that I embrace, they do not readily come to mind.

I believe the Supreme Court's abortion decree in *Roe v. Wade* (1973)[37] and invention of a right to homosexual sodomy in *Lawrence v. Texas* (2003)[38] created wretched constitutional law. I do not believe the Constitution confers a right to same-sex marriage. I oppose racial or gender preferences as offensive to the equal protection clause of the Fourteenth Amendment (second cousins of odious white, male supremacy). However, I celebrated the color-blind civil rights movement of the 1950s and 1960s, which culminated in the 1964 Civil Rights Act and the 1965 Voting Rights Act.[39] My high school valedictorian speech featured courageous Michigan housewife Viola Liuzzo, who had traveled to Alabama to register blacks to vote and was murdered by the Ku Klux Klan on March 25, 1965, while driving from Selma to Montgomery.[40]

I subscribe to Adam Smith's economic philosophy as expounded in *Wealth of Nations*, which frowns on government regulation or taxation to manipulate or distort free market choices.[41] I think minimum wage laws, government dictated pensions, price controls, or comparable worth statutes are either fatuous or injurious.

In sum, I am not a liberal craving an opportunity to attack a Republican president or the Republican Party. Indeed, all of my convictions and precepts are pure conservatism as understood by the Founding Fathers. They derive from a deep suspicion of human nature and a recognition that most of the people most of the time are motivated by a passion for money, fame, power, lust, leisure, or entertainment. My eternal verities include the following:

- unchecked power invariably degenerates into despotism;
- ambition must counteract ambition to preserve liberty;
- sunshine is the best deterrent and disinfectant;
- the wise man knows what he does not know;
- there must be Aristotelian balance and moderation in all things;
- the rule of law should be the nation's political religion;
- an educated citizenry is the cornerstone of liberty;
- no branch of government is infallible; each branch profits from scrutiny and questioning by coequal branches;
- tyranny by the majority is still tyranny;
- you should distrust any politician who says, "trust me";
- the history of liberty is a history of procedural safeguards against error or oppression;
- process is always more important than results;
- truth is more chiaroscuro than prime colors;
- there are sensible exceptions to every rule;
- no good deed goes unpunished;
- if you do not participate in governing yourself—with all its vexations and stumbles—you are no better than a vassal or serf;
- human nature is a jumble of contradictions.

A genuine conservative believes that differences over preferred policies should never stand in the way of upholding and defending the Constitution. Its diffusion and limitations of power as well as checks and balances against foolish wars or laws, or government oppression, are vastly more important than particular outcomes. The latter are provisional and can be changed by sober second thoughts, experience, and advocacy, as long as the Constitution's mechanisms for correcting mistakes remain undisturbed. An erroneous interpretation of the Constitution by the Supreme Court can be corrected by a constitutional amendment or by a subsequent decision overruling the precedent. The Fourteenth Amendment, for example, corrected the Supreme Court's error in *Dred Scott v. Sanford* (1857),[42] which held that blacks were ineligible for U.S. citizenship. However, the Supreme Court corrected *itself* by overruling its *Lochner v. New York* (1905)[43] line of cases, which disparaged economic regulation, in *National Labor Relations Board v. Jones & Laughlin Steel Co.* (1937).[44]

A Supreme Court nonconstitutional stumble can be corrected by congressional legislation. A flawed law passed by Congress can be either vetoed by the president or repealed by a subsequent Congress. A wayward executive order by the president can be superseded by a statute enacted by Congress or modified by a new executive order. President Richard M. Nixon's wage and price controls imposed in August 1971 were largely revoked in April 1974 after experience and further debate exposed its staggering flaws.[45] But crippling the Constitution's checks and balances for making decisions and investigating government wrongdoing threatens permanent overreaching and aggravating or compounding errors.

The rule of law consists of two fundamental elements: (1) a collective agreement to accept a particular result voluntarily if it results from procedures ordained by the Constitution; and (2) an equilibrium of power between the president, Congress, and the Supreme Court that consistently keeps outcomes away from extremes characterized by their disregard for minorities or the unorthodox. A statute that would make adherence to Islam a crime if passed unanimously by Congress, signed by the president, and unanimously sustained by the U.S. Supreme Court, would nevertheless be tyranny, not law, because it would fail a minimum moral yardstick inherent in the rule of law. Every citizen would be required to disobey the statute or oppose its enforcement. The post–World War II Nuremberg proceedings are informative on what threshold of morality must be satisfied to crown a government decree with the dignity of law. Consider the following exchange between court psychologist G. M. Gilbert and William Frick, a lawyer and Third Reich minister of the interior, that transpired in Frick's cell:

> Frick: Well, what do you expect a man to do when he has orders to carry out?
>
> Gilbert: If it is a question of one man's will against the lives of millions of people, I would say that one is morally obligated to kill the dictator rather than carry out such orders, if that is the only way out.
>
> Frick: A moral obligation to murder? That is a very peculiar obligation. That is a crime against social convention, you know.
>
> Gilbert: I see. Killing a murderous dictator is a crime against social convention, but war and extermination were quite legal in Nazi Germany.
>
> Frick: Oh, that is another matter.[46]

In a separate interview, Gilbert inquired of Deputy Fuhrer Herman Goering:

> Gilbert: What about killing the man who ordered the mass murder?
>
> Goering: Oh, that is easily said, but you cannot do that sort of thing. What kind of a system would that be if anybody could kill the commanding officer if he didn't like

his orders? You have got to have obedience in a military system.[47]

The rule of law nurtured by checks and balances insures that the government becomes neither too strong for the liberties of the people nor too weak to maintain its republican existence.

The Constitution should command universal reverence transcending partisan differences because of the common interest in enlightened government and the prevention of oppression or persecution. But even more important, the Constitution should unify all Americans because it secures to each citizen the inestimable right to participate in self-government. With the abolition of slavery in the Thirteenth Amendment, the Constitution acknowledges neither lords nor vassals. In its eyes, every man and woman is a king or queen, but none wears a crown—to borrow from Louisiana's former governor and senator, Huey Long.[48] The process of self-government elevates all citizens by saddling them with political responsibility and struggles over vexing or agonizing political questions: war and peace, civil rights, freedom of speech and religion, taxation and spending, and so on. Without self-government, citizens are reduced to little more than sheep, subject to the orders, whims, and caprices of a paternalistic government. The legitimacy of government only by the informed consent of the governed—at war with Plato's Republic—is America's signature contribution to civilization.

Its quest was what provoked the American Revolution. The Founding Fathers did not fight for leisure. They did not fight for creature comforts. They fought for the dignity that comes from charting your own political destiny—mistakes, miscalculations, and all. They elaborated in the Declaration of Independence that the just powers of government are derived from the consent of the governed—a natural offspring of "No Taxation without Representation."[49]

The nation's wholesale abandonment of the Constitution and conservative philosophy in favor of executive despotism and citizen vassalage is what provoked me to write this book. The abandonment started years before 9/11 but was accelerated by the abomination of that day. President Bush, Vice President Cheney, Congress, and the American people all share the blame. Congress and the American people, however, bear ultimate responsibility. The Founding Fathers expected each branch of government to seek to gain the powers of the other branches. They knew that people are typically attracted to politics because they covet power for its own sake and revel in publicity. They armed each branch and the American people (through the right to vote) with the means to defeat encroachments. The Founding Fathers anticipated President Bush's monumental constitutional usurpations and abuses born of staggering ignorance, arrogance, pettiness, and ambition for a monarch-like White House. They did not anticipate that Congress would turn invertebrate and play spectator while the president lacerated and thieved powers entrusted to the legislative branch. Congress could have prevented or stopped every constitutional violation by the Bush–Cheney duumvirate over the past seven years by brandishing the power of the purse or impeachment.

In Federalist No. 58 James Madison elaborated, "This power over the purse may, in fact, be regarded as the most complete and effectual weapon with which any constitution can arm the immediate representatives of the people, for obtaining a redress of every grievance, and for carrying into effect every just and salutary measure."[50] Congress could have enforced compliance with judicial checks on gathering foreign intelligence by targeting Americans under FISA, for example, by passing a law declaring, "No monies of the United States shall be expended to gather foreign intelligence in contravention of FISA." To overcome President Bush's authorization to torture detainees, Congress could have passed a law declaring, "No monies of the United States shall be expended to torture any detainee in the custody or control of the United States." President Bush might have vetoed the bills, but two-thirds majorities could probably have been marshaled in Congress for overrides. The vetoes would have been a confession by President Bush that he wished to retain an option to flout the law. Even if the vetoes were sustained, they would have enabled the American people to know the president's contempt for the law and to adjust their political attachments or energies accordingly.

Congress, however, has done virtually nothing to restrain the Bush–Cheney administration. Indeed, Congress has augmented the Bush–Cheney embrace of despotic powers through the Military Commissions Act of 2006,[51] the Protect America Act of 2007,[52] the Foreign Intelligence Surveillance Act Amendment of 2008, and the John Warner National Defense Authorization Act of 2006.[53] The latter act, supported by liberals and conservatives alike, passed 100–0 in the Senate.[54] It empowers the president to impose martial law in response to any "natural disaster, epidemic, or other serious public health emergency, terrorist attack or incident, or other condition."[55] The term "other condition" is not defined and can mean anything the president wants it to mean—for example, a condition of unrest provoked by opposition to the wars in Iraq or Afghanistan.

But the American people are more culpable than Congress over the nation's constitutional peril because they have declined to exercise their right to vote or their First Amendment right to petition Congress for a redress of grievances to demand corrective legislation or impeachment to end the Bush–Cheney transgressions. Congress is like a human weather vane. Its action or inaction reflects popular sentiments. The vast majority of Americans care more about the price of gasoline, food, designer clothes, or video games than they do about the constitutional waywardness of the president that threatens the freedoms of every citizen and self-government not only for the living but for those yet to be born. They devote little time to understanding or scrutinizing what their public officials are doing. They are not clamoring for a restoration of constitutional regularity, even if they *were* able to recognize it if it reappeared.

No man is an island in a democracy. Every citizen's political indifference, inertness, or irresponsibility weakens the democratic framework for all. Freedom depends on collective public review and informed evaluations of government officials. It depends on citizens who will support candidates who promise the rule of law rather than bread and circuses. It depends on voters who will demand the impeachment of the president, vice president, or other officers of the United States for high crimes and misdemeanors. If a majority subordinate freedom to personal comfort, the Constitution will collapse on everyone. The minority who struggled to sustain a constitutional order will not be saved. Everyone in a democracy is thus burdened with a moral duty to act as a sentinel for the liberty of everyone else. At present, the majority of citizens are neglecting their duty.

What Have Bush and Cheney Done?

President George W. Bush has inflated the danger of international terrorism to the equivalent of World War II or the Civil War in order to justify repeated and gratuitous invasions of individual liberties and obstructions of Congress's power to expose what the executive branch is doing. He has declared that the United States is permanently at war with global terrorists—in other words, that the war will not end until the Milky Way is purged of anyone who would wish America harm. On Septmber 20, 2001, in an address to the nation before a joint session of Congress, President Bush declared, "Our war on terror begins with Al-Qaeda, but it does not end there. It will not end until every terrorist group of global reach has been found, stopped, and defeated."[1] He has established military commissions whose proceedings combine judge, jury, and prosecutor, and use secret evidence and coerced confessions—the very definition of tyranny in the eyes of the Founding Fathers. He has suspended the Great Writ of habeas corpus, which safeguards against wrongful executive detentions, of which there have been many. Based on secret evidence and without providing access to lawyers, he has detained alleged unlawful enemy combatants, including American citizens, indefinitely at Guantanamo Bay and elsewhere—a practice that the U.S. Supreme Court held unconstitutional in *Boumediene v. Bush* (June 8, 2008).[2] He has spied on Americans on his say-so alone, which is in criminal contravention of the Foreign Intelligence Surveillance Act of 1978's (FISA) requirement of a judicial warrant. Despite congressional amendments for perceived FISA deficiencies in the aftermath of 9/11, the president nevertheless flouted the law and hid his lawlessness. Indeed, these words about massive FISA violations could not have been written if there had not been an executive branch leak to the *New York Times* that was published on December 15, 2005.[3] President Bush's hope was to evade legal and political accountability for his lawbreaking indefinitely.

He has issued executive orders that would impose financial death sentences, without notice to the accused, without an opportunity to discredit the accusation. He has thwarted congressional oversight by extravagant claims of executive privilege or state secrets. He has deceived Congress and the American people about weapons of mass destruction in Iraq and by issuing executive orders purporting to represent presidential policies but then classifying and hiding secret decisions to waive or revoke the orders. He directed, encouraged, or permitted former Attorney General Alberto Gonzales to bring the Department of Justice into disrepute with endless lies, defenses of secret government, and a skewing of prosecutorial discretion to advance a Republican Party political agenda.

Gonzales's successor, Attorney General Michael B. Mukasey, has echoed President Bush's theory of the White House *über alles*. He has voiced agnosticism on whether waterboarding, or simulated drowning, as practiced by the Central Intelligence Agency (CIA) is torture. The interrogation practice, however, has been prosecuted as a war crime by the United States since at least the Spanish-American War; and former Secretary of Homeland Security Tom Ridge, among other notables, has condemned waterboarding as torture. Director of the Federal Bureau of Investigation (FBI) Robert S. Mueller stated in a National Press Club appearance on May 16, 2008, that it was the FBI's policy "not to use coercion" in interrogations—period, with no exception for terrorism investigations.[4]

Attorney General Mukasey has questioned congressional power to regulate the state secrets privilege, which denies legal remedies for victims of constitutional wrongdoing—for example, kidnapping or torture. He has maintained that legal advice provided by the Department of Justice to CIA interrogators, no matter how patently flawed it may be, immunizes them from prosecution for torture. He has defended the power of the president to claim executive privilege for purely vice presidential communications and to refuse to permit former or current White House advisers from even appearing before Congress to testify about suspected crimes or maladministration.

President Bush has kidnapped, imprisoned, and tortured suspected terrorists abroad. He has created a climate of lawlessness in the executive branch, which emboldened CIA officials to destroy interrogation videotapes sought by the 9/11 Commission or Congress that probably provided ocular evidence of torture. He has signed bills passed by Congress while announcing his intent to disregard provisions that he maintains are unconstitutional—for example, a provision denying funds to establish permanent military bases in Iraq. He has asserted the power to break and enter homes, open mail, kidnap, and torture to gather foreign intelligence without review by any other branch. He has tacitly declared that every square inch of the United States is a battlefield appropriate for military force and military law because Al Qaeda hopes to kill Americans anywhere, and terrorists can blend into civilian populations.

He has made Americans less safe by making foreign friends reluctant to cooperate in counterterrorism gambits because they cannot receive assurances that the targets will not be tortured or abused, and by acting on the principle that any government may kill, kidnap, imprison, or abuse foreign nationals whom it claims are supporting or are sympathetic to alleged domestic or foreign terrorist organizations. Under that principle, Russian Prime Minister Vladimir Putin would be justified in kidnapping or assassinating American civilians thought to be sympathetic to Chechen rebels. A parliamentary committee in Great Britain reported that British intelligence refused to collaborate with the CIA in a covert action in 2005 because assurances against torture or maltreatment of detainees were not forthcoming. In 2008, Italy moved forward with a prosecution in absentia of 26 CIA operatives and top Italian intelligence officers complicit in the abduction of an Egyptian, Abu Omar, who was transported from Italy to Egypt and allegedly tortured. Expert FBI interrogators have refused to participate in the CIA's questioning of suspected terrorist detainees for fear of complicity in war crimes.

These indictments of the president are more troublesome than the bill of particulars that Thomas Jefferson penned against King George III in the Declaration of Independence, which justified the Revolutionary War. The king was assailed, among other things, for "depriving us, in many Cases, of the Benefits of Trial by Jury"; making "Judges dependent on his Will alone, for the Tenure of their Offices, and the Amount and Payment of their Salaries"; and, affecting "to render the Military independent of and superior to the Civil Power."[5] By the exacting standards of the Founding Fathers, President Bush's multiple crimes against the Constitution amount to impeachable misconduct under Article II, Section 4.

Alexander Hamilton characterized impeachable behavior in Federalist No. 65 as "offenses which proceed from the misconduct of public men, or in other words, from the violation or abuse of some public trust. They are of a nature which with peculiar propriety may be denominated political, as they relate chiefly to injuries done immediately to society itself."[6] And nothing is more injurious to society than to treat citizens as vassals or serfs, denying them knowledge of what their government is doing and why and not allowing any opportunity to hold government actions accountable to the law and popular will. A comparable impeachment case can be made against Vice President Richard B. Cheney, who has been the de facto president due to President Bush's acquiescence in setting national security policy—including military commissions, detentions of enemy combatants without trials or access to courts or lawyers, torture, warrantless surveillance of American citizens in violation of FISA, and a secret government that frustrates political accountability.

A rough and ready clue as to whether presidential claims or wrongdoing should be impeachable is whether parallels may be found in Aleksandr Solzhenitsyn's *One Day in the Life of Ivan Denisovich* or Arthur Koestler's *Darkness at Noon*.[7]

Impeachment, of course, is not a constitutional mandate but a matter of political discretion that is left to the House of Representatives, just as the executive branch enjoys prosecutorial discretion in determining which crimes to prosecute.[8] But there are no prudential reasons to desist from an inquiry by the House Judiciary Committee into whether the president and vice president have committed high crimes and misdemeanors. Neither enjoys any popular mandate to remain in office. President Bush's approval rating has plunged to an unprecedented 28 percent low.[9] The vice president's corresponding 18 percent approval rating ranks far below the 45 percent commanded by then–Vice President Spiro Agnew a month before his resignation in 1973 for tax evasion.[10]

Impeachment proceedings do not disable the president from defending the national security. President Nixon gave full attention to the Yom Kippur War of 1973 while Congress was investigating his complicity in the Watergate cover-up and other abuses. Neither was the nation's domestic agenda frozen during the Senate Watergate hearings followed by the House Judiciary Committee's impeachment proceedings in 1974. The Endangered Species Act of 1973 and the Budget Control and Impoundment Act of 1974, for example, were passed during Nixon's impeachment ordeal.

Similarly, President William Jefferson Clinton was impeached by the House and tried by the Senate on two counts of high crimes and misdemeanors in 1998–99 without compromising national security or a domestic agenda. He retained sufficient focus to fire rockets into Sudan and Afghanistan to retaliate for their complicity in terrorist incidents against the United States.[11] The United States Supreme Court in *Clinton v. Jones* (1997)[12] discredited the fatuous idea that a president's national security responsibilities cannot be performed if he must also defend alleged misconduct in either a judicial or legislative forum. Former CIA Director George Tenet wrote in *At the Center of the Storm*: "I never saw any evidence that Clinton's personal problems distracted him from focusing on his official duties."

A special feature of the Bush–Cheney administration makes urgent the need for a House Judiciary Committee impeachment inquiry: the repeated frustration of congressional oversight and exposure of what the executive branch is doing and why by extravagant and unprecedented claims of executive privilege or state secrets. That knowledge by citizens is indispensable to fashioning their political loyalties and judgments and to crafting remedial legislation or administrative reforms. The origins of FISA, President Gerald R. Ford's executive order against assassinations, and Department of Justice Guidelines for the FBI's investigation of domestic threats are illustrative of the importance of transparency to a Republican form of government.[13]

For many years, a succession of presidents have kept Congress and the American people in the dark about massive FBI or CIA illegal mail openings, interceptions of international telegrams, burglaries, and spying on Vietnam War protestors or others for exercising First Amendment rights. The same is true for various attempts made by the CIA—with or without presidential knowledge—to assassinate foreign leaders like Fidel Castro or Patrice Lumumba.[14] After these nefarious practices became public knowledge—either through leaks to the media or voluntary disclosures by the executive branch—Congress held extensive hearings.

The most celebrated hearings were conducted by the so-called Church Committee, named after Senator Frank Church (D-ID), which was officially titled "Senate Select Committee to Study Governmental Operations with Respect to Intelligence Activities."[15] Some Church Committee members protested that in order to investigate the nation's intelligence agencies would harm or cripple national security. But despite protracted televised hearings and voluminous reports, no evidence has ever been adduced to substantiate that claim. Congressional committees are authorized by the Constitution to convene in "executive session"[16] to safeguard intelligence sources or methods, or particular weapons systems like the Manhattan Project.[17] And regarding leaks of classified information to the media, former CIA Director George Tenet confirmed to Senator Richard Shelby that the executive branch is a far worse culprit than is Congress.[18]

The light that the media and the Church Committee shined on the nation's intelligence agencies yielded landmark laws and new administrative policies to strengthen individual liberty and the safety of the nation's leaders without compromising national security. President Ford issued Executive Order 11905, which declared: "No employee of the United States government shall engage in or conspire to engage in political assassination."[19] Speculation persists that Cuba may have assisted in the assassination of President John F. Kennedy in retaliation for repeated CIA attempts guided by then–Attorney General Robert Kennedy to assassinate Castro after the Bay of Pigs debacle in Operation Mongoose.[20]

The House and Senate established intelligence committees to oversee the intelligence community. To foreclose the defense of plausible presidential deniability and to create political accountability, the Hughes-Ryan Act of 1974 required the president to make specific findings that each planned covert action would be important to national security.[21] The Intelligence Oversight Act of 1980 required covert actions to be reported to congressional committees in the House and Senate. FISA generally required judicial warrants based on probable cause to believe the citizen was acting as an agent of a foreign power in order to target him for electronic surveillance to gather foreign intelligence, and prohibited reliance on First Amendment activity as the sole basis for probable cause.

Then Attorney General Edward Levi issued unclassified Department of Justice guidelines in 1976 governing the FBI's investigation of domestic groups, and classified guidelines governing the FBI's investigation of terrorist groups linked to a foreign power.[22] The guidelines responded to the Church Committee's findings that the FBI had maintained massive files at FBI headquarters detailing the political activities of individuals, investigated domestic political groups, and infiltrated and surveilled persons or groups based solely on political affiliation, with no legitimate criminal investigative purpose. From 1966 to 1976, for example, in the city of Chicago a staggering five thousand informants were employed by the FBI to infiltrate peaceful civic and political organizations.[23]

President Bush himself has demonstrated the salience of transparency to democratic governance and the Constitution's checks and balances. After the *New York Times* disclosed the Bush administration's warrantless domestic surveillance program targeting American citizens on American soil in contravention of FISA, Congress held numerous hearings to explore the program's legality and necessity. I was a witness at several of the hearings.[24] President Bush initially insisted that his warrantless spying was both authorized by statute and justified by his inherent constitutional power, and that Congress was impotent to restrict his power to gather foreign intelligence against American citizens.

But under the fire of harsh public and congressional criticism, then–Attorney General Gonzales "voluntarily" renounced warrantless spying on Americans in January 2007 in favor of FISA warrants whose details remain secret[25]—although they seemed to deviate from the customary Fourth Amendment's warrant standard of individualized suspicion of wrongdoing or of acting as a foreign agent. President Bush then tacitly acknowledged the power of Congress to regulate foreign intelligence collection in signing the Protect America Act of 2007, followed by the FISA Amendments Act of 2008.[26] Publicity had acted like photosynthesis on public opinion. Congress was energized to block unilateral presidential action, which forced President Bush to bend. Disclosure of the Bush administration's legal memorandum justifying torture, including waterboarding, triggered a legal retreat. The memorandum was withdrawn, and torture was renounced. Similarly, if there had not been publicity, there would have been no investigations or prosecutions of the stomach-wrenching abuses at Abu Ghraib prison in Iraq.[27]

Democratic governance wars with secret government, but President Bush champions secrecy at every turn. He has refused to permit current and former presidential advisers to appear before Congress to answer questions about suspected executive branch criminality or maladministration in conjunction with the firing of nine U.S. attorneys. Bush did permit the vice president's chief of staff and counsel David Addington and former Deputy Assistant Attorney General John Yoo to testify before the House Judiciary Committee on June 26, 2008, but the two refused to answer many questions by invoking executive privilege.

The president has concealed from Congress and the American public the number of citizens who were spied on in contravention of FISA, how they were chosen as targets, the intelligence yield that could not have been obtained if FISA had been followed, and the contemporary legal reasoning used to justify ignoring the statute, but for a snippet of a classified John Yoo memorandum shown to select members of Congress. The probability is overwhelming that President Bush is operating many secret intelligence collection programs that have not yet leaked to the public because Bush administration officials like Attorney General Gonzales have publicly hedged as to whether any exist. Finally, the president has classified and concealed executive orders that revoke or waive published orders that remain outstanding. The American people and Congress are thus left guessing as to which executive orders are in effect and which are not—reminiscent of the practice of Roman Emperor Caligula of writing laws high on walls in miniscule print to deny citizens fair warning of what was required.[28]

Congressional committees can challenge the president's privilege claims in civil actions in federal courts. Indeed, the House Judiciary Committee has done so regarding the refusals of White House Chief of Staff Joshua Bolten and former White House Counsel Harriet Miers to appear to answer questions or to respond to a request for documents over the firings of the U.S. attorneys.[29] But executive privilege suits are invariably lead-footed. By the time a final decision might be reached, the information sought by Congress would be politically stale. Thus, the Judiciary Committee's complaint was filed on March 10, 2008.[30] The executive branch opposed an expedited briefing schedule and promised to appeal any order accelerating the case on the federal district court's docket. When President Bush leaves office in January 2009, the litigation will be unresolved. There will then be little political stomach in the new Congress for continuing to fight. It will wish to give the new president a decent honeymoon, and the public will not care about the firings of U.S. attorneys by a former president residing on a ranch in Texas.

Congress enjoys the constitutional power to imprison persons who defy their subpoenas. That power was asserted in *McGrain v. Daugherty* (1927)[31] against a former attorney general. But the practice has fallen into desuetude for three-quarters of a century because of political irresolution. Congress could resurrect its contempt authority without disturbing checks and balances. Congressional detainees would retain the right to petition independent federal courts for writs of habeas corpus challenging the factual or legal foundations of their detentions.

But Congress has clearly foresworn the imprisonment option for executive branch officials. An impeachment inquiry by the

House Judiciary Committee is thus the sole vehicle for Congress and the American people to discover what President Bush has done or is doing with accompanying legal and policy explanations in the name of national security or law enforcement. To refuse to answer questions or supply information in an impeachment inquiry would be an impeachable offense itself under the precedent set by the House Judiciary Committee that voted articles of impeachment against President Richard M. Nixon.[32]

If Congress shies from impeachment to vindicate its oversight powers, its institutional weight will shrivel. Without the ability to extract information about the executive branch or to force compliance with the laws it passes, Congress's handiwork will be little more than earmarks for favored donors or political supporters. The legislature needs information from the executive branch to know whether new laws are needed or old laws are defective.

Impeachment detractors argue that the constitutional nightmare of the Bush–Cheney administration will soon be over in January 2009. They rhetorically ask, "Why go through an impeachment ordeal inevitably beset with partisan rancor for a problem with a very short shelf life?"

The short answer can be discovered in Marc Antony's funeral oration in Shakespeare's play, *Julius Caesar*: "The evil that men do lives after them. The good is oft interred with their bones."[33] If Congress does not repudiate the Bush–Cheney abuses and usurpations—perpetrated under the pretense that the nation has been forced to a permanent war footing with international terrorism threatening to bring a Caliphate to Washington, DC—a dangerous safe harbor will have been created for their successors in the White House. To paraphrase Justice Robert Jackson in *Korematsu v. United States* (1943),[34] the Bush–Cheney precedents will lie around like loaded weapons ready for use by any president who claims an urgent need.

Moreover, no president voluntarily surrenders power. Think of the major presidential candidates for 2008: Barack Obama and John McCain. Neither has pledged to take the nation off a permanent war footing. And as Cicero averred, in times of war, the law is silent.[35] Neither candidate has assailed President Bush for employing military commissions to try war crimes that could be prosecuted in civilian courts. (The hydraulic bureaucratic forces that bias military commissions against the accused have been confirmed by the disqualification of Air Force Brigadier General Thomas W. Hartman, the top legal adviser in the Office of Military Commissions, for exerting improper influence to bring "sexy" cases and use coerced testimony.[36]) Neither has denounced President Bush's practice kidnapping, imprisoning, and torturing persons abroad in a legal and political twilight zone. Neither one has pledged to repudiate President Bush's extravagant claims of executive privilege to operate secret government or state secrets to deny justice to victims of unconstitutional practices. Neither has repudiated power to initiate warfare unilaterally. (Obama's celebrated *Audacity of Hope* is virtually silent on the mushrooming of executive power.)

Indeed, Senator Hillary Clinton in a broadcast interview in May 2008 declared that if Iran attacked Israel, "[she] want[s] the Iranians to know that if [she's] the president, we will attack Iran."[37] She would deny the Congress even a cameo appearance in the decision-making process. Senator Clinton's detractors criticized the harshness of her rhetoric, not her tacit claim that the president is crowned with power to initiate war unilaterally. To permit the constitutional abuses of the Bush–Cheney administration to go unchastened, would be to give them a strong constitutional footing.

In hindsight and after sober second thoughts, liberal icon Arthur Schlesinger Jr. came to believe that an imperial presidency took root in the 1960s from a naïve belief that good people could be trusted to exercise unchecked power.[38] Then came the imperial presidency of Richard Nixon and its infamous lawlessness, which bettered the instruction of President Lyndon B. Johnson's illegal surveillances and other abuses. That type of mistake should not be repeated—that is, believing that the Bush–Cheney precedents can be tolerated because they will be succeeded by saints. As philosopher George Santayana preached, "Those who forget the past are condemned to repeat it."[39]

House Speaker Nancy Pelosi (D–CA) has ruled "impeachment off the table"[40] for President Bush and Vice President Cheney. An overriding reason is Pelosi's complicity in President Bush's major abuses through silence after she was informed of the president's illegal electronic surveillance of Americans and torture of detainees. Pelosi's anti-impeachment decree verifies British parliamentarian Edmund Burke's observation that all that is necessary for the triumph of evil is for good men and women to do nothing.[41] The Speaker has been the cief obstacle to an impeachment inquiry by House Judiciary Committee chairman John Conyers. The chairman was present during Nixon's impeachment. He is no fan of President Bush or Vice President Cheney. The most plausible explanation for his impeachment reticence is a command from higher authority. Pelosi has explained her opposition to impeachment not by reference to what is good for the country or the Constitution but by what she believes is good for the Democratic Party in 2008 and her own personal ambitions. She is subordinating Congress as an institution to her own fortunes as a Democratic Party leader. The duumvirate of Bush and Cheney has predictably been emboldened to further sneer at Congress, knowing that their grip on power is unassailable no matter how microscopic their respective approval ratings.

Pelosi cannot be saddled with the lion's share of the blame for impeachment inertia. Democrats in the House of Representatives have not repudiated her stance. Staunch House Judiciary Committee liberals such as Chairman Conyers and Subcommittee Chairman Jerald Nadler (D-NY) have not challenged Pelosi. And neither have the American people flooded Pelosi's office with protesting e-mails or phone calls. To paraphrase Pogo, we have met the enemy of impeachment to secure freedom and checks and balances, and we are they.[42]

Public enthusiasm for impeachment has been dulled because the typical known victims of President Bush's wrongdoing sport odd-sounding names evocative of Islam, or the Middle East—for example, Abu Omar, Maher Arar, Mohammed el-Masri, or Lakhdar Boumediene.[43] Consider two additional cases that have left Americans thoroughly unmoved. Sami al-Hajj, a cameraman for Al Jazeera, was released from Guantanamo Bay on May 1, 2008, after six years' of detention without charge. Imagine if Bush made you disappear into a legal black hole for six years based on his gut instinct that you were a danger.[44] Abdul Razzaq Hekmati died in Guantanamo Bay on December 30, 2007, after five years' detention without accusation or trial. No serious effort was undertaken by the U.S. military to verify the credibility of his claim that he was anti-Taliban.[45]

Americans historically have displayed indifference to injustices inflicted on those whose names, appearances, or cultures seem alien. Virtually no voice was heard to protest concentration camps for 120,000 unswervingly loyal Japanese Americans or permanent resident aliens in World War II. Two infamous U.S. Supreme Court precedents upholding the concentration camps featured Japanese names Hirabiyashi and Korematsu.[46] Americans are also suspicious of Islam as an alien force in society. Senator John McCain, Republican candidate for the White House in 2008, like 55 percent of all Americans,[47] maintains that the U.S. Constitution establishes a Christian nation—although Christianity cannot be made a condition of holding any public office, and cannot be promoted by government nor be preferred to any other religion or to atheism. The senator also betrayed his coolness toward Islam in declaring, "I just have to say in all candor that since this nation was founded primarily on Christian principles . . . personally I prefer someone who has a solid grounding in my faith."[48]

McCain's religious prejudice is confirmed by his invention of the idea that the Constitution established a Christian nation to justify his skepticism of Islam. The invention enables McCain to pretend that his prejudice is ordained by the Constitution and not freely chosen. But not a single syllable in the notes of the Constitutional Convention of 1787, the state ratification debates, or the Federalist Papers insinuates that the Constitution made the nation Christian. The Constitutional Preamble—which enumerates the purposes of the Constitution—conspicuously omits any reference to establishing a Christian nation.[49] Benjamin Franklin proposed at the Constitutional Convention to open each day's assembly with a prayer to heaven. But it failed to be adopted.[50] The Constitution established a secular state with secular instruments to arrest or mitigate the sordidness of human nature—in the spirit of Oliver Cromwell's advice to his soldiers: "Trust in God and keep your powder dry."[51] It did not establish a Christian nation as the flip side to Persia's future theocracy.

People are naturally inclined to embrace fantasies to avert unpleasant thoughts or pangs of conscience. The vast majority of Americans are silent about President Bush's constitutional excesses because they believe they will never be targeted. They should memorize the words of Martin Niemoller about why Nazi Germany confronted no popular uprising: "First they came for the Socialists, and I did not speak out—because I was not a Socialist. Then they came for the Trade Unionists, and I did not speak out—because I was not a Trade Unionist. Then they came for the Jews, and I did not speak out—because I was not a Jew. Then they came for me, and there was no one left to speak for me."[52]

President Nixon was more vulnerable to impeachment than President Bush because his list of enemies contained familiar names, including celebrities. The White House Plumbers burgled the office of Dr. Lewis Fielding, Daniel Ellsberg's psychiatrist. The Watergate burglars targeted the Democratic National Committee. Most Americans could empathize with the victims of Nixon's lawlessness.

There are undoubtedly thousands of American citizens who have been and continue to be victims of President Bush's illegal spying who would be outraged if they knew the details of the massive illegalities. In the aftermath of 9/11, the president instructed the National Security Agency (NSA) to target American citizens on American soil for electronic surveillance without judicial warrants in contravention of the FISA, pursuant to his so-called Terrorist Surveillance Program (TSP).[53] The targets remain unknown. The government cannot be compelled by the courts to disclose the spying to the victim unless a criminal prosecution is initiated based on the fruits of the illegality. With one possible exception, the government has shied from such prosecutions to maintain the illusion that what it has been doing is constitutional.[54] Under the doctrine of standing, mere suspicion that an individual or group may have suffered injury because of illegal spying is not sufficient to challenge the TSP in the federal judiciary. A Michigan federal district court decision holding the TSP unconstitutional was overturned by the U.S. Court of Appeals for the Sixth Circuit on the theory that the challengers could only speculate about whether their communications had been either intercepted or chilled.

A complementary legal barrier to identifying victims of illegal spying is the state secrets doctrine.[55] Generally speaking, it empowers the government to prevent courts from litigating claims by victims of illegal conduct if proof of the government's wrongdoing would disclose information arguably harmful to national security. At present, no alleged victim of the TSP in civil litigation has surmounted the state secrets privilege.

The president and former Attorney General Gonzales have tacitly admitted to secret spying programs in addition to the TSP that have not yet leaked to the media. The invasions of privacy will never be known unless Congress initiates an impeachment inquiry (where state secrets or executive privilege would have no sway) or brings into being a new Church Committee. The Committee succeeded in attracting broad public support that culminated in landmark legislation to bring the rule of law to the intelligence community because its hearings educated the public of the evils of secret government.

Senator Obama and Senator McCain should categorically disavow the Bush–Cheney crippling of checks and balances. Both should declare, "If I am elected president, I will not ape President Bush and sign into law a bill passed by Congress but refuse to enforce the provisions I think are constitutionally dubious. I will veto any bill that I believe contains unconstitutional provisions, and ask that the offending provisions be deleted and the revised bill be repassed. If I am elected, I will comply with laws passed by Congress to regulate the collection of foreign intelligence and seek congressional amendments if I think the laws are deficient. I will not imitate President Bush and simply ignore laws that I think are misguided or ill-crafted. I will transfer the trials of alleged war criminals before military commissions to civilian courts. I will not oppose the grant of habeas corpus to any detainee within the custody or control of the United States outside an active military zone. I will not detain without trial any American citizen as a suspected unlawful enemy combatant. I will not invoke state secrets to deny justice to victims of government illegality. I will not employ executive privilege to frustrate congressional oversight. I will not initiate war without the express authorization of Congress. And I will not deceive Congress and the American people about international dangers."

To his credit, Republican presidential nominee Senator John McCain has renounced presidential signing statements—but in the past his political promises have proven indistinguishable from a restricted railroad ticket good only for this day and this train. For example, after celebrating the need for checks and balances, he soon endorsed President Bush's view that Article II of the Constitution empowers the president to flout congressional statutes to gather foreign intelligence—at least after 9/11.

With the support of McCain and other members, Congress has also balked at challenging that alarming claim. Last August, Congress passed the Protect America Act of 2007 (PAA), which purported to limit the president's ability to collect foreign intelligence in spying on Americans or foreigners outside the United States.[56] The act was not confined to collecting foreign intelligence to defeat international terrorism. It extended to spying to obtain economic, environmental, political, or social information that might affect the foreign policy of the United States. The act placed no limitation on intercepting or keeping on file the communications of Americans on American soil if they are called by a noncitizen from abroad. It empowered the NSA to intercept international phone calls or e-mails for at least one year if the spy targets are "reasonably believed"[57] to be in a foreign country when the surveillance begins. That benchmark can be satisfied if the government develops a formula, reviewed six months later by a judge, that was not "clearly erroneous"[58] in predicting whether the target was abroad. The standard is indistinguishable from a group warrant, which the Fourth Amendment deplores because it eviscerates the fundamental right to be left alone. Think of the following analogous law: Congress enacts the hypothetical Protect against Murder Act of 2008. The bill authorizes the Department of Justice to obtain a warrant to search every home in the United States if the director of the FBI certifies that the collective searches are "reasonably likely" to lead to the arrest and prosecution of a murderer. We would all soon expect a daily visit from FBI agents snooping through our homes and bedrooms.

Congress readily capitulated to President Bush's demand to denude American citizens of privacy protections in enacting the PAA. Members were cowed by the president's threat to blame them for any future terrorist attacks if they voted in opposition. The surrender came despite President Bush's insistence that he was still crowned by the Constitution with authority to ignore the law at will and to conceal his lawlessness. Congress accepted its vassalage.

The PAA expired by its own terms after six months. President Bush sought an extension from Congress by shouting that Americans would be massacred because of a failure of intelligence if the act were not renewed. In a rare moment of strength, the House of Representatives balked. The PAA lapsed. No American died. Congress, however, replaced the PAA with the FISA Amendments Act of 2008, which retained its major privacy deficiencies.

The Constitution, of course, is not a suicide pact. But none of President Bush's usurpations and excesses has been shown to assist the foiling of international terrorism. Congress has similarly enacted oppressive laws with no demonstration of need. Favorable political optics have been sufficient. Members generally believe that any legislation with the appearance of doing something against terrorists will be rewarding. They fret that a vote against it could be twisted to mean they were in favor of terrorism. Compare that attitude with John Adams, who successfully defended British soldiers accused in the Boston Massacre despite public hostility and the loss of more than half of his law practice's clients. He later called the defense "one of the most gallant, generous, manly, and disinterested actions of my whole life, and one of the best pieces of service I have ever rendered my country."[59]

In *Hamdan v. Rumsfeld* (2006),[60] the Supreme Court declared that President Bush's unilateral creation of military commissions for the trials of war crimes was illegal. Congress responded by enacting new legislation authorizing the commissions without a crumb of evidence that they were relevant to frustrating international terrorism. During the first six years that have elapsed since 9/11, the government has prosecuted but one case before a military commission. David Hicks, a puny anonymity from Australia, pled guilty to providing material assistance to a foreign terrorist organization. He was sentenced to nine months imprisonment to be served in Australia.[61] That same crime is routinely tried in civilian courts every day without difficulty—for example, the John Walker Lindh and Jose Padilla prosecutions and convictions.[62] In July 2008, a second military commission trial began against Salim Ahmed Hamdan, who is not accused of killing a single American.

Military commissions are worrisome because they are geared to convict the innocent, whom no civilized people have an interest in punishing. Moreover, erroneous verdicts spawn resentment abroad and make foreign allies less likely to cooperate in confronting international terrorism. With military commissions, the judge, jury, and prosecutor respond to the same superior. Secret evidence, coerced testimony, and hearsay are permitted. The right to call favorable witnesses is clipped. The probability of acquittal is slim. In stark contrast: In civilian courts, the judge, jury, and prosecutor are separated. Secret evidence, coerced testimony, and hearsay are forbidden. The accused enjoys a right to confront all of the evidence against him and to secure favorable witnesses. Jury unanimity and proof beyond a reasonable doubt are required. Verdicts in civilian courts are highly reliable. The Department of Justice's terrorism prosecution scorecard is thus reassuringly mixed. A 100 percent conviction rate, as in Communist China, would signal trouble.

Take the case of Saudi computer-science student Sami Omar al-Hussayn. Attorney General John Ashcroft maintained that he was part of a "terrorist threat that is fanatical, and it is fierce."[63] Idaho Governor Dirk Kempthorne declared al-Hussayn was proof that terrorists were nesting in the heartland. But a federal jury acquitted the Saudi man of all charges of providing material assistance to a terrorist organization in June 2004.

The Supreme Court in *Rasul v. Bush* (2005)[64] held that federal habeas corpus statutes applied to unlawful enemy combatant detainees at Guantanamo Bay. Congress answered by suspending the Great Writ—a writ of habeas corpus—for noncitizen detainees in the Military Commissions Act (MCA).[65] What danger had the Great Writ created? It is not a get-out-of-jail-free card. It simply requires the executive to provide a factual and legal foundation for the detentions—an obligation that has been routine since the Magna Carta in 1215. When Congress suspended habeas corpus, the Great Writ had not occasioned the release of even one detainee—including the absurd cases of several Uighurs, whose chief threat is to Communist China.[66] The U.S. Supreme Court held the suspension unconstitutional in *Boumediene v. Bush* (2008).[67] The MCA also embraced a definition of "unlawful enemy combatant" to include persons who might stitch the britches of Osama bin Laden or sell him fruits or vegetables.[68] No explanation was given as to why persons who "materially assisted" terrorism could not be charged and prosecuted in civilian courts under the material assistance statute.

Members are supine in defending the Constitution, including their own powers, for two reasons. First, they are generally ignorant of the Constitution's antecedents, history, and philosophy. They hold no deep convictions about the dangers of constitutional wrongdoing. And without muscular convictions hardened by struggling with ideas, members instinctively shy from confronting and rebuking the president's usurpations and unconstitutional claims. The ordinary member is unschooled in the Magna Carta, the English Bill of Rights of 1688, the Stamp Act, the Declaration of Independence, the Articles of Confederation, the Constitutional Convention of 1787, the Federalist Papers, the Gettysburg Address, the Constitution itself, and landmark Supreme Court rulings.

Congress also plays spectator to the president's unconstitutional encroachments and abuses because members routinely subordinate the Constitution to party loyalty. That hierarchy violates the constitutional stipulation in Article VI, Section 3: "The Senators and Representatives . . . shall be bound by Oath or Affirmation, to support this Constitution."[69] But when members calculate, they figure what is good for the party, not what is good for the nation's constitutional dispensation. During the first six years of the Bush presidency, the Republican-controlled Congress declined to issue even one subpoena to the executive branch. Congressional oversight became comatose not because the Bush administration was irreproachable—think of Hurricane Katrina—but because Republican members believed that embarrassing a Republican president would be bad for the party. As one

Republican member in the House of Representatives lamented to me confidentially, a majority of Republicans are ready to drink the Kool-Aid[70] for President Bush, and a majority equate truth with political expediency.

President Dwight D. Eisenhower's nominee for secretary of defense, Charles Wilson, former head of General Motors, testified to the Senate Armed Services Committee in 1952, "For years I thought that what was good for our country was good for General Motors, and vice versa. The difference did not exist."[71] He was roundly decried. But members of Congress have been trumpeting a companion slogan, "What's good for my Party is good for the country." Statesmanship and maintaining the Constitution's checks and balances are foreign to their personal or party agendas. With the takeover of Congress by the Democratic Party in 2007, oversight has been awakened from its Republican slumber. Subpoenas have been issued to the executive branch; but none have been enforced over the objection of President Bush—for example, subpoenas for the testimonies or documents of former White House Counsel Harriet Miers, and Chief of Staff Joshua Bolten. Congress has desisted from new legislation or political retaliation to overcome President Bush's assertions of privilege.

Congressional cowardice or complicity, however, does not exonerate President Bush's constitutional wrongdoing. The president takes an oath to preserve, protect, and defend the Constitution of the United States, irrespective of the actions of coequal branches of government. And a modicum of self-restraint is required by the president, as well as Congress, if the system is to avoid capsizing. Without self-restraint, for example, President George Washington could have killed the Supreme Court at its conception by refusing to nominate justices. And conversely, Congress could have killed the presidency by refusing to appropriate money for any executive officer but the president. In modern times, Attorney General Edward Levi under President Gerald Ford set a splendid example of self-restraint in March

1976 in promulgating written guidelines for the FBI in dealing with counterintelligence surveillance investigations and restrictions on seeking access to reporters' sources or confidential information.

The American people should be awakened to their duty to uphold and defend the Constitution of the United States from its current peril by forcing corrective action on the president and Congress. Citizens should make defense of the Constitution and checks and balances a deciding factor for presidential and congressional candidates, every bit as much as the National Rifle Association members make gun control a deciding factor for their ballots. The power of public opinion remains invincible. It forced Harriet Miers to withdraw her Supreme Court nomination and prompted Attorney General Alberto Gonzales's resignation. Public opinion was decisive in President Nixon's downfall. Within two weeks of Nixon's Saturday Night Massacre during the Watergate investigation, Western Union reported 450,000 citizen telegrams to the White House and the Watergate Special Prosecution Force protesting the firing of Special Prosecutor Archibald Cox.[72]

President Grover Cleveland elaborated in his first inaugural,

But he who takes the oath today to preserve, protect, and defend the Constitution of the United States only assumes the solemn obligation which every patriotic citizen—on the farm, in the workshop, in the busy marts of trade, and everywhere—should share with him. The Constitution which prescribes his oath, my countrymen, is yours. . . . Every citizen owes to the country a vigilant watch and close scrutiny of its public servants and a fair and reasonable estimate of their fidelity and usefulness. Thus is the people's will impressed upon the whole framework of our civil polity—municipal, State, and Federal; and this is the price of our liberty and the inspiration of our faith in the Republic.[73]

If the struggle to retain the Constitution and our democracy is to succeed, citizens must also acquire an understanding of constitutional philosophy and its unwritten code of moderation. They should carefully read the Declaration of Independence, the Constitution, the Federalist Papers, George Washington's Farewell Address, Alexis de Tocqueville's *Democracy in America*, and President Abraham Lincoln's Gettysburg Address and Second Inaugural. They should especially appreciate that their rights, as elaborated in the Declaration, are unalienable. They are not at the sufferance of the president or Congress. They should visit the nation's capitol to receive inspiration and courage from the Washington Monument, the Jefferson Memorial, and the Lincoln Memorial. They should return home to scold any official—high or low—who violates the Constitution in either letter or spirit.

Edward Gibbon insisted in *The Decline and Fall of the Roman Empire* that "History is little more than the register of crimes, follies, and misfortunes of mankind."[74] But history is biography. We, the people of the United States, hold the power to discredit Gibbon.

THREE

Looking Backward

I still vividly remember the evening of October 20, 1973, as a young Department of Justice lawyer in the office of legal counsel. I had taken an oath a few months earlier to defend and support the Constitution for which so many had given or risked the ultimate measure of devotion—at Cemetery Ridge, Omaha Beach, Guadalcanal, and sister battlefields. And the Constitution itself, which made the sacrifices worth giving, had been fashioned and maintained by men of moral courage, wisdom, and a sense of honor. My heroes included George Washington, James Madison, Thomas Jefferson, Alexander Hamilton, Abraham Lincoln, John Marshall, Oliver Wendell Holmes, and Louis Brandeis. Most of all, I admired Washington. He repudiated an offer of kingship during the Revolutionary War, and at the constitutional convention, he admonished, "Let us raise a standard to which the wise and honest may repair."[1]

As a law clerk, I helped draft the opinion in *National Treasury Workers Union v. Nixon* (1973),[2] in which the U.S. Court of Appeals for the District of Columbia Circuit held President Richard M. Nixon legally accountable for violating the Federal

Pay Comparability Act. The president had claimed absolute immunity from suit, only a slight variation of King Louis XIV's boast, "I am the state."[3] A new danger to the Constitution was unfolding before my eyes, and the stakes were high.

I was watching Robert Pierpoint of CBS news report the so-called Saturday Night Massacre from the White House lawn. President Nixon had ordered Attorney General Elliot Richardson to fire Watergate Special Prosecutor Archibald Cox in an effort to conceal his complicity in the Watergate cover-up. Richardson had resigned. Deputy Attorney General William Ruckelshaus had also resigned rather than fire Cox. Acting Attorney General Robert H. Bork then removed the special prosecutor. FBI agents sealed off the offices and files of Cox's prosecution team. The offices of Richardson and Ruckelshaus were also sealed. People were worried that America had witnessed its equivalent of the burning of the Reichstag in 1933.

The events that precipitated the Saturday Night Massacre underscored its challenge to the Constitution. In an April 30, 1973, televised address, Nixon had announced the resignations of Attorney General Richard Kleindienst, White House Chief of Staff H. R. Haldeman, and White House adviser John Ehrlichman, as well as the firing of White House Counsel John Dean because of ongoing investigations of Watergate-related crimes.[4] The president also announced the nomination of then–Secretary of Defense Richardson for attorney general. He would enjoy discretion to appoint a special prosecutor to investigate Watergate. Even before his Senate confirmation hearings, Richardson announced he would do so, and Nixon offered the Senate the opportunity to evaluate and unofficially confirm his designee before the appointment became final. During the confirmation hearings, Richardson, Cox, and the Senate Judiciary Committee negotiated guidelines that would govern Cox's independence and authority. In sum, the Cox appointment and terms of service were a product of executive-legislative collaboration—even though the constitutional responsibility for faithfully executing the laws belongs to the president.

The guidelines gave Cox full authority to investigate and prosecute "all offenses arising out of the 1972 presidential election for which the special prosecutor deems it necessary and appropriate to assume responsibility, allegations involving the president, members of the White House staff, or presidential appointees, and any other matters which he consents to have assigned to him by the Attorney General."[5] The guidelines also secured Cox's independence: "In exercising this authority, the special prosecutor will have the greatest degree of independence that is consistent with the attorney general's statutory accountability. . . . The attorney general will not countermand or interfere with the special prosecutor's decisions or actions. The special prosecutor will determine whether and to what extent he will inform or consult with the attorney general about the conduct of his duties and responsibilities. The special prosecutor will not be removed from his duties except for extraordinary improprieties."[6]

Special prosecutors were historically ingenious devices to overcome the conflict of interest inherent when the executive branch investigates itself. They were employed to investigate the Whiskey Ring under President Ulysses S. Grant, the Teapot Dome under President Calvin Coolidge, and tax scandals under President Harry Truman.[7] Special prosecutors exemplified checks and balances at its best—voluntary action taken by one branch to check itself through legally binding regulations ensuring the independence of an internal review. Since Dr. Bonham's Case in 1610,[8] Anglo-American law had frowned on the idea that one branch could sit as a judge in a case to which it was a party.

In conducting his investigation, Special Prosecutor Cox issued a subpoena to the president for copies of presidential documents and taped conversations recorded in the Oval Office. President Nixon balked, but the United States Court of Appeals for the District of Columbia Circuit ruled in favor of Cox in *Nixon v. Sirica* (1973).[9] Nixon then offered what came to be known as the Stennis Compromise in lieu of complying with the court order. Under the alternate plan, the aging and semi-alert U.S. Senator John C. Stennis (D-MS) would review and summarize the tapes for the special prosecutor. Cox refused and insisted on compliance with the court decree. Infuriated by the idea that the president is subject to the law, and fearful of his undoing, President Nixon then instructed Attorney General Richardson to discharge Cox in violation of the special prosecutor's independence charter.

Richardson resigned rather than participate in an obstruction of justice. Deputy Attorney General Ruckelshaus followed suit. Solicitor General Bork then became acting attorney general under the department's regulations and fired Cox. He had been prevailed upon to stay by Richardson and Ruckelshaus, to keep the department operating. The Saturday Night Massacre suggested that President Nixon might succeed in derailing the Watergate investigation, eviscerating checks and balances, and stabbing the Constitution in the back.

The U.S. Supreme Court declared in *Ex parte Milligan* (1866)[10] that no official was above the law, even during the Civil War exigencies that threatened the nation's very existence. Speaking through Justice David Davis, the Court elaborated,

> The Constitution of the United States is a law for rulers and people, equally in war and in peace, and covers with the shield of its protection all classes of men, at all times and under all circumstances. No doctrine involving more pernicious consequences was ever invented by the wit of man than that any of its provisions can be suspended during any of the great exigencies of government. Such a doctrine leads directly to anarchy or despotism, but the theory of necessity on which it is based is false, for the government, within the Constitution, has all the powers granted to it which are necessary to preserve its existence, as has been happily proved by the result of the great effort to throw off its just authority.[11]

Yet President Nixon was acting and speaking like Stuart monarchs in Great Britain before the Glorious Revolution of 1688.[12] President Nixon later famously harrumphed to David Frost in a postresignation interview, "When the president does it, that means it is not illegal."[13] He similarly insisted that no court could review his decision to keep presidential communications secret no matter how crucial to law enforcement or congressional oversight. He could order assassinations, burglaries, wiretappings, obstructions of justice, or violations of law with impunity. His constitutional duty to take care that the laws be faithfully executed was advisory only.

I thought that if President Nixon were not impeached by the House of Representatives, convicted by the Senate, and removed from office for high crimes and misdemeanors, the Constitution would crumble over the ensuing decades. Its celebrated checks and balances, Bill of Rights, and Civil War Amendments would bow to a supreme leader. The nation would have come full circle since throwing off the yolk of King George III in 1776. A hereditary king would have been replaced by an elected despot.

I recalled that at the conclusion of the Constitutional Convention in 1787 Benjamin Franklin had encountered a Mrs. Powell who inquired, "Well Doctor what have we got, a republic or a monarchy?" "A republic," he replied, "if you can keep it."[14] The task of keeping the republic, I recognized, is saddled on every generation of Americans. I contemplated whether I should care if the Constitution collapsed; I anticipated that the future would be grim.

The revolutionary idea of the Founding Fathers was that the chief mission of the state was to make men and women free to pursue their ambitions and to develop their faculties steeled by the responsibilities of self-government, not to build global empires or to aggrandize the president. They immortalized their electrifying idea in the Declaration of Independence: "We hold these Truths to be self-evident, that all Men are created equal, that they are endowed by their Creator with certain inalienable

Rights, that among these are Life, Liberty, and the Pursuit of Happiness—That to secure these Rights, Governments are instituted among Men."[15] Individual liberties were not at the sufferance of the president or Congress but were conferred as natural rights and protected by a Constitution.

With the Constitution replaced by a supreme executive authority, the state's mission would be perverted into expanding the powers of government and chronically concocting excuses for war. The Founding Fathers worried over the incentive of the executive branch to exaggerate national danger to justify usurping power in the name of national security. James Madison, father of the Constitution and president of the United States during the War of 1812, warned,

> Of all the enemies to public liberty, war is, perhaps, the most to be dreaded, because it comprises and develops the germ of every other. . . . War is the parent of armies; from these proceed debts and taxes; and armies, and debts, and taxes are the known instruments for bringing the many under the domination of the few. In war, too, the discretionary power of the Executive is extended; its influence in dealing out offices, honors, and emoluments is multiplied; and all the means of seducing the minds, are added to those of subduing the force, of the people. The same malignant aspect in republicanism may be traced in the inequality of fortunes, and the opportunities of fraud, growing out of a state of war, and in the degeneracy of manner and morals, engendered in both. No nation can preserve its freedom in the midst of continual warfare.
>
> War is in fact the true nurse of executive aggrandizement. In war, a physical force is to be created; and it is the executive will, which is to direct it. In war, the public treasuries are to be unlocked; and it is the executive hand which is to dispense them. In war, the honors and emoluments of office are to be multiplied; and it is the executive patronage under which they are to be enjoyed; and it is the executive brow they

are to encircle. The strongest passions and most dangerous weaknesses of the human breast, ambition, avarice, vanity, the honorable or venal love of fame, are all in conspiracy against the desire and duty of peace.[16]

Madison also wrote in 1798, the year of the infamous Alien and Sedition Acts and an undeclared war with France, that "Perhaps it is a universal truth that the loss of liberty at home is to be charged to provisions against danger, real or pretended, from abroad."[17]

The Vietnam War folly had vindicated Madison's prescience about the inclination of the president to manufacture justifications for war, for war to bloat executive power, and for foreign conflict to engender the loss of freedom at home. Among other things, President Lyndon B. Johnson lied about an alleged second North Vietnamese attack on destroyers USS *Maddox* and USS *C. Turner Joy* to justify the open-ended Gulf of Tonkin Resolution. On November 30, 2005, the National Security Agency (NSA) released hundreds of pages of previously secret documents on the 1964 Gulf of Tonkin incident. The release showed that NSA historian, Robert J. Hanyok, had authored an article in 2001 asserting that the agency's intelligence officers had "deliberately skewed"[18] the evidence provided to presidential advisers and the public in order to falsely suggest that North Vietnamese ships had attacked American destroyers on August 4, 1964. The historian reported that 90 percent of the relevant communication intercepts had been withheld. In 1995, retired Vietnamese General Nguyen Giap categorically denied the attack to former Secretary of Defense Robert McNamara. And a taped conversation of the latter released in 2001 reveals McNamara voicing doubts to President Johnson that the attack had even occurred.

The August 7, 1964, Gulf of Tonkin Resolution—the child of the executive's misrepresentations—crowned President Johnson with carte blanche authority to initiate war against North Vietnam: "Consonant with the Constitution of the United States and the Charter of the United Nations and in accordance with its obligations under the Southeast Asia Collective Defense Treaty, the United States is, therefore, prepared, as the president determines, to take all necessary steps, including the use of armed force, to assist any member or protocol state of the Southeast Asia Collective Defense Treaty requesting assistance in defense of its freedom."[19] With the war came massive military spending, budget deficits, additional taxes, and the draft.

President Johnson also exploited the Vietnam War to justify spying on his critics at home, deluded by the conviction that they must be receiving foreign funding. Public officials are customarily convinced of their infallibility. They are equally fervent that all their detractors are driven by corrupt motives. President Johnson repeatedly misled the country and Congress over the prospects of success in Vietnam. As California Senator Hiram Johnson earlier remarked, "The first casualty of war is truth."[20] That observation corroborated the insight of Sam Johnson, who wrote in *The Idler* more than a century before, "Among the calamities of war may be jointly numbered the diminution of the love of truth, by the falsehoods which interest dictates and credulity encourages."[21] The light at the end of the tunnel was an optical illusion.

President Nixon concealed from Congress the 1969–70 secret bombings of Cambodia and the falsification of military records in conjunction with the war. He invoked the conflict as an excuse to seek suppression of the Pentagon Papers in *New York Times v. United States* (1971)[22] and permitted the burglary of a psychiatrist's office (that of Dr. Lewis Fielding) under the banner of national security.

Vietnam, I thought, was no aberration. President Franklin D. Roosevelt had lied about an alleged Nazi submarine attack on the USS *Greer* on September 4, 1941, to provoke U.S. entry into World War II. British Prime Minister Winston Churchill, upon his return to London in August 1941 from meeting with President Roosevelt, informed his cabinet, "Roosevelt had said that he would wage war, but not declare it, and that he would become more and more provocative."[23] Churchill further claimed that he and FDR had arranged a system for escorting supply convoys, and that the American president had directed the Navy to shoot Nazi submarines on sight to "force" an incident.[24]

Then-Congressman Abraham Lincoln suspected that President James K. Polk had misrepresented Mexican aggression against U.S. soldiers on American soil to justify the Mexican-American War. He introduced "spot resolutions" insisting that the president precisely identify the spot at which a drop of American blood had been shed.[25] Congressman Lincoln exhorted, "Let him answer fully, fairly, and candidly. Let him answer with facts and not with arguments. Let him attempt no evasion, no equivocation."[26] Polk left Lincoln's challenge unanswered.

Madison lectured that to "chain the dogs of war," the Constitution "has accordingly with studied care vested the question of war to the Legislature."[27] James Wilson, a future justice of the Supreme Court, praised the Constitution before the Pennsylvania Ratifying Convention because of its barriers to the initiation of war: "This system will not hurry us into war; it is calculated to guard against it. It will not be in the power of a single man, or a single body of men, to involve us in such distress, for the important power of declaring war is vested in the legislature at large."[28] If the Constitution did not check executive power, presidents would discover excuses to place the nation on a permanent war footing. Presidents are inclined toward war, not only to aggrandize power but also to engender popular support or to leave their footprints in the sands of time. They thrill at the prospect of calling their opponents unpatriotic or traitors, and frightening the people into docility with war measures—for example, suspending the Great Writ of habeas corpus or supplanting civilian tribunals with those of the military. And President George W. Bush, according to White House Press Secretary Scott McClellan in *What Happened*, believed that "only a wartime president is likely to achieve greatness, in part because the epochal upheavals of war provide the opportunity for change of the kind Bush hoped to achieve. In Iraq, Bush saw his opportunity to create a legacy of greatness."[29]

I also surmised that majorities would systematically tyrannize or discriminate against minorities without constitutional checks. Human nature abounds with racial, ethnic, religious, and gender bigotry. I remembered the maltreatment of persons left outside the original Constitution who were made vulnerable to predation by white males: blacks, women, and American Indians. The former had been enslaved and brutalized. The Fugitive Slave Act of 1850 insulted the rule of law. For example, commissioners appointed to summarily adjudicate fugitive slave disputes received $10 for a ruling favoring a purported slave owner, but only $5 for an adverse decision. Moreover, the testimony of the fugitive was inadmissible. Harriet Beecher Stowe's character Simon Legree in *Uncle Tom's Cabin* was more truth than exaggeration.[30] Chief Justice Roger B. Taney declared for the Supreme Court in *Dred Scott v. Sanford* (1857)[31] that blacks had no rights that whites were bound to respect, and that both free and enslaved blacks were excluded from U.S. citizenship.

Even with the Civil War and the ratification of the Thirteenth, Fourteenth, and Fifteenth Amendments abolishing slavery and guaranteeing racial equality under the law, blacks had been brutalized by Jim Crow laws for a century.[32] The signature of Jim Crow laws was lynching; disenfranchisement; and racial discrimination in transportation, employment, education, housing, and government services. As recently as the 1960s, Public Safety Commissioner of Birmingham, Alabama, Bull Connor turned fire hoses and police attack dogs on unarmed, nonviolent protest marchers; and Selma, Alabama, Sheriff Jim Clark employed cattle prods against black youths.

Women had fared better than blacks outside the Constitution, but that still left much room for abuses or subjugation. Abigail Adams pleaded with her husband and future President John Adams without result: "In the new code of laws which I suppose it will be necessary for you to make, I desire that you would remember the ladies, and be more generous and favorable to them than your ancestors. Do not put such unlimited power into the hands of husbands. Remember all men would be tyrants if they could."[33]

The Supreme Court in *Bradwell v. Illinois* (1873)[34] upheld the exclusion of women from the practice of law. In a concurring opinion, Justice Joseph Bradley condescendingly wrote,

> The civil law, as well as nature herself, has always recognized a wide difference in the respective spheres and destinies of man and woman. Man is, or should be, woman's protector and defender. The natural and proper timidity and delicacy which belongs to the female sex evidently unfits it for many of the occupations of civil life. The constitution of the family organization, which is founded in the divine ordinance, as well as in the nature of things, indicates the domestic sphere as that which properly belongs to the domain and function of womanhood. The harmony, not to say the identity, of interests and views which belong, or should belong, to the family institution is repugnant to the idea of a woman adopting a distinct and independent career from that of her husband. So firmly fixed was this sentiment in the founders of the common law that it became a maxim of that system of jurisprudence that a woman had no legal existence separate from her husband, who was regarded as her head and representative in the social state; and, notwithstanding some recent modifications of this civil status, many of the special rules of law flowing from and dependent upon this cardinal principle still exist in full force in most States. One of these is, that a married woman is incapable, without her husband's consent, of making contracts which shall be binding on her or him. This very incapacity was one circumstance which the Supreme Court of Illinois deemed important in rendering a married woman incompetent fully to perform the duties and trusts that belong to the office of an attorney and counselor.[35]

In 1872, Susan B. Anthony was arrested and indicted in Albany for voting. The following year, she was tried and fined $100 with costs after the judge instructed the jury to deliver a guilty verdict. The constitutionality of denying women the franchise was sustained by the U.S. Supreme Court in *Minor v. Happersett* (1874).[36] Women gained protection against the tyranny or prejudices of men with both the ratification of the Nineteenth Amendment guaranteeing equality in the franchise, and the Supreme Court's decision in *Reed v. Reed* (1971)[37] and its progeny giving teeth to the Fourteenth Amendment's prohibition on gender discrimination.

The Trail of Tears and the Sand Creek Massacre were emblematic of the plunder and oppression of American Indians by the Anglo-Saxon majority. Treaties were flouted, land and gold were stolen, and Indians were routinely beaten or killed from the outset of the United States. General Philip Henry Sheridan reputedly declared at Fort Cobb (Indian territory in 1869), "The only good Indians I ever saw were dead."[38] American Indians did not acquire citizenship until 1920.

I further recalled that even groups within the Constitution's nominal protection have suffered odious and sustained discrimination. An inexhaustive list would include Roman Catholics, Jews, Mormons, Asian Americans, and the Irish. I remembered the 120,000 Japanese Americans during World War II who were herded into concentration camps based on the racist and unsubstantiated canard of General John DeWitt that they were loyal to Emperor Hirohito.[39] The Supreme Court sanctioned this racism in *Hirabayashi v. United States* (1943)[40] and *Korematsu v. United States* (1944).[41] Alexis de Tocqueville had warned against the tyranny of the majority in American Democracy and maintained that a constitutional separation of powers was best calculated to thwart that evil.[42]

I also conjectured that freedom of speech and press would shrivel without the Constitution. Public officials and popular majorities invariably seek to punish expression that they find offensive or obnoxious. The Sedition Act of 1798, for example, was enacted by a Federalist Congress to criminalize speech that was intended to bring Congress, Federalist President John Adams, or the Federalist government into disrepute. It provided,

> That if any person shall write, print, utter or publish . . . any false, scandalous, and malicious writing or writings against the government of the United States, or either House of the Congress of the United States, or the president of the United States, with the intent to defame [them], or to bring them [into] contempt or disrepute; or to excite against them [the] hatred of the good people of the United States, . . . then such person . . . shall be punished by a fine not exceeding two thousand dollars, and by imprisonment not exceeding two years.[43]

The Sedition Act conspicuously omitted punishment of speech that traduced Republican Vice President Thomas Jefferson and cynically lapsed on the day that he replaced President Adams in the White House.

Without the Constitution, I wagered, laws that punish speech that is critical of public officials or public measures would multiply—for example, the war in Vietnam or President Nixon's détente with the Soviet Union. Legislative majorities would prohibit speech that they found offensive or disagreeable, ushering in an era reminiscent of the Pope's "Index of Forbidden Books."[44] Chaucer, Shakespeare, and Balzac would be prime candidates for banishment. Pro-life states would prohibit pro-choice speech and vice versa. Some states would prohibit Darwin, while others would prohibit the book of Genesis.

Politicians would ordain historical or scientific truths to the detriment of knowledge and wisdom. I recalled the trial of Galileo,[45] the Scopes Trial,[46] and Trofim Lysenko's false theory of the inheritability of acquired characteristics.[47] Soviet dictator Joseph Stalin had outlawed opposition to Lysenko in 1948 and had imprisoned his detractors.[48] I knew, however, that freedom of speech is the lifeblood of enlightenment and everything that makes life worth living.

Speaking in 399 BCE before the Athenian jury that had convicted him of heresy and sedition, Socrates avowed that his responsibility was "to let no day pass without discussing goodness and all other subjects about which you hear me talking and examining both myself and others."[49] He insisted that this activity, "is really the very best thing that a man (or woman) can do, and that life without this sort of examination is not worth living."[50]

Justice Oliver Wendell Holmes lectured in dissent in *Abrams v. United States* (1919)[51]:

> Persecution for the expression of opinions seems to me perfectly logical. If you have no doubt of your premises or your power and want a certain result with all your heart you naturally express your wishes in law and sweep away all opposition. . . . But when men have realized that time has upset many fighting faiths, they may come to believe even more than they believe in the very foundations of their own conduct that the ultimate good desired is better reached by free trade in ideas—that the best test of truth is the power of the thought to get itself accepted in the competition of the market, and that truth is the only ground upon which their wishes safely can be carried out.[52]

Justice Louis Brandeis further elaborated the nexus between free speech, individual happiness, and representative government in *Whitney v. California* (1927)[53]:

> Those who won our independence believed . . . liberty to be the secret of happiness and courage to be the secret of liberty. They believed that freedom to think as you will and to speak as you think are means indispensable to the discovery and

spread of political truth; that without free speech and assembly, discussion would be futile; that with them, discussion affords ordinarily adequate protection against the dissemination of noxious doctrine; that the greatest menace to freedom is an inert people; that public discussion is a political duty; and that this should be a fundamental principle of the American government.[54]

Thomas Jefferson understood that freedom of the press is more important to securing liberty than government itself. He thus sermonized, "The basis of our government being the opinion of the people, the very first object should be to keep that right; and were it left to me to decide whether we should have a government without newspapers, or newspapers without a government, I should not hesitate a moment to prefer the latter."[55]

Without the Constitution, I anticipated that some religions would be favored over others in both schools and public life. State churches would be established, and citizens would be taxed to support religions they opposed. Religion would infect secular public school curricula, and there would be multiple new editions of the Scopes Trial.

I thought, the Fourth Amendment's protection of privacy would shrink. The amendment proscribes unreasonable searches and seizures, and ordinarily requires a warrant issued by a neutral magistrate based on probable cause to believe that criminal mischief is afoot in order to justify the government's intrusion into private enclaves. The Founding Fathers understood that the right to be left alone is the liberty most cherished by civilized people. It fosters spontaneity, creativity, and assertiveness that make citizens sturdy, independent, and fulfilled. William Pitt, Earl of Chatham, passionately amplified on this right in the House of Commons in 1763, an address which echoed throughout the American Colonies, which were then harassed by obnoxious writs of assistance: "The poorest man may in his cottage bid defiance to all the forces of the Crown. It may be frail; its roof may shake; the wind may blow through it; the storm may enter; the rain may enter; but the King of England cannot enter—all his force dares not cross the threshold of the ruined tenement."[56] But without the Constitution, the government could routinely break and enter homes, intercept phone conversations, open mail, and detain to harass political or personal enemies or detractors. The citizenry would be cowed into silence, and the country would stride eerily toward East Germany under the watch of the Stasi.[57]

Without the Constitution, I believed that Supreme Court and subordinate judges would be made removable by the president to enable retaliation for adverse rulings. I recalled one of the indictments of King George III in the Declaration of Independence: "He has made Judges dependent on his Will alone, for the Tenure of their Offices, and the Amount and Payment of their Salaries."[58] Judicial decisions would come to resemble a collection of political maneuvers informed by ulterior motives. Law and politics would converge.

I believed secret government would flourish because the executive could conceal information from Congress and the American people. Darkness rather than light invites lawlessness, unethical scheming, and maladministration. The Nixon administration was a classic example: the secret bombing of Cambodia,[59] the Huston Plan for domestic burglaries,[60] illegal electronic surveillance and mail openings, and the White House Plumbers, who planned and executed the burglary of the offices of Daniel Ellsberg's psychiatrist.

I imagined government would resort to anonymous witnesses, secret evidence, and nonunanimous verdicts to convict in criminal prosecutions. Trials would come to imitate the Star Chamber or the Spanish Inquisition.[61] Bills of attainder that inflict punishment on political opponents or critics by legislative decree would multiply.

Without the Constitution, I conjectured that the nation's economy would nosedive. States would enact legislation favorable to local industry and hostile to interstate enterprises. Out-of-state businesses would lack lobbying clout. The efficiencies and competition that come from nationwide markets would be lost. Moreover, legislatures could be expected to pass laws upsetting private contracts—for example, saddling small businesses with prohibitive health insurance, pension, or environmental obligations. The uncertain and fluctuating legal landscape would dampen investment and employment opportunities. James Madison rhetorically inquired in Federalist No. 62, "What prudent merchant will hazard his fortunes in any new branch of commerce when he knows not that his plans may be rendered unlawful before they can be executed? What farmer or manufacturer will lay himself out for the encouragement given to any particular cultivation or establishment, when he can have no assurance that his preparatory labors and advances will not render him a victim to an inconsistent government?"[62]

Without the Constitution, I surmised that the wealthiest states might attempt to secede, thus provoking a second Civil War or a nonviolent dissolution of the Union. Nations and peoples readily neglect Benjamin Franklin's wisdom that if you do not hang together, then you are likely to hang separately.[63] And with a splintering of the nation, foreign countries would exploit rivalries among the new anemic statelets, reminiscent of the fragile and disjointed Union under the Articles of Confederation. Alexander Hamilton bemoaned in Federalist No. 15 that under the articles, "There is scarcely anything that can wound the pride or degrade the character of an independent nation which we do not experience."[64]

I firmly believed that without the Constitution's checks and balances, domestic and foreign policies would be chronically ill-conceived. Checks and balances are the scientific method for discovering political truths and for subordinating rashness to prudence. No single branch or official is infallible. Endogamous thinking is fatal. The wish is father to the thought. I remembered the example of President John F. Kennedy's Bay of Pigs debacle attempting to overthrow Cuba's Fidel Castro. The president and his credentialed advisers had convinced themselves that Cubans were coiled for a popular revolt. But a public opinion survey conducted in the spring of 1960 by Lloyd A. Free of the Institute for International Social Research at Princeton (no adulator of Castro) found that Cubans were optimistic about the future and dreaded a return of Cuban dictator Fulgencio Batista. Hadley Cantril, an associate of Free, later observed, "This study on Cuba showed unequivocally not only that the great majority of Cubans supported Castro, but that any hope of stimulating action against him or exploiting a powerful opposition in connection with the United States invasion of 1961 was completely chimerical, no matter what Cuban exiles said or felt about the situation, and that the fiasco and its aftermath, in which the United States became involved, was predictable."[65]

Vetting by coequal branches detects errors, and adds information and perspectives. Of all the sciences, political science is the most difficult to master. Its axioms are elusive and contingent; the future routinely outfoxes current certitudes. Checks and balances do not insure against folly but substantially diminish its likelihood.

I further believed that the Constitution fortified a collective state of mind or political culture as important as the Constitution itself: a reverence for the rule of law; an understanding that the history of liberty is a history of procedural safeguards; a willingness to sacrifice creature comforts and pleasures for the public good; a preference for humility over hubris; a fierce sense of individual dignity; a respect for dissent and the dissenter; an eagerness to accommodate minorities; and a tolerance of the unorthodox or unconventional, and independent thinking. I fully concurred with Thomas Jefferson's admonition: "In questions of power let no more be said of confidence in man but bind him down from mischief by the chains of the Constitution."[66]

I considered the possibility that freedom and unity could flourish in the United States without the Constitution. Great

Britain and Israel, for example, both lack constitutions yet are recognized as free and democratic. The Irish, however, were oppressed in Great Britain until independence was secured after a bloody rebellion in 1922. And the Arab people of Israel, who comprise 20 percent of the population, are second-class citizens. As a matter of theory, all of the rights protected by the Constitution could be equally protected by a political culture that would visit retribution on violators through elections or public obloquy. But it seemed to me improbable that a political culture that accepted the vandalizing of the Constitution with equanimity would lift a finger to protect rights after they had been stripped of constitutional dignity.

I remembered that British statesman William Ewart Gladstone rhapsodized on the centennial of the Constitution, "I have always regarded that Constitution as the most remarkable work known to me in modern times to have been produced by the human intellect, at a single stroke (so to speak), in its application to political affairs."[67] I was convinced that the collective wisdom of the 55 delegates to the Constitutional Convention in 1787 would never be matched in a culture that adulated brainless movie stars and witless professional athletes. The parade of post-Constitution horribles that traversed my mind and Lord Gladstone's praise solidified my conviction that the Constitution was a political jewel worth keeping, and that President Nixon's impeachment was imperative—but I hesitated.

The intellectual and political energy necessary for success would be formidable. No president had been impeached since Andrew Johnson in 1868. And history had come to perceive that impeachment as an illegitimate effort by the Radical Reconstruction Congress to cripple the executive branch by controlling the president's Cabinet.[68] An effort to impeach and convict President Nixon might fail.

Moreover, his multiple sins had left the Constitution wounded but not dead. Precedents would have been established that would destroy checks and balances, transparent government, and the rule of law on an installment plan. The Constitution would not be in danger of instant collapse. I recalled that Alaric the Great had sacked Rome in 410 CE, centuries after Rome had begun its decay as chronicled in Edward Gibbon's work, *The History of the Decline and Fall of the Roman Empire*.[69] The Romans whose insouciance, vices, and silence had occasioned the decline had died long before Alaric. It was their posterity that suffered at the hands of the barbarians. Similarly, if my fellow American citizens and I, not to mention officeholders, neglected to impeach, convict, and remove President Nixon from office, the Constitution would have trembled, but the final destruction would not arrive until we were safely in our graves. Why should I expend time and effort to save the Constitution just to benefit those yet to be born? The latter neither votes nor makes campaign contributions. They would not pay fees for defending the Constitution, nor would they be present to prick my conscience.

But I recalled that the only reason I was enjoying the excitement of self-government and the unalienable rights enshrined in the Declaration of Independence was because countless Americans had marched to heroic drummers with courage, a sense of duty, and honor in action. In the words of Thomas Paine, they were not summer soldiers or sunshine patriots.[70] I thought of Valley Forge, Gettysburg, Omaha Beach, and Iwo Jima. I remembered that Socrates had unreluctantly taken the hemlock to free the mind from tyranny. I was ashamed that I had even contemplated shirking a self-evident obligation.

With fresh energy and conviction, I slaved in the office of legal counsel in preparing a comprehensive memorandum that explored the history and earmarks of impeachable offenses under Article II, Section 4 of the Constitution. It provides, "The President, Vice President, and civil Officers of the United States, shall be removed from Office on Impeachment for, and Conviction of, Treason, Bribery, or other high Crimes and Misdemeanors."[71] The legal and political commentary was relatively sparse because only one president had ever been impeached and that had been more than a century earlier.

I played a minor invisible and inaudible foot soldier's role in the national campaign to force President Nixon from office. I remember standing with admiration on the balcony overlooking the Great Hall of Justice witnessing Attorney General Richardson's explanation for his resignation. I was electrified by the American people and public officials in their resolute defense of the Constitution against the most powerful leader in the world.

President Nixon was foiled; Special Prosecutor Leon Jaworski was appointed to replace Cox. President Nixon backed down from his announced intent to flout the federal court of appeals order in *Nixon v. Sirica*, which required the disclosure of presidential tapes and documents to a grand jury. Indictments, trials, and convictions were forthcoming against the president's inner circle for obstruction of justice and related crimes.

The House Judiciary Committee voted three articles of impeachment against President Nixon. The articles are useful benchmarks for determining whether President Bush has committed impeachable offenses.

Article I pivots on the president's oath of office and unflagging constitutional duty to faithfully execute the laws. It makes clear that the president must assist and not sabotage the detection of crimes or maladministration by Congress and criminal prosecutions by duly constituted law enforcement authorities, and must not deceive the American people or Congress to conceal wrongdoing or escape political accountability. In other words, presidential lies to Congress or the public about what the president has done, is contemplating, or knows may amount to impeachable offenses. Article I charges,

> In his conduct of the office of President of the United States, Richard M. Nixon, in violation of his constitutional oath faithfully to execute the office of President of the United States

and, to the best of his ability, preserve, protect, and defend the Constitution of the United States, and in violation of his constitutional duty to take care that the laws be faithfully executed, has prevented, obstructed, and impeded the administration of justice, in that:

On June 17, 1972, and prior thereto, agents of the Committee for the Re-election of the President committed unlawful entry of the headquarters of the Democratic National Committee in Washington, District of Columbia, for the purpose of securing political intelligence. Subsequent thereto, Richard M. Nixon, using the powers of his high office, engaged personally and through his close subordinates and agents, in a course of conduct or plan designed to delay, impede, and obstruct the investigation of such illegal entry; to cover up, conceal and protect those responsible; and to conceal the existence and scope of other unlawful covert activities.

The means used to implement this course of conduct or plan included one or more of the following:

1. making false or misleading statements to lawfully authorized investigative officers and employees of the United States;

2. withholding relevant material evidence or information from lawfully authorized investigative officers and employees of the United States;

3. approving, condoning, acquiescing in, and counseling witnesses with respect to giving false or misleading statements to lawfully authorized investigative officers and employees of the United States and false or misleading testimony in duly instituted judicial and congressional proceedings;

4. interfering or endeavoring to interfere with the conduct of investigations by the Department of Justice of the United States, the Federal Bureau of Investigation, the office of Watergate Special Prosecution Force, and Congressional Committees;

5. approving, condoning, and acquiescing in, the surreptitious payment of substantial sums of money for the purpose of obtaining the silence or influencing the testimony of witnesses, potential witnesses or individuals who participated in such unlawful entry and other illegal activities;

6. endeavoring to misuse the Central Intelligence Agency, an agency of the United States;

7. disseminating information received from officers of the Department of Justice of the United States to subjects of investigations conducted by lawfully authorized investigative officers and employees of the United States, for the purpose of aiding and assisting such subjects in their attempts to avoid criminal liability;

8. making or causing to be made false or misleading public statements for the purpose of deceiving the people of the United States into believing that a thorough investigation had been conducted with respect to allegations of misconduct on the part of personnel of the executive branch of the United States and personnel of the Committee for the Re-election of the President, and that there was no involvement of such personnel in such misconduct; or

9. endeavoring to cause prospective defendants, and individuals duly tried and convicted, to expect favored treatment and consideration in return for their silence or false testimony, or rewarding individuals for their silence or false testimony.

In all of this, Richard M. Nixon has acted in a manner contrary to his trust as President and subversive of constitutional government, to the great prejudice of the cause of law and justice and to the manifest injury of the people of the United States.[72]

Article II establishes that a president is impeachable for using executive branch agencies or units for illicit or unauthorized purposes—for example, tax audits, illegal electronic surveillance, or burglaries that violate the constitutional rights of citizens—and for neglecting to investigate suspected crimes committed by subordinate executive branch officers or agents. It declares,

> Using the powers of the office of President of the United States, Richard M. Nixon, in violation of his constitutional oath faithfully to execute the office of President of the United States and, to the best of his ability, preserve, protect, and defend the Constitution of the United States, and in disregard of his constitutional duty to take care that the laws be faithfully executed, has repeatedly engaged in conduct violating constitutional rights of citizens, impairing the due and proper administration of justice and the conduct of lawful inquiries, or contravening the laws governing agencies of the executive branch and the purposes of these agencies.
>
> This conduct has included one or more of the following:
>
> 1. He has, acting personally and through his subordinates and agents, endeavored to obtain from the Internal Revenue Service, in violation of the constitutional rights of citizens, confidential information contained in income tax returns for purposes not authorized by law, and to cause, in violation of the constitutional rights of citizens, income tax audits or other income tax investigations to be initiated or conducted in a discriminatory manner.
> 2. He misused the Federal Bureau of Investigation, the Secret Service, and other executive personnel in violation or disregard of the constitutional rights of citizens, by directing or authorizing such agencies or personnel to conduct or continue electronic surveillance or other investigations for purposes unrelated to national security, the enforcement of laws, or any other lawful function of his office; he did direct, authorize, or permit the use of information obtained

thereby for purposes unrelated to national security, the enforcement of laws, or any other lawful function of his office; and he did direct the concealment of certain records made by the Federal Bureau of Investigation of electronic surveillance.

3. He has, acting personally and through his subordinates and agents, in violation or disregard of the constitutional rights of citizens, authorized and permitted to be maintained a secret investigative unit within the office of the President, financed in part with money derived from campaign contributions, which unlawfully utilized the resources of the Central Intelligence Agency, engaged in covert and unlawful activities, and attempted to prejudice the constitutional right of an accused to a fair trial.

4. He has failed to take care that the laws were faithfully executed by failing to act when he knew or had reason to know that his close subordinates endeavored to impede and frustrate lawful inquiries by duly constituted executive, judicial and legislative entities concerning the unlawful entry into the headquarters of the Democratic National Committee, and the cover-up thereof, and concerning other unlawful activities including those relating to the confirmation of Richard Kleindienst as Attorney General of the United States, the electronic surveillance of private citizens, the break-in into the offices of Dr. Lewis Fielding, and the campaign financing practices of the Committee to Re-elect the President.

5. In disregard of the rule of law, he knowingly misused the executive power by interfering with agencies of the executive branch, including the Federal Bureau of Investigation, the Criminal Division, and the Office of Watergate Special Prosecution Force, of the Department of Justice, and the Central Intelligence Agency,

> in violation of his duty to take care that the laws be
> faithfully executed.
>
> In all of this, Richard M. Nixon has acted in a manner
> contrary to his trust as President and subversive of constitu-
> tional government, to the great prejudice of the cause of law
> and justice and to the manifest injury of the people of the
> United States.[73]

Article III is arguably the most important. It establishes the
principle that invoking executive privilege to refuse to answer
questions or to provide documents in an impeachment inquiry
is itself an impeachable offense. The impeachment power would
be toothless if the president could conceal incriminating information, which characteristically is within his exclusive custody
or control. Furthermore, self-government and congressional
oversight of the executive branch is a farce if the people and
members of Congress are prevented from knowing what the
president is doing and why. Accordingly, Article III assails President Nixon's unresponsiveness to the Committee's subpoenas:

> In the conduct of the office of President of the United States,
> Richard M. Nixon, contrary to his oath faithfully to execute
> the office of President of the United States and, to the best
> of his ability, preserve, protect, and defend the Constitution
> of the United States, and in violation of his duty to take care
> that the laws be faithfully executed, has failed without lawful
> cause or excuse to produce papers and things as directed by
> duly authorized subpoenas issued by the Committee on the
> Judiciary of the House of Representatives on April 11, 1974,
> May 15, 1974, May 30, 1974, and June 24, 1974, and will-
> fully disobeyed such subpoenas. The subpoenaed papers and
> things were deemed necessary by the Committee in order to
> resolve by direct evidence fundamental factual questions relat-
> ing to Presidential direction, knowledge or approval of actions
> demonstrated by other evidence to be substantial grounds for

impeachment of the President. In refusing to produce these papers and things Richard M. Nixon, substituting his judgment as to what materials were necessary for the inquiry, interposed powers of the Presidency against the lawful subpoenas of the House of Representatives, thereby assuming to himself functions and judgments necessary to the exercise of the sole power of impeachment vested by the Constitution in the House of Representatives.

In all of this, Richard M. Nixon has acted in a manner contrary to his trust as President and subversive of constitutional government, to the great prejudice of the cause of law and justice, and to the manifest injury to the people of the United States.[74]

Before the three articles were presented to the full House of Representatives for debate and voting, the U.S. Supreme Court in *United States v. Nixon* (1974)[75] rejected President Nixon's claim of executive privilege to withhold from Special Prosecutor Jaworksi 64 tapes and related documents that exposed his efforts to obstruct justice. The president bowed to the Supreme Court's decree. The tapes implicated President Nixon in obstruction of justice. His impeachment in the House and conviction in the Senate became a foregone conclusion. Republican Senator Barry Goldwater (AZ), an arch-conservative and erstwhile presidential candidate in 1964, conveyed the unwelcome news to the president and urged resignation. To escape further embarrassment and humiliation, President Nixon reluctantly accepted the advice and resigned on August 9, 1974. I was electrified by the broadcast of Nixon's White House departure. Thinking of Churchill, I hymned, "This has been one of America's finest hours. The Constitution had been saved for the moment by a combination of statesmanship and an aroused public refusing to accept vassalage."

The Nixon impeachment precedent would have been far stronger if the full House had debated and voted articles of impeachment, and if the Senate had held a trial. The televised proceedings would have instructed the public about the Constitution. An ignorant citizenry will be oblivious to constitutional violations and usurpations. The televised Senate Watergate hearings had performed yeoman's service on that score, including former White House counsel John Dean's "cancer on the presidency"[76] testimony and White House adviser John Ehrlichman's chilling defense of President Nixon's authority to commit burglary or other crimes. President George Washington elaborated in the first presidential address to Congress on the State of the Union,

> To the security of a free constitution [knowledge] contributes in various ways . . . by teaching the people themselves to know, and to value their own rights; to discern and provide against invasions of them; to distinguish between oppression and the necessary exigencies of lawful authority, between burdens proceeding from a disregard to their convenience and those resulting from the inevitable exigencies of society; to discriminate the spirit of liberty from that of licentiousness, cherishing the first, avoiding the last, and uniting a speedy but temperate vigilance against encroachments, with an inviolable respect to the laws.[77]

President Nixon never acknowledged his multiple crimes against the Constitution. President Gerald Ford's pardon frustrated a possible criminal trial, which would have offered another opportunity to teach the American people about the Constitution's rule of law, checks and balances, and celebration of transparency over secret government.

I believed, nevertheless, that Nixon's resignation would deter future presidents from sneering at the rule of law and the presidential oath or affirmation prescribed in Article II, Section 1 of the Constitution: "I do solemnly swear (or affirm) that I will faithfully execute the office of president of the United States, and will to the best of my Ability, preserve, protect and defend the Constitution of the United States."[78]

I proved a poor prophet.

Impeachment returned to the political stage with President William Jefferson Clinton. He presented less danger to our constitutional system than did Richard Nixon, but the impeachment clause is not reserved for the worst offenders. It reaches all official misconduct that seriously erodes the rule of law or cripples checks and balances.

I did not vote for President Clinton. But I strongly supported his right to appoint executive officers or judges of his philosophical persuasion irrespective of the opposition of a Republican controlled Senate. I held the same constitutional conviction in serving as associate deputy attorney general under President Ronald Reagan. The Appointments Clause of the Constitution, including the Senate's confirmation role, was intended to enable the president to speak with a single voice and thus to control the views of his subordinates to promote political accountability. The president could be blamed for failures and given kudos for successes. I thus criticized Republican senators for blocking the nomination of Bill Lann Lee as assistant attorney general for civil rights in the Department of Justice. I further deplored Republican maneuvering to block Senate votes on Clinton's judicial nominees.

On the other hand, I strenuously supported President Clinton's impeachment for lying about his relationship with Monica Lewinsky a second time before a grand jury; refusing to confess that lying under oath violated his presidential oath and duty to take care that the laws be faithfully executed; and declining to answer questions submitted by the House Judiciary Committee in its impeachment inquiry. I championed impeachment not because the president was a Democrat (Vice President Al Gore would have acceded to the presidency if impeachment succeeded), but because I believed the Constitution and the rule of law is too precious to be crucified on a cross of presidential lies under oath.

President Clinton was a lawyer, not a legal ingénue. During his January 1997 deposition in the Paula Jones civil suit, he could have refused to answer embarrassing questions about Monica Lewinsky to protect his privacy or otherwise. Adverse inferences could have been drawn from the president's silence, but he would not have violated his constitutional obligation to eschew lying under oath. But the president lied and obstructed justice. In *Jones v. Clinton* (E.D. Ark. 1999),[79] Judge Susan Webber Wright held President Clinton in civil contempt and amplified, "[T]here simply is no escaping the fact that the president deliberately violated this Court's discovery Orders and thereby undermined the integrity of the judicial system. Sanctions must be imposed, not only to redress the president's misconduct, but to deter others who might themselves consider emulating the president of the United States by engaging in misconduct that undermines the integrity of the judicial system."[80]

Even the first lie under oath would not have justified impeachment if President Clinton had confessed his wrongdoing and expressed remorse for violating his obligation to take care that the laws be faithfully executed. A confession would have avoided creating a noxious legal precedent that the president is above the law. As noted earlier, he teaches the people by example. If he becomes a lawbreaker, the rule of law is endangered. That explains why the Constitution saddles the president with the responsibility of faithfully executing, not circumventing, the laws.

President Clinton chose not to confess. Indeed, he disparaged his critics through his wife, Hillary Clinton, and others as members of a right-wing conspiracy. After eight months had elapsed since his initial lie, President Clinton repeated his prevarication about his relations with Lewinsky before a federal grand jury. He quibbled over the meaning of the words "is" and "alone."[81] And the president again declined to apologize for his lies and misleading statements.

When the House Judiciary Committee commenced an impeachment inquiry, the president refused to answer relevant questions. Clinton's nonresponsiveness seemed a carbon copy of President Nixon's stonewalling to the Committee in 1974 that had justified the third article of impeachment.

The two articles ultimately voted against President Clinton by the House of Representatives seemed to me to be justified by the Nixon precedent. The gravamen was lying and obstructing justice in a civil case, to which the president was a party. President Nixon had been accused by the House Judiciary Committee of comparable misconduct in an attempt to obstruct a criminal proceeding. To be sure, criminal cases are more important to the rule of law than civil litigation. Furthermore, Nixon was implicated in a political crime against the Democratic Party. Clinton was covering up sexual infidelity and licentiousness. But those distinctions simply showed that Nixon was more impeachable than Clinton, not that Clinton's impenitent lies under oath failed to meet the high crimes and misdemeanors threshold. Perjury and obstruction of justice are exceptionally worrisome offenses, especially when committed by role models like the president or his inner circle. To paraphrase Justice Brandeis in *Olmstead v. United States* (1928),[82] the president is the potent and omnipresent teacher. He teaches the people by his example, and if he becomes a lawbreaker, he invites every man to become a law unto himself.[83] This explains Scooter Libby's stiff prison sentence imposed by U.S. District Judge Reggie Walton before President George W. Bush's controversial commutation. The U.S. Supreme Court explained in *ABF Freight System, Inc v. NLRB* (1994),[84] "False testimony in a formal proceeding is intolerable. We must neither reward nor condone such a 'flagrant affront' to the truth—seeking function of adversary proceedings."[85]

The first article of impeachment against President Clinton echoed President Nixon's lies to cover-up Watergate. It charged,

In his conduct while President of the United States . . . in violation of his constitutional oath to faithfully execute the office of President . . . he has . . . undermined the integrity of his office . . . betrayed his trust as President . . . and acted in a manner subversive of the rule of law by:

- willfully corrupting and manipulating the judicial process of the United States for his personal gain and exoneration;
- willfully committing perjury by providing false and misleading testimony to the grand jury in relation to his relationship with an employee;
- willfully committing perjury by providing false and misleading testimony to the grand jury in relation to prior perjurious testimony in a civil rights action brought against him;
- allowing his attorney to make false and misleading statements in the same civil rights action; and,
- attempting to influence witness testimony to slow discovery of evidence in that civil rights action.[86]

The second article of impeachment resembled the obstruction of justice allegations in the impeachment articles against Nixon:

President William Jefferson Clinton has [in the Paula Jones Case] prevented, obstructed, and impeded the administration of justice by:

- encouraging a witness to give a perjurious affidavit;
- encouraging a witness to give false testimony if called to the stand;
- allowing and/or encouraging the concealment of subpoenaed evidence;

- attempting to sway a witness testimony by providing a job for that witness;
- allowing his attorney to make misleading testimony;
- giving false or misleading information to influence the testimony of a potential witness in a Federal civil rights action; and,
- giving false ore misleading information to influence the testimony of a witness in a grand jury investigation.[87]

To my dismay, the Senate summarily acquitted President Clinton. The Constitution had only suffered a flesh wound, but it was a wound nonetheless. My chagrin stemmed from these lines ascribed to Sir Thomas More in *A Man for All Seasons*:

The law Roper, the law. I know what's legal, not what's right. And I'll stick to what's legal. . . . I'm not God. The currents and eddies of right and wrong, which you find such plain-sailing, I can't navigate, I'm no voyager. But in the thickets of the law, oh there I'm a forester. . . . What would you do? Cut a great road through the law to get after the Devil? . . . And when the last law is down, and the Devil turned round on you—where would you hide, Roper, the laws all being flat? . . . This country's planted thick with laws from coast to coast—Man's laws, not God's—and if you cut them down . . . d'you really think you could stand upright in the winds that would blow them? . . . Yes, I'd give the Devil benefit of law, for my own safety's sake.[88]

I was happy with President George W. Bush's defeat of Vice President Al Gore in 2000. The latter had shamelessly defended President Clinton's multiple lies under oath.

Then came September 11, 2001. It put to the test the cardinal constitutional principles that informed the Nixon and Clinton impeachments. It further demonstrated that defending the Constitution is the never-ending task and obligation of the American people. There is never a time for complacency.

FOUR

Setting the Stage

Contrary to Vice President Richard B. Cheney's claims, President George W. Bush entered office with the powers of the presidency at their zenith in both foreign and domestic affairs.[1] Congress had surrendered vast powers over war and peace to the president. The last occasions in which Congress played an instrumental role in foreign policy were over the League of Nations[2] after World War I and the Neutrality Acts[3] in the 1930s.

The War Powers Resolution of 1973,[4] enacted with the aim of confining the president's authority to initiate and continue military hostilities, had been reduced to sound and fury. The resolution purported to place a 60-day limit on the president's deployment of the military to conduct hostilities, which was subject to congressional extensions. But during that interim, the president could blunder into a military quagmire—as is the case with Iraq today—with no viable exit option. Furthermore, the resolution tacitly acknowledged an inherent constitutional power in the President to initiate warfare for 60 days without authorization from Congress—which contradicted the intent of the Founding Fathers.

Moreover, Section 2's limitation on the president's authority to wage war was illusory. It provided, "The constitutional powers of the President, as Commander-in-Chief to introduce the United States Armed Forces into hostilities, or situations where imminent involvement in hostilities is clearly indicated by the circumstances, are exercised only pursuant to (1) a declaration of war, (2) specific statutory authorization, or (3) a national emergency created by at attack upon the United States, its territories or possessions, or its armed forces."[5]

But those congressional restraints were eclipsed by Section 8(d)'s declaration that the resolution did not intend to challenge the president's claim to unilateral war-making power: "Nothing in this joint resolution (1) is intended to alter the constitutional authority of Congress or of the President."[6] Congress should have written a statute that explicitly prohibited the president from initiating warfare in any circumstance without prior congressional authorization and criminalized the expenditure of any funds of the United States to deploy the military in violation of the war prohibition.

The president entered office empowered to revoke treaties unilaterally without the participation of the Senate. The U.S. Supreme Court had determined in *Goldwater v. Carter* (1979)[7] that President Jimmy Carter was justified in unilaterally terminating the Taiwan Defense Treaty to placate Communist China. President Bush employed that authority to terminate the U.S. Anti-Ballistic Missile Treaty with Russia in 2003. Congress had delegated sweeping authority to the president to freeze assets or financial transactions to achieve national security objectives under the International Emergency Economic Powers Act (IEEPA). The Supreme Court held in *Dames & Moore v. Regan* (1981)[8] that the IEEPA justified President Carter's blocking the removal or transfer of "all property and interests in property of the Government of Iran, its instrumentalities and controlled entities and the Central Bank of Iran which are or become subject to the jurisdiction of the United States."[9]

One year earlier in *Snepp v. United States* (1980),[10] the Supreme Court upheld the power of the president to require Central Intelligence Agency (CIA) officials to submit all writing to the agency for prepublication review of classified information and to capture the profits made by any violations.

The Clark Amendment, which ended funding for the CIA's covert operations in Angola in 1975, had not been repeated or emulated by succeeding Congresses.[11] Neither did the Bush–Cheney administration confront second editions of the notorious Boland Amendments, which occasioned the Iran-Contra Affair and clipped President Ronald Reagan's assistance to the Nicaraguan resistance that was fighting Daniel Ortega's Sandanistas. Congress similarly chose not to place limits on military advisers in countries beset by guerillas aided by Cuba or Russia, as had been done earlier for El Salvador.[12]

The Supreme Court in *Immigration and Naturalization Service v. Chadha* (1983)[13] had invalidated the legislative veto (a congressional mechanism to block or force executive action by the vote of one chamber or both chambers, or by a congressional committee, a legislative tool that circumvented the president's qualified veto power). Legislative vetoes had been used, among other things, to block controversial arms sales.

Congress had accepted open-ended authority for President George H. W. Bush to war against Manuel Noriega in Panama and against Saddam Hussein in Iraq, and for President William Jefferson Clinton to employ military force against Serbia's Slobodan Milošević in Bosnia and Kosovo.[14] The Foreign Intelligence Surveillance Act of 1978 (FISA),[15] which generally required judicial warrants to justify targeting American citizens on American soil for electronic surveillance or physical searches to gather foreign intelligence, had elicited no presidential complaints that the statute was impairing national security over the succeeding 23 years. Virtually every warrant application had been granted by the Foreign Intelligence Surveillance Court. The president's authority to kidnap foreigners abroad and transport them for trial in the United States had been affirmed by the Supreme Court in *United States v. Alvarez-Machain* (1992).[16] The Fourth Amendment's protection against unreasonable searches and seizures, the Court also held in *United States v. Verdugo-Urdiquez* (1990),[17] generally did not extend outside the United States, at least regarding noncitizens.

In sum, President Bush stood at the commanding heights of national security powers at his first inauguration in January 2001. And his vast powers in both foreign and domestic affairs had been fortified by the Supreme Court's decision in *Nixon v. Fitzgerald* (1982),[18] which held that the president was absolutely immune from damage suits for presidential acts, and by the lapse of the Independent Counsel Act that had so bedeviled President Clinton.[19]

The abominations on September 11, 2001, were not caused by national security constraints on President Bush, a conclusion supported by the 9/11 Commission. They were dastardly criminal acts that might have been thwarted by shrewd application of customary investigatory and prosecutorial tools. Indeed, Zacarias Moussaoui—the so-called twentieth hijacker—was detained, prosecuted, and sentenced to life imprisonment through the ordinary criminal justice system.[20] Terrorist Ramzi Yousef had been earlier prosecuted and convicted for the 1993 bombing of the World Trade Center.[21] José Padilla, who had initially been detained as an enemy combatant, was later charged and convicted on August 16, 2007, in a federal civilian court, of conspiring to provide and providing material assistance to a foreign terrorist organization.[22]

The 9/11 terrorist attacks in particular and international terrorism generally fall short of the threshold of national danger customarily required to justify war powers—for example, military commissions, indefinite detentions of enemy combatants, or the suspension of habeas corpus. Not every gruesome or frightening crime of violence constitutes an act of war.

Timothy McVeigh killed hundreds of people in the Oklahoma City bombing, yet the mass murder did not place the nation on a war footing. Mr. McVeigh was tried, convicted, and sentenced to death in the civilian criminal justice system.[23] Al Qaeda bombed U.S. embassies in Kenya and Tanzania in 1998.[24] Americans were killed and wounded. The culprits in the murders were prosecuted and punished in the ordinary course of law enforcement.

The American deaths caused by international terrorism have not reached levels associated with war. Approximately three thousand people died on September 11, 2001, a number greater than Pearl Harbor's grisly casualty toll.[25] But not a single additional American has been killed by a terrorist attack in the United States in more than six years, leaving a death rate of five hundred per year. (American war deaths in Afghanistan and Iraq since September 11, 2001, approximate four thousand, but only a tiny fraction of that number can be attributed to Al Qaeda.)[26]

During that same period, annual murders in the United States averaged more than 16,000, or a rate 32 times as great as the corresponding terrorist carnage.[27] Yet the United States is not at war with murderers. The criminal justice system is not said to be ineffective because it fails to deter or to thwart 16,000 murders annually. It is no more persuasive to argue that subjecting international terrorists to criminal justice by civilian courts does not work because the convictions of Ramzi Yousef, and the Kenya and Tanzania embassy terrorists did not deter the events of 9/11.

War ordinarily occasions civilian sacrifices by the nation in support of military troops. President Bush has asked virtually nothing of civilians in the conflict with international terrorism and the wars in Iraq and Afghanistan. Brave men and women in the voluntary armed forces and their families and friends are doing all of the heavy lifting.

The Constitution authorizes Congress to suspend the Great Writ of habeas corpus in times of "rebellion" or "invasion," presumptive earmarks of war.[28] (The Great Writ entitles detainees held on the president's say-so alone to challenge the factual or legal foundation for their detentions before an impartial and independent magistrate.) Neither 9/11 nor subsequent international terrorist acts have entailed an invasion or rebellion. Thus, the U.S. Supreme Court held in *Boumediene v. Bush* (June 12, 2008)[29] that Congress was powerless to suspend the Great Writ for enemy combatant detainees at Guantanamo Bay.

A threat to national sovereignty is a prominent proxy of war—for example, the Civil War or World War II. The conflict with international terrorism, in contrast, raises no threat to the sovereignty of the United States. On November 13, 2001, President Bush issued a military order that asserted that Al Qaeda and sister terrorist organizations "possess both the capability and the intention to undertake further terrorist attacks against the United States that, if not detected and prevented, will cause mass deaths, mass injuries, and massive destruction of property, and may place at risk the continuity of the operations of the United States Government."[30] The Soviet Union posed a vastly greater danger to the United States during the cold war, but that ever-present threat to U.S. sovereignty did not justify the exercise of presidential war powers.

War customarily carries a benchmark for a termination of hostilities: an enemy surrender, a truce, or a peace treaty. While traditional wars have carried no automatic time limit at their inceptions, ordinary limits on the political, economic, and military capacity for armed conflict have made perpetual war unthinkable. The conflict with international terrorism, however, defies any termination benchmark. Neither President Bush nor his champions have attempted to articulate a level of terrorist threat or violence that would signal the end of the "war" with international terrorism. The president and Congress have endorsed the idea that the terrorist war will continue as long as one terrorist anywhere on the planet threatens to kill an American. Under that definition, the nation will be in perpetual war, a condition anathema to freedom. No president will ever say that the risk of an international terrorist attack had plunged to zero and risk embarrassment or humiliation within hours.

No convincing evidence has emerged indicating that international terrorism defies defeat by the application of criminal justice in civilian courts and the treatment of terrorists as criminals. Individuals have been prosecuted and convicted for terrorist acts or for providing material assistance to a terrorist organization. Terrorist conspiracies have been detected and thwarted in their pre-embryonic stages. The Classified Information Procedures Act of 1980[31] enables the prosecution of terrorists without disclosing intelligence sources or methods. The 9/11 Commission did not recommend military justice in lieu of criminal justice just to defeat a second edition of 9/11.

Detractors of criminal justice assert that terrorist plots require more time to investigate than other crimes. Accordingly, the government should be entitled to detain terrorist suspects for months, if not years, before trial. Spain and France authorize up to four years of pretrial detentions.[32] But no convincing evidence has been forthcoming showing that international terrorism is more difficult to investigate than international drug trafficking, smuggling, or organized crime rings. To be sure, international terrorism is a much more dangerous crime. The failure to detect a terrorist is more threatening to society than a failure to detect a smuggler of undocumented aliens.

But identifying terrorist suspects is also more troublesome than identifying drug traffickers or smugglers or organized crime figures. The Bush administration defines a terrorist or enemy combatant as any person who provides support or encouragement to a terrorist organization,[33] which could be stretched to include speech that voices sympathy for some of the aims of Al Qaeda—for example, a removal of U.S. troops from the Middle East or a cessation of U.S. support for Israel. Thus, the percentage of false positives in identifying terrorist suspects is probably much higher than the corresponding percentages for other crimes. Glaring injustices are risked by protracted periods of pretrial detention of suspected terrorists that will find their way to Al Jazeera television and to Al Qaeda recruitment stations. Americans are again made less safe.

Terrorism is also said to confound criminal justice because plots must be foiled in their infancy, when evidence of guilt is sparse, to avoid the possibility of them ripening into gruesome successes. Accordingly, detentions should be permitted indefinitely without accusation. But sparse evidence of guilt points also to innocence. Moreover, to a hammer, everything is a nail; and to a spy, anything unorthodox, unconventional, or disagreeable is treason. The mental temperament of a spy is suspicion. James Angleton, for example, the fabled CIA chief of counterintelligence who served for decades, maintained that every Soviet defector was a double agent and that Soviet moles were rife within the CIA itself.[34] With this as a key example, the risk of misidentifying enemy combatants is thus high. The problem is compounded by the routine infiltration of terrorists into civilian populations.

To abandon the requirement of concrete evidence of wrongdoing to justify detentions or punishments is to embrace a military-police state and turn the Declaration of Independence on its head. The Declaration states that governments are instituted among men to secure the unalienable rights of individuals to life, liberty, and the pursuit of happiness, not to exercise arbitrary power.[35]

Terrorist investigations involve global evidence trails that traverse many countries and require the cooperation of other governments. But the same can be said of international drug trafficking or smuggling investigations. And the latter may be more difficult to thwart because law enforcement officials are regularly bribed by drug traffickers or smugglers to desist from collaboration with the FBI (Federal Bureau of Investigation) or CIA. Moreover, friendly democratic governments will partner with the United States in counterterrorism covert actions or intelligence sharing only if procedural and substantive safe-guards against abuses are observed. Great Britain, Italy, and Germany are illustrative cases of this.

Jack Goldsmith, former assistant attorney general for the office of legal counsel in the Department of Justice under President Bush, maintains that "sometimes the government simply lacks evidence enough to convict a terrorist even though clear evidence shows that the terrorist is a danger to society. The rationale for detention—prevention of possible future harm to society—is the same as traditional non-criminal detentions for the mentally incompetent and people with infectious diseases."[36] Mr. Goldsmith's argument is chilling, like a chapter from Aleksandr Solzhenitsyn's *Gulag Archipelago*.[37] The law of conspiracy and the law of attempt enable the government to prosecute terrorists before any harmful terrorist activity. José Padilla, for example, was convicted of conspiracy to provide material assistance to a terrorist organization in a civilian court.[38] The Lackawanna Six, a handful of Arab Americans who attended an Al Qaeda camp, were convicted of providing material support to Al Qaeda before any threat to the United States had germinated.[39] Goldsmith is proposing that the law go beyond conspiracy or attempts to punish persons who are a "danger to society." But every person has the potential of committing a terrorist act. Everyone holds the possibility of future harm to society. Goldsmith is clueless as to what evidence distinguishes inherent dangerousness that should be left unpunished from dangerousness that should trigger punishment.

Detentions based on the possibility of future harm are life sentences. Not even a saint could disprove a microscopic possibility of committing a future antisocial act. "Danger to society" detentions are unlike quarantining persons with infectious diseases. A disease may be cured, and quarantine leaves the freedom of the detainee undisturbed except for direct contact with other humans who might become infected. The mentally incompetent can be detained only if the government proves by clear and convincing evidence that the detainee is a danger to himself or others. The government must periodically review any initial dangerous finding to justify continuing detention. In contrast, danger-to-society detentions based on a potential for terrorism are permanent.

In addition, there has been no persuasive evidence since 9/11 that international terrorism requires abandoning civilian justice for military justice. Only two American citizens and one resident alien have been held as unlawful enemy combatants. There has been but one trial and one guilty plea before a military commission.[40] President Abraham Lincoln during the Civil War rhetorically asked Congress on July 4, 1861, "Is there, in all republics, this inherent and fatal weakness? . . . Must a government, of necessity, be too strong for the liberties of its own people, or too weak to maintain its own existence?"[41] At least in the United States, the answer is "no."

If the United States is at war with international terrorism everywhere in the world, military power can be employed anywhere to capture and kill individuals suspected of terrorism on the president's say-so alone, despite the inevitability of cruel collateral damage. This idea is vivified by a May 23, 2008, report in *The Washington Post* on civilian casualties in the Iraqi war:

> On Wednesday, eight people, including two children, were killed when a U.S. helicopter opened fire on a group of Iraqis traveling to a U.S. detention center to greet a man who was being released from custody, Iraqi officials said.
>
> The U.S. military said in a statement that it had targeted men linked to a suicide bombing network. "Unfortunately, two children were killed when the other occupants in the vehicle, in which they were riding, exhibited hostile intent," the statement said.
>
> "It's not Hollywood and it's not 110 [percent] perfect," said Col. Timothy J. Edens, the commander of the 12th Combat Aviation Brigade, of the accuracy of his unit's strikes. "It

is as precise as very hard-working soldiers and commanders can make it. These criminals do not operate in a clean battle space. It is occupied by civilians, law-abiding Iraqis."

Those civilians include people like Zahara Fadhil, a 10-year-old girl with a tiny frame and long brown hair. Relatives said she was wounded by a missile on April 20 at approximately 8 p.m. in Baghdad's Shiite enclave of Sadr City. . . . "[U.S. troops] kill people," she said. Lying in bed, she gasped for air before continuing. "They should leave Iraq now."[42]

The Constitution is not a suicide pact. Self-preservation is the law of every nation. But nothing in the state of constitutional law or the facts concerning international terrorism indicates a justification for abandoning customary constitutional norms and principles in responding to the danger.

FIVE

The Foreign Intelligence Surveillance Act

In 1970 the nation was in upheaval over Vietnam. At Kent State University and Jackson State University, college students were shot as they protested the war. The streets brimmed with antiwar demonstrators. President Richard M. Nixon believed revolutionary violence was afoot. On June 5 he summoned the heads of intelligence agencies to the Oval Office. There he instructed them to join a committee to prepare a threat assessment, identify current restraints on intelligence collection, and present options for their relaxation.

The result was the so-called Huston Plan, named after a junior White House aide, Tom Charles Huston. It recommended, among other things, illegal mail openings, burglaries, illegal, warrantless electronic surveillance, and the recruitment of college campus spies in the hope of finding foreign influence on Vietnam War detractors in the United States. President Nixon approved the assault on the rule of law and citizen privacy, and the plan was dispatched for implementation to the FBI,

CIA, and military intelligence agencies. American journalist Theodore White observed that, if it had been enacted, the Huston Plan would have empowered the federal government to reach "all the way to every mailbox, every college campus, every telephone, every home."[1] Five days after his approval, President Nixon revoked the plan at the insistence of FBI Director J. Edgar Hoover and Attorney General John Mitchell, although neither was customarily squeamish about infringements on civil liberties.

The Huston Plan, nevertheless, was implemented piecemeal, and in different moods and tenses. Egil Krogh, former deputy assistant to President Nixon, recently recounted his involvement in a national security burglary, which fit the Huston Plan like a glove, in a column he authored for the *International Herald Tribune*:

> In early August 1971, I attended a secret meeting in Room 16, a hideaway office in the basement of the Old Executive Office Building, across the street from the White House. Huddled around the table were G. Gordon Liddy, a former FBI agent; E. Howard Hunt, a former CIA agent; and David R. Young Jr., a member of the National Security Council staff . . .
>
> Two months earlier, [t]he *New York Times* had published the classified Pentagon Papers, which had been provided by Daniel Ellsberg. Nixon had told me he viewed the leak as a matter of critical importance to national security. He ordered me and others, a group that would come to be called the "plumbers," to find out how the leak had happened and keep it from happening again.
>
> Hunt urged us to carry out a "covert operation" to get a "mother lode" of information about Ellsberg's mental state, to discredit him, by breaking into the office of his psychiatrist, Dr. Lewis Fielding. . . .
>
> I listened intently. At no time did I or anyone else there question whether the operation was necessary, legal[,] or

moral. Convinced that we were responding legitimately to a national security crisis, we focused instead on the operational details. . . .

On September 3, 1971, burglars broke into Fielding's Beverly Hills office to photograph the files, but found nothing related to Ellsberg.

The premise of our action was the strongly held view within certain precincts of the White House that the president and those functioning on his behalf could carry out illegal acts with impunity if they were convinced that the nation's security demanded it. . . .

With the Fielding break-in, some of us in the Nixon White House crossed the Rubicon into the realm of lawbreakers. In November 1973, I pleaded guilty to criminal conspiracy in depriving Fielding of his civil rights, specifically his constitutional right to be free from an unwarranted search. . . .

In early 2001, after George W. Bush was inaugurated, I sent the new White House staff a memo explaining the importance of never losing their personal integrity. In a section addressed specifically to White House lawyers, I said that integrity required them constantly to ask, is it legal? And I recommended that they rely on well-established legal precedent and not some hazy, loose notion of what phrases like "national security" and "commander in chief" could be tortured into meaning.[2]

The White House scoffed at Krogh's personal history lesson and forgot the discredited Huston Plan and the origins of the Foreign Intelligence Surveillance Act of 1978 (FISA), a statute provoked by decades of presidential spying abuses, which included Nixon's. The Church Committee wrote,

Our findings and the detailed reports which supplement this volume set forth a massive record of intelligence abuses over the years. Through the use of a vast network of informants, and through the uncontrolled or illegal use of intrusive techniques—ranging from simple theft to sophisticated electronic surveillance—the Government has collected, and then used improperly, huge amounts of information about the private lives, political beliefs and associations of numerous Americans.[3]

The Committee further concluded that "intelligence activities have undermined the constitutional rights of citizens and they have done so primarily because checks and balances designed by the framers of the Constitution to assure accountability have not been applied."[4] FISA's chief feature was judicial supervision of electronic surveillance (and physical searches after a 1994 amendment) targeting American citizens to gather foreign intelligence.[5] The strength of congressional concern to protect citizen privacy found expression in making FISA violations criminal.

In the aftermath of 9/11, however, President George W. Bush instructed the National Security Agency (NSA) to intercept the e-mails and phone conversations of American citizens on American soil on his say-so alone, in direct criminal contravention of FISA—President Bush's so-called Terrorist Surveillance Program (TSP).[6] (A leak from the executive branch to the *New York Times* led to public and congressional knowledge of the illegal spying on December 16, 2005.)[7]

The canard that 9/11 could have been foiled if FISA had not handcuffed the collection of foreign intelligence must be exposed. President Bush has never made that claim; the 9/11 Commission did not make that claim. And these are the words of Mark M. Lowenthal, assistant director of central intelligence and vice chairman of the National Intelligence Council from 2002 to 2005:

No one has yet revealed the one or two or [ten] things that, had they been done differently, might have prevented the attacks. In my view, and in the view of many of my colleagues, even missed "operational opportunities" identified by the 9/11 Commission would have done little more than force [A]l Qaeda to send different terrorists into the United States, especially considering the legal rules in play at that time. Even if every "dot" had been connected, they would not have led to the tactical intelligence needed to stop these four planes on that Tuesday morning.

This is a profoundly disturbing message to send. Political leaders and the public would rather believe that [A]l Qaeda's attacks exploited flaws that have been found and fixed, letting us all return to our pre-9/11 feeling of safety.[8]

President Bush's FISA crimes continued for more than five years until Attorney General Alberto Gonzales abandoned the TSP in favor of FISA warrants in January 2007.[9] There were no mitigating circumstances for the crimes. If President Bush thought that FISA was handcuffing his ability to collect foreign intelligence that was needed to thwart another 9/11, he could have obtained the necessary amendments from Congress. Congress has amended FISA on numerous occasions since September 11, 2001, to accommodate President Bush, including the Patriot Act.[10] If President Bush believed that the urgency of the 9/11 situation required that he act immediately without waiting for congressional amendments, he could have sought congressional ratification of his illegal spying akin to congressional ratification of President Abraham Lincoln's suspension of the Great Writ of habeas corpus during the Civil War.

But President Bush did neither. And putting aside the criminality of the TSP, Bush has failed to adduce a crumb of evidence that FISA, with its various amendments, was deficient. President Bush's crimes were not intended to protect Americans but rather to set a precedent that would make the president a king in national security affairs. Indeed, as Bush's own Justice Department was effusing over FISA's nimbleness and muscularity to the Senate Intelligence Committee, Bush was absurdly insisting on the need for criminal violations of the law to protect Americans.[11] The president's cynical attitude was captured in a chilling remark by David Addington, Vice President Cheney's counsel: "We're one bomb away from getting rid of that obnoxious [FISA] court."[12]

President Bush's countless FISA crimes are sufficient, standing alone, to justify his impeachment, conviction, and removal for high crimes and misdemeanors. On a constitutional plane, they are indistinguishable from President Nixon's complicity in the Watergate cover-up and illegal spying, which triggered his impeachment proceedings. The rule of law is the signature of the American Republic, as underscored by President Lincoln in 1838:

> Let reverence for the laws, be breathed by every American mother, to the lisping babe, that prattles on her lap—let it be taught in schools, in seminaries, and in colleges; let it be written in Primers, spelling books, and in Almanacs;—let it be preached from the pulpit, proclaimed in legislative halls, and enforced in courts of justice. And, in short, let it become the political religion of the nation; and let the old and the young, the rich and the poor, the grave and the gay, of all sexes and tongues, and colors and conditions, sacrifice unceasingly upon its altars.[13]

Until September 11, 2001, more than 23 years since 1978, presidents had collected foreign intelligence subject to FISA without complaining that national security had been compromised. That interval included periods of high danger and tragedy: the cold war generally, the Islamic Revolution in Iran, the Soviet invasion of Afghanistan, the U.S. invasion of Panama, the 1993 World Trade Center bombings, the conflicts in Bosnia and Serbia, the Kenya and Tanzania embassy bombings, Communist Chinese threats to invade Taiwan, and so on.

Furthermore, the 9/11 Commission saw no need to alter FISA in recommending a menu of reforms to defeat international terrorism. And 9/11 did not alter prevailing international tele-communications networks. But even if Bush had discerned genuine FISA deficiencies after 9/11, the Constitution required that he ask Congress for amendments in lieu of flouting the law. And in the aftermath of 9/11, Congress and the American people would have supported anything Bush proposed. But the day it becomes acceptable for the president to disobey any law he believes to be imprudent is the day the Republic has yielded to dictatorship.

President Bush violated FISA as part of his scheme with Vice President Richard B. Cheney to cripple congressional power over national security matters. The president correctly predicted that Congress would shy from rebuking him over his FISA crimes, which would set a precedent for the idea that no other branch may second-guess the president's national security decisions. The president also claimed unchecked power to open citizens' mail, break and enter homes, kidnap, or torture to gather foreign intelligence, which includes economic information about foreign nations or organizations. On matters of separation of powers, past political practices between the branches are nine-tenths of the law. Historical custom was the foundation for the Supreme Court's recognition of a qualified executive privilege in *United States v. Nixon* (1974).[14]

President Bush also asserted constitutional authority to conceal from Congress and the American people in perpetuity the existence of the NSA's criminal violations of FISA and sister secret spying programs. At this very moment, Congress knows little if anything more about President Bush's criminal encroachments on the right of citizens to be left alone than what has been leaked to the media by the executive branch: how many Americans have been spied on without warrants, how individuals were selected as spy targets, what was done with the information collected, what percentage of targets yielded useful counterterrorism information, whether the information collected could also have been intercepted with a FISA warrant, or whether a specific terrorist act or plot was thwarted because of the warrantless surveillance program. The congressional leadership was informed of the general outline of the TSP under injunctions of absolute secrecy, including current House Speaker Nancy Pelosi and Congresswoman Jane Harmon (D-CA).[15] The injunctions, however, were constitutionally unenforceable. Under the Speech or Debate Clause, the members could have disclosed the criminal violations on the floor of Congress or in a committee hearing with impunity.[16] Yet all remained silent, which made them politically if not legally complicit in Bush's crimes. That explains why a Democrat-controlled Congress has shied from holding President Bush accountable for flouting FISA. All that is necessary for the triumph of evil is for good men and women to do nothing.[17]

President Bush's FISA crimes and his government's unacknowledged secret spying programs clearly constitute crimes against society that the Founding Fathers conceived as impeachable offenses. Citizen privacy has been invaded and a database has probably been collected with the potential for blackmail, intimidation, and political retaliation. That is the lessen of the Church Committee hearings about unchecked intelligence collection.[18] The knowledge that the government is spying and building files on citizens from the president's say-so alone chills political dissent, boldness, and spontaneity—all of which enrich democratic discourse, the political process, and the pursuit of happiness. The retribution visited on Ambassador Joseph Wilson and his wife Valerie Plame for the ambassador's exposing of the president's lie about an Iraqi quest to purchase uranium in Niger is a dark parable known to every U.S. citizen.[19] George Orwell taught in 1984 that omnipresent spying and dossiers are the earmarks of tyranny. He himself was spied on by the British secret service as a potential national security threat.[20]

The Founding Fathers revolted from Great Britain over less obnoxious invasions of privacy than the TSP. The Fourth Amendment was calculated to prevent the U.S. government from aping the British king.[21] It was provoked by writs of assistance, or court orders, that authorized customs officers to conduct generalized searches for smuggled goods within any suspected premises. In February 1761, James Otis declaimed against the writs as "a power that places the liberty of every man in the hands of every petty officer."[22] Otis amplified,

> Now, one of the most essential branches of English liberty is the freedom of one's house. A man's house is his castle; and whilst he is quiet, he is as well guarded as a prince in his castle. This writ, if it should be declared legal, would totally annihilate this privilege. Customs-house officers may enter our houses when they please; we are commanded to permit their entry. Their menial servants may enter, may break locks, bars, and everything in their way; and whether they break through malice or revenge, no man, no court can inquire. Bare suspicion without oath is sufficient.[23]

John Adams later declared that in Otis's oration, "then and there was the first scene of the first act of opposition to the arbitrary claims of Great Britain. Then and there the child of Independence was born."[24]

General search warrants were first cousins to writs of assistance. They were indefinite as to the persons to be arrested or the places to be searched. They were condemned in Great Britain by Lord Camden in 1765 in *Entick v. Carrington*, a decision acclaimed by the U.S. Supreme Court in *Boyd v. United States* (1886) as "landmarks of English liberty . . . one of the permanent monuments of the British Constitution."[25] The facts of the case were informative of the fragility of privacy when executive power is left unchecked. The British secretary of state, Lord Halifax, issued a general search warrant authorizing messengers to search for John Entick and to seize his private papers and books. Entick's writings had assailed the Crown. He supported John Wilkes, the famous editor of the *North Briton*, whose scorn for the Crown had provoked retaliatory arrests, searches, and seizures. Entick obtained a damage judgment for trespassing occasioned by the general warrant. In sustaining the jury verdict, Lord Camden amplified that unchecked executive authority to break and enter homes would mean that "the secret cabinets and bureaus of every subject in this kingdom would be thrown open to the search and inspection of a messenger, whenever the secretary of state shall see fit to charge, or even to suspect, a person to be the author, printer, or publisher of a seditious libel."[26]

The colonial wrath toward general warrants and writs of assistance culminated in the Fourth Amendment. It provides, "The right of the people to be secure in their persons, houses, papers, and effects, against unreasonable searches and seizures, shall not be violated, and no Warrants shall issue, but upon probable cause, supported by oath or affirmation, and particularly describing the place to be searched, and the persons and things to be seized."[27] FISA added teeth to the amendment by making warrantless spying on Americans a criminal offense: "A person is guilty of an offense if he intentionally—(1) engages in electronic surveillance under color of law except as authorized by statute."[28]

The president's claim of inherent constitutional power to disregard FISA or any other law that regulates national security attacks the rule of law itself. It echoes President Nixon's assertion that he was above the law and that the burglary of the office of Daniel Ellsberg's psychiatrist ordered by Nixon's subordinate, John Ehrlichman, would have been legal if done by the president directly. In testimony delivered to the Senate Judiciary Committee, then–Attorney General Alberto Gonzales refused to concede that Congress could restrict the president's inherent Article II authority to gather foreign intelligence[29]; and, in a presidential signing statement issued in conjunction with the Detainee Treatment Act of 2005, President Bush asserted authority to inflict cruel, inhumane, or degrading treatments of detainees in direct violation of federal laws and treaties under a banner of national security.

Other than his quest for an omnipotent presidency, President Bush has never explained why he chose to commit FISA crimes rather than to seek FISA amendments. Congress is authorized to hold secret sessions and to enact classified laws under Article I, Section 5, Clause 3.[30] And Congress was eager to pass any legislation presented by the president on the heels of 9/11. Its members were no less worried about a second edition of 9/11 than he was. Indeed, Congress has amended FISA on numerous occasions since 9/11 to accommodate the heightened danger and new communications technologies, including the Patriot Act. The latest amendment, FISA Amerndments Act of 2008, was enacted last summer.

President Bush then compounded his FISA crimes with secrecy.

When Congress commenced hearings on the TSP after the leak to the *New York Times*, the president invoked executive privilege of state secrets to deny disclosure of legal advice to the president and the NSA, and details of the TSP generally. Despite skeletal disclosures to the congressional leadership and later the House and Senate Intelligence Committees, Congress has been unable to assess the utility of the spying, the need for FISA criminal prosecutions, or the need for new laws. The public was denied knowledge of what President Bush was doing to them and therefore could not adjust their political calculations to voice protest or support for the TSP.

Suppose that he had publicly announced the TSP in a nationwide televised address from the Oval Office as follows: "My fellow Americans, today I have directed the NSA to gather foreign intelligence by spying on Americans whom I believe are connected with Al Qaeda. I am conducting the spying in contravention of FISA because I believe it unconstitutionally ties my hands in trying to protect you from another 9/11." That hypothetical presidential address would have comported with political and legal accountability under the Constitution without giving Al Qaeda or other international terrorists information that would enable them to evade electronic surveillance. They knew the United States was spying on them with or without FISA warrants at the time of 9/11 because FISA itself is a public document and the universe of spying that requires warrants is tiny. In any event, international terrorists are indifferent as to the legal theory employed to target them for surveillance. Indeed, President Bush himself confirmed that publicizing the TSP did not harm national security because he continued to operate the TSP after the *New York Times* disclosure.[31]

President Bush's claim that he was forced to the TSP because FISA was crippling his ability to gather foreign intelligence on international terrorists is preposterous, which explains why he returned to FISA warrants in January 2007 without suggesting any foreign intelligence loss. FISA does not apply to more than 99 percent of the foreign intelligence operations of the NSA or its sister foreign intelligence agencies. It is generally triggered only when the target of the electronic surveillance or physical search is an American citizen who holds a reasonable expectation of privacy under the Fourth Amendment. The U.S. Supreme Court declared in *United States v. Verdugo Urdiquez* (1990)[32] that the amendment generally has no application outside the United States as applied to noncitizens or inside the United States as applied to transients. Thus, FISA leaves U.S. intelligence agencies free to spy on foreign targets abroad, which provide the overwhelming proportion of foreign intelligence. For example, the NSA may ordinarily vacuum clean every communication exchange between Al Qaeda members located outside the United States without a warrant.

There is an exception, however. FISA has been interpreted to apply to a wire communication between foreign points if it is intercepted while transiting the United States even when the communicants lack any reasonable expectation of privacy protected by the Fourth Amendment. FISA should have been amended at the behest of congressional leadership or the president to confine its protections to persons in the United States or citizens abroad with reasonable expectations of privacy in their communications. The amendment would have simply provided: "A warrant under FISA shall not be required if its only trigger is that a communication has been intercepted in the United States." Its enactment would not have required disclosing classified sources or methods.

A FISA warrant is not difficult to obtain. The government must demonstrate probable cause to believe the target is an agent of a foreign government or implicated in international terrorism. A significant motive of the spying must be foreign intelligence, which includes anything that might bear on international terrorism, foreign affairs, or diplomacy generally—for example, the dollar reserves of Iranian banks. Furthermore, procedures must be implemented to minimize the acquisition and retention, and prohibit the dissemination, of nonpublicly available information concerning U.S. persons consistent with the need of the United States to obtain, produce, and disseminate foreign intelligence information and to detect and prosecute crime. Minimization procedures are necessary to prevent the government from creating permanent files or databases unrelated to foreign intelligence that could be employed to blackmail, embarrass, or intimidate citizens or resident aliens.[33] During FISA's lifetime, approximately twenty thousand warrants have been issued and but a handful have been denied. FISA also authorizes spying before obtaining a warrant for 72 hours in cases of emergency and for 15 days in the event of war.[34]

Like President Nixon in Watergate, President Bush lied and deceived the American people about the TSP in order to prevent congressional inquiries or public evaluation of what he was doing. After the *New York Times* publication, the president declared the next day in his weekly radio address, "In the weeks following the [9/11] terrorist attacks on our Nation, I authorized the National Security Agency, consistent with U.S. law and the Constitution, to intercept the international communications of people with known links to Al Qaeda and related terrorist organizations. Before we intercept these communications, the government must have information that establishes a clear link to these terrorist networks."[35]

President Bush's statements were disingenuous. FISA warrants can be readily obtained to spy on persons with "known links" to Al Qaeda. There would be no need for the TSP if its targets were confined to known terrorists or their active supporters. If the number of international terrorist targets had ballooned after 9/11, President Bush could have asked Congress to enlarge the number of FISA judges or Department of Justice personnel authorized to approve FISA applications. In any event, President Bush did not say he resorted to the TSP because the resources for FISA warrants were deficient, and neither was the TSP necessary for speed. As previously explained, in emergencies FISA spying can begin and continue for 72 hours before a warrant is issued. On July 31, 2002, the Department of Justice testified to the Senate Intelligence Committee that FISA was nimble, flexible, and impeccable in enabling terrorist conspiracies to be detected in their embryonic stages. The department opposed lowering the FISA threshold for obtaining a warrant. The 9/11 Commission did not recommend altering FISA to prevent international terrorism, a tacit endorsement of its efficacy. The truth seems to have been that President Bush embraced the TSP because he wanted to spy indiscriminately without judicial or legislative oversight to establish presidential omnipotence in national security matters.

Bush's acknowledgment of the warrantless TSP conducted by the NSA demonstrated the deceit in his previous assertions that all wiretaps were authorized by court orders. On April 20, 2004, President Bush delivered a speech in Buffalo, in which he volunteered, "Now, by the way, any time you hear the United States government talking about a wiretap, it requires—a wiretap requires a court order. Nothing has changed by the way. When we're talking about chasing down terrorists, we're talking about getting a court order before we do so."[36]

On July 14, 2004, in Wisconsin, President Bush reiterated, "Any action that takes place by law enforcement requires a court order. In other words, the government can't move on wiretaps or roving wiretaps without getting a court order."[37] In Columbus, Ohio, on June 9, 2005, President Bush for a third time offered reassuring words, "Law enforcement officers need a federal judge's permission to wiretap a foreign terrorist's phone, a federal judge's permission to track his calls, or a federal judge's permission to search his property. Officers must meet strict standards to use any of these tools. And these standards are fully consistent with the Constitution of the U.S."[38]

When these representations were made, the president knew the TSP was operating without warrants to gather foreign intelligence. In the manner of President William Jefferson Clinton's quibbling over the meanings of the words "is" and "alone,"[39] President Bush might retort that he was speaking only of warrants issued in support of law enforcement and meant to imply nothing about warrants to gather foreign intelligence. But Bush knew that such a law enforcement–foreign intelligence distinction would have been lost on a lay audience. Moreover, FISA permits the initiation of spying for both foreign intelligence and law enforcement purposes—for example, spying to detect espionage. President Bush was eager to mislead the American people and Congress about wiretapping to forestall oversight hearings that could have uncovered his FISA crimes and end the TSP, as publicity ultimately did. President Nixon similarly prevaricated with the American people after the Watergate burglary by maintaining that White House counsel John Dean had "conducted a complete investigation of all leads which might involve any members of the White House staff."[40] The investigation was a concoction. The public lie formed the basis of an impeachment article against Nixon.

President Bush's radio address also described the mechanism by which the TSP was authorized and reviewed:

The activities I authorized are reviewed every 45 days. Each review is based on a fresh intelligence assessment of terrorist threats to the continuity of our government and the threat of catastrophic damage to our homeland. During each assessment, previous activities under the authorization are reviewed. The review includes approval by our Nation's top legal officials, including the Attorney General and Counsel to the President. I have reauthorized this program more than 30 times since the September 11th attacks, and I intend to do so for as long as our Nation faces a continuing threat from Al Qaeda and related groups.

The NSA's activities under this authorization are thoroughly reviewed by the Justice Department and NSA's top legal officials, including NSA's General Counsel and Inspector General. Leaders in Congress have been briefed more than a dozen times on this authorization and the activities conducted under it. Intelligence officials involved in this activity also receive extensive training to ensure they perform their duties consistent with the letter and intent of the authorization.[41]

The president's statements were both misleading and incomplete. He declined to disclose that then–Acting Attorney General James Comey refused to sign off on the TSP's legality in March 2004 for reasons that remain classified.[42] White House officials Andrew Card and Alberto Gonzales then raced to the hospital bedside of ailing Attorney General John Ashcroft in hopes of overruling Comey. Ashcroft balked, and the White House then altered the TSP to satisfy Comey in ways that also remain classified.[43] Furthermore, President Bush failed to explain what benchmarks were employed by his lawyers and intelligence gurus to determine whether to extend the TSP. It speaks volumes that President Bush nowhere insinuates that the TSP was inaugurated because FISA was flawed.

Attorney General Gonzales later asserted that the TSP intercepts "contents of communications where . . . one party of the communication is outside the United States"[44] and the government has "a reasonable basis to conclude that one party of the communication is a member of Al Qaeda, affiliated with Al Qaeda, or a member of an organization affiliated with Al Qaeda, or working in support of Al Qaeda."[45] The attorney general avowed, "This [program] is not about wiretapping everyone. This is a very concentrated, very limited program focused on gaining information about our enemy."[46] President Bush added that the government's "international activities strictly target al Qaeda and their known affiliates,"[47] "the government does not listen to domestic phone calls without court approval,"[48] and the government is "not mining or trolling through the personal lives of millions of innocent Americans."[49]

The statements of the president and the attorney general defy credulity. The gist of their nonsense is that the TSP is employed to spy on Americans without warrants to gather foreign intelligence only when the government possesses information sufficient to obtain FISA warrants, which would make the TSP superfluous—in other words, that the spying only targets "Al Qaeda and their known affiliates." President Bush's omission of any TSP success stories also speaks to its embrace solely to aggrandize the White House. If the TSP were in any way superior to FISA, the president would have instantly declassified or leaked TSP intelligence coups to the media and Congress. That tactic was employed by the president in signing the Military Commissions Act of 2006 to justify the CIA's secret prisons and coercive interrogations of presumed terrorists in Eastern or Central Europe, which had leaked to *The Washington Post* and had encountered sharp criticism: "The CIA program helped us identify terrorists who were sent to case targets in the United States, including financial buildings in major cities on the East Coast. And the CIA program helped us stop the planned strike on U.S. Marines in Djibouti, a planned attack on the U.S. consulate in Karachi, and a plot to hijack airplanes and fly them into Heathrow Airport and Canary Wharf in London."[50]

Regarding Bush's denial of warrantless data mining, on May 11, 2006, *USA Today* reported that the NSA has been secretly collecting domestic phone call records of tens of millions of Americans from data provided by private phone companies.[51] The purpose is to analyze calling patterns in hopes of identifying terrorists.

The Bush-Gonzales statements also discredit the need for the TSP. FISA warrants are obtained to intercept domestic to domestic communications—for example, a call between two Al Qaeda members smuggled into the United States to conduct a terrorist attack. But FISA procedures for obtaining a warrant are identical whether or not the communication to be intercepted is purely domestic or features a foreign sender or recipient. If FISA is satisfactory for gathering foreign intelligence for domestic-to-domestic communications, it is equally satisfactory for intercepting domestic-to-foreign communications or vice versa. Indeed, the interceptions of domestic-to-domestic calls in international terrorist investigations are the most urgent because they would be the most likely to have a connection to an imminent attack on American soil, such as the domestic-to-domestic calls of the 9/11 hijackers.

On January 10, 2007, Attorney General Gonzales wrote to Senate Judiciary Committee Chairman Patrick Leahy (D-VT) that "a Judge of the Foreign Intelligence Surveillance Court issued orders authorizing the government to target for collection international communications into or out of the United States where there is probable cause to believe one of the communicants is a member or agent of Al Qaeda or associated terrorist organizations."[52] The attorney general added that "any electronic surveillance that was occurring as part of the [TSP] will now be conducted subject to approval of the Foreign Intelligence Surveillance Court."[53]

The FISA court's order has not been publicized. The attorney general's letter suggests that warrants are issued based on individualized suspicions that the targets are Al Qaeda members. But continued secrecy prevents any confidant conclusion. The order has been shared with some members of Congress who have been enjoined from discussing its contents. The January 10 letter, moreover, excludes any concession that the president's constitutional authority to gather foreign intelligence can be restricted in any way by FISA or other statutes. In other words, the president is entitled to gather foreign intelligence without warrants, irrespective of FISA court orders.

President Bush's defenders insist that even if FISA crimes were perpetrated, a better intelligence product emerged from the TSP to protect the American people. That claim is unsupported by credible evidence. Furthermore, the TSP intelligence was probably distorted for political purposes to inflate the international terrorist danger in order to justify a condition of permanent war. With regard to "cooking" the intelligence books, Tim Weiner in *Legacy of Ashes* quotes the blunt observation of the CIA's John Huizenga, who captained the office of national estimates in 1971:

> In retrospect, you see, I really do not believe that an intelligence organization in this government is able to deliver an honest analytical product without facing the risk of political contention. By and large, I think the tendency to treat intelligence politically increased over this whole period. And it's mainly over issues like Southeast Asia and the growth of Soviet strategic forces that were extremely divisive politically. I think it's probably naïve in retrospect to believe what most of us believed at one time . . . that you could deliver an honest analytical product and have it taken at face value. . . . I think that intelligence has had relatively little impact on the policies that we've made over the years. Relatively none. In certain[,] particular circumstances, perhaps insights and facts that were provided had an effect on what we did. But only in a narrow range of circumstances. By and large, the intelligence effort did not alter the premises with which political leadership came

to office. They brought their baggage and they more or less carried it along. Ideally, what had been supposed was that . . . serious intelligence analysis could . . . assist the policy side to re-examine premises, render policy making more sophisticated, close to the reality of the world. Those were the large ambitions which I think were never realized.[54]

FISA was no congressional lark to vex the president. It responded to the experience with unchecked executive spying—the best test of truth.

Attorney General Edward Levi chronicled the legal history of intelligence collection before the Church Committee on November 6, 1975. The chronicle demonstrated the inexorable tendency of unchecked spying to balloon, the propensity of secret spying to lawlessness, and the deterrence to intelligence wrongdoing created by publicity or oversight. He testified as follows:

As I read the history, going back to 1931 and undoubtedly prior to that time, except for an interlude between 1928 and 1931 and for two months in 1940, the policy of the Department of Justice has been that electronic surveillance could be used without a warrant in certain circumstances. . . .

On May 21, 1940, President Franklin Roosevelt issued a memorandum to the Attorney General stating his view that electronic surveillance would be proper under the Constitution where "grave matters involving defense of the nation" were involved. The President authorized and directed the Attorney General "to secure information by listening devices [directed at] the conversation of other communications of persons suspected of subversive activities against the Government of the United States, including suspected spies." The Attorney General was requested "to limit these investigations so conducted to a minimum and to limit them insofar as possible to aliens."[55]

Attorney General Levi did not disclose whether the request for spying minimization was honored, which seems a dubious proposition. Subversive activities could include any speech disparaging the United States protected by the First Amendment. Furthermore, intelligence agents cannot readily distinguish between aliens and citizens by appearance, voice inflection, or otherwise.

Warrantless wiretapping and electronic surveillance predictably climbed in frequency. Attorney General Levi continued,

> On July 17, 1946, Attorney General Tom C. Clark sent President [Harry] Truman a letter reminding him that President [Franklin D.] Roosevelt had authorized and directed Attorney General Jackson to approve "listening devices [directed at] the conversation or other communications of persons suspected of subversive activities against the Government of the United States, including suspected spies" . . . Attorney General Clark recommended that the directive "be continued in force in view of the "increase in subversive activities" and "a very substantial increase in crime."[56]

The attorney general provided no evidence to substantiate the purported rise in "subversive activities." Nor did he explain why a jump in crime was relevant because President Franklin D. Roosevelt had only authorized warrantless spying to detect subversion. The reference to crime indicates that the use of wiretaps and electronic surveillance was expanding beyond intelligence collection and into law enforcement. That conclusion later became inescapable.

To return to Attorney General Levi's narrative:

> [T]he policy against Attorney General approval, at least in general, of trespassory microphone surveillance was reversed by Attorney General Herbert Brownell on May 20, 1954, in

a memorandum to Director Hoover instructing him that the Bureau was authorized to conduct trespassory microphone surveillances. The Attorney General stated that: "Considerations of internal security and the national safety are paramount and therefore, may compel the unrestricted use of this technique in the national interest."[57]

A memorandum from Director Hoover to the deputy attorney general on May 4, 1961, described the Bureau's practice since 1954 as follows:

> In the internal security field, we are utilizing microphone surveillances on a restricted basis even though trespass is necessary to assist in uncovering the activities of Soviet intelligence agents and Communist Party leaders. In the interests of national safety, microphone surveillances are also utilized on a restricted basis, even though trespass is necessary, in uncovering major criminal activities. We are using such coverage in connection with our investigations of the clandestine activities of top hoodlums and organized crime. From an intelligence standpoint, this investigative technique has produced results unobtainable through other means. The information so obtained is treated in the same manner as information obtained from wiretaps, that is, not from the standpoint of evidentiary value but for intelligence purposes.[58]

The Hoover memorandum confirms that warrantless surveillance that began with targeting primarily suspected alien subversives soon expanded into targeting U.S. citizens implicated in crimes unrelated to subversion. Attorney General Levi's testimony continued,

> Subsequently, in September 1965, the Director of the FBI wrote the Attorney General and referred to the—*** present atmosphere, brought about by the unrestrained and injudicious

use of special investigative techniques by other agencies and departments, resulting in Congressional and public alarm and opposition to any activity which could in any way be termed an invasion of privacy. As a consequence, we have discontinued completely the use of microphones.[59]

The attorney general responded in part as follows:

The use of wiretaps and microphones involving trespass present more difficult problems because of the inadmissibility of any evidence obtained in court cases and because of current judicial and public attitude regarding their use. It is my understanding that such devices will not be used without my authorization, although in emergency circumstances they may be used subject to my later ratification. At this time I believe it desirable that all such techniques be confined to the gathering of intelligence in national security matters, and I will continue to approve all such requests in the future as I have in the past. I see no need to curtail any such activities in the national security field."[60]

These exchanges make clear that executive branch restraints on intelligence collection came from Congress and the public, not from executive scruples about invading privacy or the Fourth Amendment.

As Attorney General Levi's testimony demonstrated, the executive branch collected foreign intelligence with virtually no congressional or judicial oversight until the hearings conducted by Senator Frank Church (D-ID) in 1975–76 under the aegis of the Select Committee to Study Governmental Operations with Respect to Intelligence Activities. The Church Committee revealed major abuses. Its hearings were prompted by a front-page *New York Times* story authored by Seymour Hersh on December 22, 1974.[61] Hersh wrote that "a check of the CIA's domestic files ordered last year . . . produced evidence of dozens of other illegal activities . . . beginning in the nineteen fifties, including break-ins, wiretapping, and the surreptitious inspection of mail."[62]

Then–CIA Director James Schlesinger had commissioned the agency's "family jewels"[63] compilation in a May 9, 1973, directive after discovering that Watergate burglars E. Howard Hunt and James McCord received cooperation from the Agency in executing "dirty tricks"[64] for President Nixon. The directive commanded senior CIA officials to report immediately on any current or past agency activities that might fall outside the CIA's authority:

> I have ordered all senior operating officials of this Agency to report to me immediately on any activities now going on, or that have gone on in the past, which might be construed to be outside the legislative charter of this Agency [which forbids domestic spying]. I hereby direct every person presently employed by CIA to report to me on any such activities of which he has knowledge. I invite all ex-employees to do the same. Anyone who has such information should call . . . and say that he wishes to tell me about "activities outside CIA's charter."[65]

On June 21, 2007, CIA Director General Michael Hayden announced the declassification of the full 693-page file on the agency's illegalities prepared in response to the Schlesinger Directive.[66] The documents revealed 25 years of CIA violations until the Church Committee and sequel reforms forced transparency. Here are a few examples:

- In 1964, a Russian defector was brought to the United States. He was imprisoned and interrogated for two years because of CIA suspicion that the defector could have been a double agent. Then–CIA Director William Colby opined that the defector's confinement "might be regarded as a violation of the kidnapping laws."[67]

- In 1963, the CIA wiretapped two columnists—Robert Allen and Paul Scott—following a column that disclosed national security information.[68]
- From February 15 to April 12, 1972, "personal surveillances"[69] were conducted by the CIA on Jack Anderson and members of his staff (Les Whitten, Britt Hume, and Mr. Spear). The physical surveillances were triggered by Jack Anderson's series of articles disclosing the "tilt toward Pakistan"[70] policy of the United States in the 1972 Pakistan-India conflict.
- Between October 1971 and January 1972, the CIA conducted a physical surveillance of *Washington Post* reporter Mike Getler.[71]
- In 1971, the CIA broke into the business premises of a former employee and attempted to break into her residence in a search for CIA documents that she may have taken with her. The CIA found nothing.[72]
- In July 1970, the CIA broke into an office occupied by a former defector who was "on contract"[73] to the CIA looking for CIA documents.
- Between 1953 and 1973, the CIA's Counterintelligence Staff screened and opened mail to and from the Soviet Union traveling through the Kennedy Airport Mail Depot.[74]
- From 1969 to October 1972, the Far East Division of the CIA reviewed, in San Francisco, mail going to and from the People's Republic of China.[75]
- Beginning in 1967, the CIA initiated a program to identify possible foreign links to American Vietnam War dissidents. Both Presidents Lyndon B. Johnson and Richard M. Nixon were convinced that war protestors were receiving foreign money and support. Under the program, the CIA alerted persons abroad to identify the foreign contacts of American dissidents. The CIA placed some agents in the peace movement in the United States to burnish credentials for travel abroad. Information was gathered on the domestic activities

of various peace organizations. The program generated names of more than 9,900 Americans. CIA Director Colby considered it "worthless" from an intelligence standpoint."[76] Colby informed President Gerald R. Ford, "On the dissidents, the major effort was to check if there were any foreign connections. But we held it so close there was unease within the Agency—was it really done for the foreign connections or was it anti-dissident?"[77]

The CIA's family jewels are informative about the need for FISA and how intelligence agencies operate when unchecked by either Congress or the judiciary. Spies are inclined to subordinate the law to spying and to view with suspicion political dissidents. Intelligence agencies are likely to persist in spying programs, despite their worthlessness, and respond to White House requests to search for intelligence that would advance a partisan political agenda. President Bush probably persisted with the TSP in the hopes of substantiating his argument that Al Qaeda is as great a threat to Western civilization as were the enemies of the United States in World War II. He voluntarily abandoned the TSP in January 2007. The most probable explanation was that the warrantless spying was worthless. Bush never misses an opportunity to declare that everything he is doing is making the American people safer from a terrorist attack.

The Church Committee held hearings on twenty years of illegal mail openings by the CIA and FBI. Chairman Church observed in opening an October 21, 1975, hearing,

> Today and through the rest of the week, we wish to resume our inquiry into the question of why the Federal Government has been opening the mail of American citizens for over two decades. It is a policy fundamentally at odds with freedom of expression and contrary to the laws of the land. . . . As a case study, mail opening reveals the most revealing look at

the inner life of the CIA and the FBI. In the instance of the CIA . . . the evidence suggests their mail program was allowed to continue despite the harshest criticism of it from investigators within the CIA Inspector General's Office, and despite the fact that it was not very productive in terms of intelligence information.[78]

The mail openings persisted despite CIA knowledge of its illegality. The program continued despite gathering generally useless intelligence. A report by the inspector general, which overstated the program's utility, amplified, "Most of the offices we spoke to find it occasionally helpful, but there is no recent evidence of it having provided significant leads of information which have had positive operational results. The Office of Security has found the material to be of very little value. The positive intelligence derived from this source is meager."[79]

Congressional oversight and regulation of intelligence is essential both because intelligence agencies are disinclined to cease spying that proves useless, and because spies are inclined to violate the laws in the name of intelligence collection knowing that in a post-9/11 environment, bureaucracies reward anything done in the name of preventing another 9/11. No intelligence official in the Bush administration has been punished for spying too much.

The Church Committee also disclosed misconduct by the NSA, which also carries lessons for appraising unchecked executive-branch spying: mission creep. The NSA's initial task was the acquisition of foreign intelligence by targeting noncitizens. But NSA Director Lew Allen Jr. testified,

Beginning in 1967, requesting agencies provided names of persons and organizations, some of whom were U.S. citizens, to the NSA in an effort to obtain information which was available in foreign communications as a by-product of our normal foreign intelligence mission.

The purpose of the lists varied, but all possessed a common thread in which the NSA was requested to review information available through our usual intercept sources. The initial purpose was to help determine the existence of foreign influence on specified activities of interest to agencies of the U.S. Government, with emphasis then on Presidential protection and on civil disturbances occurring throughout the Nation.

Later, because of other developments, such as widespread national concern over such criminal activity as drug trafficking and acts of terrorism, both domestic and international, the emphasis came to include these areas. Thus, during this period, 1967–1973, requirements for which lists were developed in four basic areas: international drug trafficking; Presidential protection; acts of terrorism, and possible foreign support or influence on civil disturbances.

In the sixties there was Presidential concern voiced over the massive flow of drugs into our country from outside the United States. Early in President Nixon's administration, he instructed the CIA to pursue with vigor intelligence efforts to identify foreign sources of drugs and the foreign organizations and methods used to introduce illicit drugs into the United States. The BNDD, the Bureau of Narcotics and Dangerous Drugs, in 1970 asked the NSA to provide communications intelligence relevant to these foreign aspects, and BNDD provided watch lists with some U.S. names. International drug trafficking requirements were formally documented in [United States Intelligence Board] requirements in 1971.

As we all know, during this period there was also heightened concern by the country and the Secret Service over Presidential protection because of President Kennedy's assassination. After the Warren Report, requirements lists containing the names of U.S. citizens and organizations were provided to NSA by Secret Service in support of their efforts to protect the President and other senior officials. Such requirements were later incorporated into USIB documentation. At that time, intelligence derived from foreign communications was regarded as a valuable tool in support of Executive protection.

About the same time as the concern over drugs or shortly thereafter, there was a committee established by the President to combat international terrorism. This committee was supported by an inter-departmental working group with USIB representatives. Requirements to support this effort with communications intelligence were also incorporated into USIB documentation.[80]

On November 6, 1975, the Church Committee investigated the NSA's operation SHAMROCK. It entailed three decades of the NSA's illegal interception and distribution of certain international telegrams. Chairman Church elaborated,

SHAMROCK was the cover name given to a message-collection program in which the Government persuaded three international telegraph companies, RCA Global, ITT World Communications, and Western Union International, to make available in various ways certain of their international telegraph traffic to the U.S. Government. For almost 30 years, copies of most international telegrams originating in or forwarded through the United States were turned over to the National Security Agency and its predecessor agencies. . . . At the outset, the purpose apparently was only to extract international telegrams relating to certain foreign targets. Later, the Government began to extract the telegrams of certain U.S. citizens. . . . In the early 1960s, there was a change in technology, which had a significant impact on the way in which SHAMROCK was run. RCA Global and ITT World Communications began to store their international paid message traffic on magnetic tapes, and these were turned over to NSA. Thereafter, the telegrams were selected in precisely the same way in which NSA selects its information from other sources. This meant, for example, that telegrams to or from, or even mentioning, U.S. citizens whose names appeared on the watch list in the late sixties and early seventies, would have been sent to NSA analysts, and many would subsequently be disseminated to other agencies. . . .

Of all the messages made available to NSA each year, it is estimated that NSA in recent years selected about 150,000 messages a month for NSA analysts to review. Thousands of these messages in one form or another were distributed to other agencies in response to "foreign intelligence requirements."[81]

Only a handful of officials in the executive branch over the past 30 years had apparently been aware of the SHAMROCK operation. Dr. Louis Tordiella testified that to the best of his knowledge, no president since Truman had been informed of it: "SHAMROCK terminated by order of the Secretary of Defense on May 15, 1975."[82]

Senator Gary Hart added,

Project SHAMROCK is improper it seems to me for many reasons, including, first, that it appears unlawful under section 605 of the Communications Act of 1934, and the fourth amendment, although there is no case exactly in point. Second, it placed the Government in a position to request illegal acts of the companies, contrary to the proper role of the executive to see that the laws are faithfully executed. Third, it resulted in the Government promising the companies immunity from criminal prosecution to obtain the cooperation. It raised the possibility . . . that the companies might some day terminate their participation unless the Government granted some benefit, withheld some penalty, or halted some investigation. It resulted in the invasion of privacy of American citizens whose private and personal telegrams were intercepted as a result of their being on the NSA's watch list from 1967–1973.[83]

SHAMROCK began with the interception of international telegrams relating to foreign targets, but expanded into interceptions relating to targeted citizens. The spying program tumbled into lawlessness with no outside vetting.

Congress enacted FISA precisely because of substantiated fears that the executive branch would indiscriminately spy on Americans—especially critics of the president's policies—without a judicial check and regular congressional oversight. Executive self-restraint was not sufficient. A report by the House of Representatives elaborated, "In the past several years, abuses of domestic national security surveillances have been disclosed. This evidence alone should demonstrate the inappropriateness of relying solely on executive branch discretion to safeguard civil liberties. This committee is well aware of the substantial safeguards respecting foreign intelligence electronic surveillance currently embodied in classified Attorney General procedures, but this committee is also aware that over the past thirty years there have been significant changes in internal executive branch procedures, and there is ample precedent for later administrations or even the same administration loosening previous standards."[84]

Congress also rejected the idea that the president enjoyed inherent constitutional authority to gather foreign intelligence outside the constraints of FISA—a power that would make a mockery of checks and balances, and the long history of executive spying wrongdoing. In FISA's repeal of a law that had insinuated the contrary, the Senate Select Committee on Intelligence explained that its action "eliminate[ed] any congressional recognition or suggestion of inherent Presidential power with respect to electronic surveillance."[85] The report added that FISA's declaration that its procedures provided the "exclusive means" to gather foreign intelligence through electronic surveillance "puts to rest the notion that Congress recognizes an inherent Presidential power to conduct such surveillances in the United States outside of the procedures contained in chapters 119 and 120."[86]

Demonstrating President Bush's FISA Crimes

President George W. Bush, through Attorney General Alberto Gonzales, has conceded that the Terrorist Surveillance Program (TSP) contradicted the Foreign Intelligence Surveillance Act of 1978 (FISA). He currenly argues, nevertheless, that the TSP was legally authorized by the Authorization for Use of Military Force (AUMF) and that FISA unconstitutionally encroaches on the president's inherent power to gather foreign intelligence. Both arguments are sophomoric and were late in coming—part of what Attorney General Gonzales styled a "dynamic" as opposed to a "static" process of legal reasoning.[1]

The maiden justification for the TSP was prepared contemporaneously with its commencement when then–Deputy Assistant Attorney General for the office of legal counsel John C. Yoo scribbled together a memorandum arguing that FISA had no application whatsoever to national security spying. FISA unambiguously declares that it provides the "exclusive means by which electronic surveillance . . . and the interception of domestic wire, oral and electronic communications may be conducted."[2]

But Yoo's memorandum argued, "[u]nless Congress made a clear statement in the Foreign Intelligence Surveillance Act that it sought to restrict presidential authority to conduct warrantless searches in the national security area—which it has not—then the statute must be construed to avoid [such] a reading."[3]

The deputy assistant attorney general must have neglected to read FISA. In a section entitled "Authorization during Time of War,"[4] the statute provides, "Notwithstanding any other law, the President, through the Attorney General, may authorize electronic surveillance without a court order under this subchapter to acquire foreign intelligence information for a period not to exceed [15] calendar days following a declaration of war by Congress."[5] In other words, contrary to Yoo's statement, FISA explicitly addresses how it should apply in the national security area, whose core is war. Moreover, FISA's definition of foreign intelligence—which demarcates its ambit—expressly references national security affairs:

> Foreign intelligence information means—
> (1) information that relates to, and if concerning a United States person is necessary to, the ability of the United States to protect against—
>   (A) actual or potential attack or other grave hostile acts of a foreign power or an agent of a foreign power;
>   (B) sabotage or international terrorism by a foreign power or an agent of a foreign power; or
>   (C) clandestine intelligence activities by an intelligence service or network of a foreign power or by an agent of a foreign power; or
> (2) information with respect to a foreign power or foreign territory that relates to, and if concerning a United States person is necessary to—
>   (A) the national defense or the security of the United States.[6]

Even the Bush White House later became embarrassed at Yoo's nonsense. In May 2008, Brian A. Benczkowski, principal deputy attorney general in the office of legislative affairs, wrote Democratic Senators Sheldon Whitehouse (RI) and Diane Feinstein (CA) that the Bush administration had abandoned Yoo's FISA memo: "The 2001 [Yoo] statement addressing FISA does not reflect the current analysis of the Department."[7]

Before addressing President Bush's current statutory and constitutional contentions, a brief excursion into how a president ought legally to handle unforeseen and potentially catastrophic dangers is appropriate. We should never forget the legitimate, intense fear in the hours after the 9/11 abominations that Al Qaeda might have planned a series of sequel horrors.

John Locke acknowledged in his *Second Treatise on Civil Government*—a virtual bible for the Founding Fathers—that the law cannot anticipate every danger that may confront a nation, which the executive cannot prudently ignore. In such emergencies, the executive is entitled to contradict the law for the public good. But retroactive legislative ratification was indispensable to prove the purity of the executive's motives.

9/11 created a Locke-like emergency for President Bush and the nation. Thousands of people had been murdered by religious fanatics. A fog of uncertainty persisted as to whether hundreds or thousands of Al Qaeda sleeper cells might be coiled to strike again. President Bush could not have been reproached if he had ordered the National Security Agency (NSA) to violate FISA with indiscriminate vacuum cleaner–type spying for a limited period after 9/11 to determine the breadth or imminence of the Al Qaeda threat in the United States and then asked Congress to retroactively ratify the emergency spying, which it certainly would have done. President Bush had a clear precedent staring him in the face.

As the Civil War erupted, President Abraham Lincoln unilaterally suspended the Great Writ of habeas corpus without the consent of Congress. A federal circuit decree issued by then–Chief

Justice of the United States Roger Brooke Taney in *Ex parte Merryman* (1861) held that Lincoln's unilateral suspension was unconstitutional. President Lincoln did not obey the judicial decree but reported his actions to Congress, which retroactively ratified what he had done.

The Constitution provided President Bush a clear legal roadmap for the TSP, but he inexcusably chose a criminal path. President Bush argues that foreign intelligence collection is an executive power, and under the unitary executive theory of the Constitution, Congress is thus powerless to regulate that White House authority. The argument is patently flawed.

Article I, Section 8, Clause 18 of the Constitution empowers Congress "to make all Laws which shall be necessary and proper for carrying into Execution . . . all . . . Powers vested by this Constitution in the Government of the United States or in any Department or Officer thereof" (Necessary and Proper Clause).[8] It thus authorizes Congress to enact necessary and proper laws to govern every constitutional power assigned to the president. Take the Appointments Clause, Article II, Section 2, Clause 2.[9] It provides that the president "shall nominate, and by and with the Advice and Consent of the Senate, shall appoint Ambassadors, other public Ministers and Consuls, Judges of the supreme Court, and all other Officers of the United States, whose Appointments are not herein otherwise provided for, and which shall be established by Law."[10] Under the clause, the president holds the power to appoint the attorney general. But pursuant to the Necessary and Proper Clause, Congress by statute could require that the attorney general possess a law degree and be licensed to practice law to insure a minimum level of competence. The Appointments Clause confers on the president power to appoint officials to independent agencies. But pursuant to the Necessary and Proper Clause,[11] Congress can (and has) stipulate that no more than a bare majority of agency commissioners can be members of the same political party to promote an ideological balance in the agency's operations.

Chief Justice John Marshall, in *McCulloch v. Maryland, 17 U.S. 316* (1819),[12] explained the breadth of discretion that Congress enjoys in addressing contingencies and circumstances unforeseen and unforeseeable by the Founding Fathers:

A constitution, to contain an accurate detail of the subdivisions of which its great powers will admit, and of all the means by which they shall be carried into execution, would partake of the prolixity of a legal code, and could scarcely be embraced by the human mind. It would, probably, never be understood by the public. Its nature, therefore, requires, that only its great outlines should be marked, its important objects designated, and the minor ingredients which compose those objects, be deduced from the nature of the objects themselves. . . . [W]e must never forget that it is a *constitution* we are expounding. . . . [The Necessary and Proper Clause] is made in a constitution, intended to endure for ages to come, and consequently, to be adapted to the various *crises* in human affairs. To have prescribed the means by which government should, in all future time, execute its powers, would have been to change, entirely, the character of the instrument, and give it the properties of a legal code. It would have been an unwise attempt to provide, by immutable rules, for exigencies which, if foreseen at all, must have been seen dimly, and which can best be provided for as they occur. To have declared, that the best means shall not be used, but those alone, without which the power given would be nugatory, would have been to deprive the legislature of the capacity to avail itself of experience, to exercise reason, and to accommodate its legislation to circumstances. . . . [W]e think the sound construction of the constitution must allow to the national legislature that discretion, with respect to the means by which the powers it confers are to be carried into execution, which will enable that body to perform the high duties assigned to it, in the manner most beneficial to the people. Let the end be legitimate, let it be within the scope of the constitution, and all means which are appropriate, which are plainly adapted to that end, which are not prohibited, but consist with the letter and spirit of the constitution, are constitutional.[13]

FISA fits the *McCulloch* understanding of the Necessary and Proper Clause like a glove. When the Constitution was ratified, the Founding Fathers could not have imagined the emergence of the United States as a global superpower and an imperial presidency possessed of the technological means of intercepting the communications of every American without detection. In 1886, President Woodrow Wilson authored a book entitled *Congressional Governance: A Study in American Government*, a testament to the then-ascendance of the legislative branch over the executive. In 1929, as secretary of state under President Herbert Hoover, Henry L. Stimson was presented with a batch of Japanese telegrams deciphered by an American code-breaking organization—the Black Chamber. The secretary ended the funding with the rebuke: "Gentlemen do not read each other's mail."[14] In 1967, the U.S. Supreme Court brought the Fourth Amendment into modern times by extending its protection to the privacy of conversations in *Katz v. United States* (1967).[15] Decades earlier in *Olmstead v. United States* (1928),[16] the Supreme Court had denied Fourth Amendment protections to conversations because its text mentions only "persons, houses, papers, and effects."[17]

The Church Committee hearings brought to light executive-branch spying abuses and crimes beyond the contemplation of the Founding Fathers. They also vindicated their fear of unchecked power and distrust of human nature. In enacting FISA, Congress did precisely what McCulloch said the Necessary and Proper Clause intended: it availed itself of experience, exercised reason, and accommodated its legislation to circumstances. FISA's legitimate goals are to fortify the Fourth Amendment's protection of privacy, and the First Amendment's protection of free speech and association from executive-branch transgressions. The liberties protected by both amendments had been chronically abused during 40 years of unchecked executive power over foreign intelligence collection. And FISA's requirement of a judicial warrant based on probable cause to justify executive-branch spying on Americans was plainly adapted to the legitimate objectives of the law. Absolute power by the president over foreign intelligence had proven a formula for lawlessness and misconduct irrespective of the party in power or the personality of the president for more than four decades. FISA, moreover, was not an instance of Congress aggrandizing its own powers over foreign intelligence collection. It left the task to the president and the federal judiciary.

U.S. Circuit Judge Richard A. Posner writes, "FISA was a legislative reaction (indeed overreaction) to executive branch abuses."[18] He insists that a changed cultural environment more respectful of civil liberties has antiquated the statute: "The point is not that human nature has changed, since the days when J. Edgar Hoover ran roughshod over civil liberties; it hasn't. It's the environment in which law enforcement and intelligence personnel work that has changed reducing the risk of abuse of private information by its governmental custodians at the same time that the menace of terrorism has increased."[19] Posner adds, "Although there is a history of misuse by the FBI, the CIA, and local police forces of personal information collected ostensibly for law enforcement and intelligence purposes, it is not a recent history. The legal and bureaucratic controls over such misuse are much tighter today than they used to be."[20] The judge's argument, however, is unconvincing.

Intelligence abuses are frequently orchestrated by the president or his political appointees, not by trained bureaucrats. Ambassador Joseph Wilson and his wife Valerie Plame, for example, were defamed through intelligence leaks from President Bush's inner circle, including Vice President Richard B. Cheney, Chief of Staff Scooter Libby, and Karl Rove, President Bush's Rasputin. Furthermore, the incentives for law enforcement and intelligence personnel since September 11, 2001, are to spy more and pay less heed to civil liberties. Even before 9/11, Wen Ho Lee's life had been ruined by government leaks falsely identifying him as a Chinese Communist spy. It was the same case for Stephen Hatfill, a so-called person of interest in the FBI's anthrax investigation. On November 3, 2006, the *New York Times* reported that FBI Director Robert S. Mueller had issued a stern message to the bureau's thirty thousand employees against leaking confidential information after recent news articles disclosed criminal investigations involving congressional incumbents, especially House Republicans. The leaks could have affected the Democratic capture of the 110th Congress. Furthermore, the Department of Justice's inspector general documented widespread misuse and maladministration in the issuance of National Security Letters by the FBI. Eric Lichtblau in *Bush's Law*[21] recounts the Department of Defense's post-9/11 spying on war protestors ridiculously claimed to by threats to military bases. Posner cites no instance of disciplinary action against an intelligence officer for spying beyond his orbit.

Customary civil or criminal deterrents to spying excesses are weak. Civil suits may be frustrated by the state secrets doctrine, which prevents plaintiffs from proceeding if proving the identity or methods of the wrongdoers might expose an intelligence source or method. Criminal liability may be averted or absolved by presidential pardons, or retroactive immunity enacted by Congress. Think of President Ronald Reagan's pardons of Ed Miller and Mark Felt for illegal burglaries. President Bush commuted the sentence of Scooter Libby for perjury and obstruction of justice in the Valerie Plame leak debacle. The Military Commissions Act exonerated violations of the War Crimes Act of 1997 by CIA officers implicated in torture or cruel, inhumane, or degrading treatment of detainees. The FBI's and CIA's intelligence wrongdoings receded from their historical high watermark because of statutes like FISA. That understanding is a reason for retaining the laws, not for their relaxation. And it should never be forgotten that to the president and his appointees intelligence collection is politics by other means.

The FBI's investigation of the leak to the *New York Times* of President Richard M. Nixon's secret bombing of Cambodia in 1969 is emblematic.[22] It began with wiretaps on Morton Halperin, an aide to National Security Adviser Henry Kissinger. It expanded to persons whom Kissinger suspected were undermining his White House influence. Two months of wiretaps and bugs yielded nothing, but Kissinger insisted on their continuance to enable the suspects to establish a "pattern of innocence"[23]—a concept worthy of Franz Kafka's *The Trial*.

The bureaucratic mentality of the spy was captured in the following FBI headquarters response to its New York office's conclusion that surveillance of a civil rights leader should cease because an investigation had unearthed no evidence of Communist sympathies: "The bureau does not agree with the express belief of the New York office that Mr. X is not sympathetic to the party cause. While there may not be any direct evidence that Mr. X is a Communist, neither is there any direct substantial evidence that he is anti-Communist."[24] In other words, it is the mental inclination of spies and the intelligence community to overreach because their job is to spy not to protect privacy interests.

The Cambodia secret bombing leak investigation soon degenerated into collecting political intelligence—for example, a planned magazine article by Clark Clifford critical of Nixon's Vietnam War policy. In all, the FBI employed technical means against 17 individuals. The information retained concerned sex lives, drug use, drinking habits, mental problems, marital disputes, vacation plans, and social contacts.

FISA was clearly a "necessary and proper" answer to this long train of presidential spying abuses, but that does not end the constitutional inquiry. The Necessary and Proper Clause was not intended as an exception to the Constitution's separation of powers. James Madison explained the doctrine in Federalist

No. 47: "where the *whole* power of one department is exercised by the same hands which possess the *whole* power of another department, the fundamental principles of a free constitution, are subverted."[25] Madison further amplified in Federalist No. 48, "the powers properly belonging to one of the departments, ought not to be directly and completely administered by either of the other departments. It is equally evident, that neither of them ought to possess directly or indirectly, an overruling influence over the others in the administration of their respective powers."[26]

The dispositive constitutional question regarding FISA is whether it endows the legislature or judiciary with an "overruling influence"[27] over the president's authority with respect to foreign intelligence. To ask the question is to answer it. At most, FISA lightly regulates but a microscopic portion of the president's foreign intelligence targets. That explains why no president complained about restrictions for more than 23 years until President Bush. Indeed, FISA was expanded under President William Jefferson Clinton to include physical searches.

FISA leaves more than 99 percent of the president's authority to gather foreign intelligence untouched. Its judicial warrant requirement is ordinarily triggered only if the target is an American citizen with a reasonable expectation of privacy in the communications that would be intercepted. The NSA has acknowledged that its targets are overwhelmingly aliens abroad, who enjoy neither Fourth Amendment nor FISA protection. As Robert L. Deitz, general counsel of the NSA, testified on September 6, 2006,

> [B]y far the bulk of the NSA's surveillance activities take place overseas, and these activities are directed entirely at foreign countries and foreign persons within those countries. All concerned agree, and to my knowledge have always agreed, that the FISA does not and should not apply to such activities. . . . In addition, even as it engages in its overseas mission, in the

course of targeting the communications of foreign persons overseas, NSA will sometimes encounter information to, from or about U.S. persons. Yet this fact does not, in itself, cause the FISA to apply to NSA's overseas intelligence activities, and to my knowledge no serious argument exists that it should.[28]

In other words, FISA regulates only a tiny crumb of the president's foreign intelligence authority. Even in that domain, the statute does not bar the president from collecting foreign intelligence but simply requires that the collection be authorized by a judicial warrant based on probable cause. The judicial warrant requirement is an exceptionally modest limitation; it is not insurmountable. FISA judges have granted more than 99 percent of warrant applications submitted by the Department of Justice.

Conclusive proof that FISA does not burden the president's collection of foreign intelligence comes from the testimony of James A. Baker, counsel for intelligence policy, before the Senate Select Committee on Intelligence on July 31, 2002, as President Bush was continuing his criminal violations of FISA:

Let me first, however, report in this open forum what, in more detail, we have reported to our oversight committees on the Hill: Congress, in enacting the USA PATRIOT Act, Pub. L. 107-56 (2001), and the Intelligence Authorization Act for Fiscal Year 2002, Pub. L. 107-108 (2001), provided the Administration with important new tools that it has used regularly, and effectively, in its war on terrorism. The reforms in those measures have affected every single application made by the department for electronic surveillance or physical search of suspected terrorists and have enabled the government to become quicker, more flexible, and more focused in going "up" on those suspected terrorists in the United States. One simple but important change that Congress made was to lengthen the time period for us to bring to court applications in support of Attorney General–authorized emergency FISAs.

This modification has allowed us to make full and effective use of FISA's pre-existing emergency provisions to ensure that the government acts swiftly to respond to terrorist threats.[29]

Another remarkable feature of Baker's testimony was the department's declination to endorse a proposed amendment by Republican Senator Mike DeWine (OH), which would have lowered the FISA threshold for spying on noncitizens from probable cause to reasonable suspicion. Baker highlighted the absence of evidence that the probable cause standards had created any problems:

> The practical concern involves an assessment of whether the current "probable cause" standard has hamstrung our ability to use FISA surveillance to protect our nation. We have been aggressive in seeking FISA warrants and, thanks to Congress's passage of the USA PATRIOT Act, we have been able to use our expanded FISA tools more effectively to combat terrorist activities. It may not be the case that the probable cause standard has caused any difficulties in our ability to seek the FISA warrants we require, and we will need to engage in a significant review to determine the effect a change in the standard would have on our ongoing operations. If the current standard has not posed an obstacle, then there may be little to gain from the lower standard and, as I previously stated, perhaps much to lose.[30]

What Baker's testimony confirms is the eagerness of politicians in a post-9/11 world to abandon cherished civil liberties, such as the right to privacy, to create an appearance of toughness on terrorism. That explains Senator Barak Obama's shift from opposition to support for a new FISA law that would endorse group warrants anathematized by the Founding Fathers.[31]

Proof beyond a reasonable doubt that FISA does not impair the president's collection of foreign intelligence comes from the

TSP itself. It requires the government to obtain FISA warrants to intercept domestic-to-domestic communications—the most likely to involve tactical intelligence needed to frustrate specific terrorist plots. It excuses a FISA warrant only where one communicant in the conversation is abroad. But the standards and rules for obtaining FISA's warrants in both situations are identical. If warrants are workable for domestic-to-domestic interceptions, as the TSP program tacitly acknowledges, then the same is true for international communications.

Al Qaeda is but a shadow of the Soviet Union as it stood when FISA was enacted in 1978. The Soviet invasion of Afghanistan was only one year away. The Cuban missile crisis was still in recent memory. The Soviet Union brandished thousands of nuclear warheads and delivery vehicles, Multiple Independently Targetable Reentry Vehicles (MIRVs), submarines, long-range bombers, and a formidable Red Army. It enjoyed a vast industrial base, oil supplies, and sister resources to support a prolonged hot war. The Soviet Union also sported first-rate scientists capable of developing sophisticated chemical and biological weapons. The United States' need for instant and reliable foreign intelligence to thwart a nuclear attack by the Soviet Union was of the highest order. If FISA did not handcuff the president in meeting the Soviet danger—and no president has made that claim—then, *a fortiori*, the statute does not encumber the president in foiling Al Qaeda's loathsome aims.

Finally, President Bush himself tacitly affirmed that FISA does not compromise his ability to collect foreign intelligence when he abandoned the TSP in favor of FISA warrants in January 2007. To be sure, technologies for communicating have advanced since 1978. But Congress has amended FISA on numerous occasions since September 11, 2001, to insure against technological obsolescence.

It might be argued that foreign intelligence collection became an instrument of war after 9/11 engulfed the United States in a perpetual conflict with international terrorism. But that argument would not diminish the constitutionality of FISA. Congress has routinely regulated the president's conduct of wars far more intrusively than FISA constrains foreign intelligence collection. As part of a strategy to force President Nixon to scale back or end the U.S. military presence in Indochina, Congress enacted four major appropriations measures. In late December 1970, Congress passed the Supplemental Foreign Assistance Appropriations Act. It prohibited the use of funds to introduce U.S. ground combat troops into Cambodia or to provide U.S. advisers to or for Cambodian military forces.

In late June 1973, Congress approved the second Supplemental Appropriations Act for FY1973. It declared, "None of the funds herein appropriated under this act may be expended to support directly or indirectly combat activities in or over Cambodia, Laos, North Vietnam, and South Vietnam by United States forces, and after August 15, 1973, no other funds heretofore appropriated under any other act may be expended for such purpose."[32] That prohibition was carried forth in the June 30, 1973, Continuing Appropriations Resolution for FY1974. In December 1974, Congress passed the Foreign Assistance Act of 1974, which capped American personnel in Vietnam at four thousand within six months of enactment and three thousand after one year.

In late September 1994, Congress passed the Department of Defense Appropriations Act for FY1995. It stipulated, "None of the funds appropriated by this Act may be used for the continuous presence in Somalia of United States military personnel after September 30, 1994."[33] Congress similarly decreed through Title IX of the Department of Defense Appropriations Act for FY1995 that "no funds provided in this Act are available for United States military participation to continue Operation Support Hope in or around Rwanda after October 7, 1994, except for any action that is necessary to protect the lives of United States citizens."[34]

Both Attorney General Alberto Gonzales in testimony before the Senate Judiciary Committee and former Deputy Assistant Attorney General John Yoo in his book *War by Other Means* have affirmed that Congress could constitutionally terminate the NSA's warrantless surveillance program through the power of the purse.[35] The text of such a statute would provide, "No funds of the United States may be expended to gather foreign intelligence in contravention of the Foreign Intelligence Surveillance Act."

The encroachment on the president's foreign intelligence authority is the same whether effectuated through the power of the purse or through FISA. An encroachment by any other name is still an encroachment. To argue, as do Attorney General Gonzales and former Deputy Assistant Attorney General Yoo, that the Constitution makes a distinction between the two is to exalt form over substance.

Finally, the Supreme Court has endorsed the concurring opinion of Justice Robert Jackson in *Youngstown Sheet & Tube v. Sawyer* (1952)[36] that the president's constitutional authorities are at their ebb when he acts contrary to an explicit congressional statute. That is precisely the case with FISA, which asserts that the president shall not proceed unilaterally in collecting foreign intelligence. It declares in Section 2511(2)(f) of the federal criminal code, "[P]rocedures in this chapter or chapter 121 and the Foreign Intelligence Surveillance Act of 1978 shall be the exclusive means by which electronic surveillance, as defined in section 101 of such Act, and the interception of domestic wire, oral, and electronic communications may be conducted."[37]

The constitutionality of FISA establishes that President Bush is guilty of FISA crimes unless Congress created a FISA exception for the TSP. Attorney General Gonzales published a Department of Justice White Paper, which makes that claim on January 19, 2006.[38] Among other things, the White Paper argues that the Authorization to Use Military Force (AUMF) enacted by Congress on September 14, 2001, authorized the TSP as an exception to FISA. The argument is frivolous.

The AUMF authorized the president to "use all necessary and appropriate force against those nations, organizations, or persons he determines planned, authorized, committed, or aided the terrorist attacks"[39] of 9/11 in order to prevent "any future acts of international terrorism against the United States."[40] The AUMF says nothing about electronic surveillance. In particular, the authorization does not even hint at making an exception to FISA's express terms for electronic surveillance during wartime. The latter declares, "Notwithstanding any other law, the President, through the Attorney General, may authorize electronic surveillance without a court order under this title to acquire foreign intelligence information for a period not to exceed fifteen calendar days following a declaration of war by the Congress."[41]

In other words, FISA contemplated wartime circumstances identical or comparable to 9/11 and provided legislation accordingly. The president enjoys a 15-day window to conduct electronic surveillance without any judicial check at the outset of the emergency. The window offers the president time to ask for a legislative extension if necessary for national security. FISA's wartime provision with its 15-day window did not technically apply to 9/11, because Congress never declared war on international terrorism through the AUMF. Congress probably required declarations of war in FISA to encourage presidents to desist from presidential wars, which would not qualify for the FISA window. In any event, FISA addresses electronic surveillance in wartime, and the ordinary rule of statutory construction makes a later-enacted general statute (AUMF) subordinate to an earlier-enacted specific statute (FISA).

Statutory interpretation seeks to honor the intent of Congress. No member who voted for the AUMF voiced any intent to supersede FISA—neither did President Bush when he signed the AUMF. Indeed, the first time that the AUMF argument surfaced was in the department's White Paper more than four years after the AUMF's enactment. Its first argument—abandoned at some unknown later date—was that FISA had no application to the TSP because it must be construed as inapplicable to national security spying.

Furthermore, Congress expressed its grave concern about departing from FISA by imposing criminal sanctions for intentional violations. It declares, "A person is guilty of an offense if he intentionally—(1) engages in electronic surveillance under color of law except as authorized by statute; or (2) discloses or uses information obtained under color of law by electronic surveillance, knowing or having reason to know that the information was obtained through electronic surveillance not authorized by statute."[42]

The criminal prohibition is complemented by a civil liability provision for victims of FISA violations. FISA's criminal and civil sanctions underscore that Congress intended that exceptions to the privacy interest protected by FISA could be made only expressly, not by implication or unwritten hints. And that understanding is confirmed by Section 201(b) of FISA: "[P]rocedures in this chapter and the Foreign Intelligence Surveillance Act of 1978 shall be the exclusive means by which electronic surveillance, as defined in section 101 of such Act, and the interception of domestic, wire, oral, and electronic communications may be conducted."[43]

If the AUMF meant what the department argued—that is, that it intended to authorize the president to gather foreign intelligence irrespective of preexisting congressional restrictions—it would mean that the AUMF also empowered the president to violate federal laws prohibiting breaking and entering homes, opening mail, kidnapping, or torture without any congressional discussion—a baldly absurd conclusion. And it would mean that these cardinal restrictions on gathering foreign intelligence were repealed forever because the AUMF authorizes perpetual warfare against international terrorism. It is preposterous to think that Congress would have effectuated such a revolution in the law of foreign intelligence collection in the cryptic language of the AUMF.

President Bush's behavior betrays his disbelief about his own legal defense of the TSP. He could have obtained an early judicial ruling on its constitutionality. He could have directed the attorney general to present a FISA court with the fruits of TSP spying in seeking a FISA warrant. Nothing has ever leaked from a FISA court. Under the law, unconstitutionally seized evidence may not be used to justify a warrant. Thus, the FISA court would have been required to determine the constitutionality of the TSP in passing on the FISA warrant.

But President Bush has fiercely resisted any judicial review of the TSP for the simple reason that he knows it would be ruled as illegal. There are no mitigating factors in President Bush's FISA crimes that would justify withholding impeachment. He has not sought ratification through retroactive legislation. He has not apologized. He has not voiced contrition. He has not renounced this unitary executive theory of presidential supremacy. Neither can President Bush's motivation to do everything imaginable to reduce the risk of another 9/11 be accepted as exculpatory.

In the aftermath of 9/11 the president pledged that "[w]e will direct every resource at our command—every means of diplomacy, every tool of intelligence, every tool of law enforcement, every financial influence, and every weapon of war—to the destruction of and to the defeat of the global terrorist network."[44] The pledge sounded fetching. Who would be opposed to diminishing the risk of a second edition of 9/11 and open himself to the accusation of being soft on terrorism?

But remember that during the Vietnam War, it was said that cities had to be destroyed to save them. President Bush seems similarly to be insisting that checks and balances, and protections against government abuses, must be destroyed to save the United States from international terrorism and to reduce the risk of another 9/11. But as the Supreme Court remarked in *United States v. Robel* (1967),[45] "[i]t would indeed be ironic if, in the name of national defense, we would sanction the subversion of . . . those liberties . . . which make the defense of the Nation worthwhile."[46] And to do everything in the effort of diminishing the probability of another terrorist incident would be to destroy the reason for the United States. It would mean imprisoning or detaining every American without any court review or congressional authorization. It would mean kidnapping and torturing citizens to gather foreign intelligence on the president's say-so alone. It would mean secret government and secret laws.

Freedom requires accepting a prudent level of risk necessary for it to breathe. That is the thrust of the Fourth Amendment's protection of the right to be left alone. It was the thrust of the Founding Fathers' opposition to general writs of assistance that enabled customs officers to snoop through every home in search of smuggled goods.

There is a risk involved in refusing to permit policemen on every corner or in every home. There is a risk involved in the presumption of innocence. It would be easier to disappear suspected terrorists into dungeons without trials. There is a risk in public trials as opposed to secret proceedings reminiscent of the British Star Chamber. Public trials enable international terrorists to know what incriminating evidence was collected against one of their own and to scrutinize their terrorist networks for vulnerabilities. However, a great nation does not stoop to ape its barbarian opponents.

Vice President Cheney fashioned a "one percent" risk standard for the president's national security policies: "If there's a one percent chance [Al Qaeda does possess a nuclear program] you have to pursue it as if it were true."[47] But a one percent standard is irreconcilable with freedom. It would authorize searches, detentions, and punishments of citizens at the whim of the president. Joseph Stalin and Mao Tse-Tung would be smiling.

SEVEN

Secret Government

Secret government is highly disfavored under the Constitution. John Adams sermonized in "A Dissertation on the Canon and Feudal Law" (1765),[1] "[L]iberty cannot be preserved without a general knowledge among the people, who have a right . . . to knowledge . . . and a desire to know; but besides this, they have a right, an indisputable, unalienable, indefeasible, divine right to that most dreaded and envied kind of knowledge, I mean, of the characters and conduct of their rulers."[2]

Yet President George W. Bush has reveled in secret government by invoking executive privilege or state secrets to frustrate congressional or private oversight of executive-branch actions—for example, the manipulation of U.S. attorneys to skew law enforcement or secret spying programs that invade the privacy of Americans and, in the case of the Terrorist Surveillance Program (TSP), are flagrantly criminal.[3] Secrecy is a clear and present danger to the Republic. The Report of the Commission on Protecting and Reducing Government Secrecy (Moynihan Commission) lectured, "Excessive secrecy has significant consequences for the national interest when, as a result, policymakers are not fully informed, government is not held accountable for its actions, and the public cannot engage in informed debate."[4]

The executive branch, however, craves secrecy, because it enables the president to lie or distort information in order to frighten Congress and the people into following his adventures, to conceal ineptness, and to perpetrate crimes with impunity. It was thus predictable that the Moynihan Commission would further observe, "The classification system . . . is used too often to deny the public an understanding of the policymaking process, rather than for the necessary protection of intelligence activities and other highly sensitive matters."[5] The executive is disinclined to support transparency because it subjects the president to congressional and public accountability or second-guessing. The president benefits from transparency to this extent: it scuttles ill-conceived ideas or plans by exposing them to outside vetting. But presidents generally believe in executive branch infallibility, which cannot be improved by outside review.

In debating challenger Senator John Kerry (D-MA), for example, President Bush insisted that he could not think of a single bad or wrong decision he had made.[6] Thus, presidents prefer intellectual endogamy to transparency even if it leads to monumental errors, as in post–Saddam Hussein Iraq. Executive privilege is a narrow exception to the constitutional rule of transparency. The words are mentioned nowhere in the Constitution's text. The idea was nowhere referred to in the constitutional convention debates or the Federalist Papers. The phrase refers to an asserted inherent constitutional authority of the president to conceal direct and indirect presidential advice or communications from Congress or the judiciary.

President Bush has invoked the privilege to prohibit current and former White House advisers—including political adviser Karl Rove, former White House Counsel Harriet Miers, and Chief of Staff Joshua Bolten—from even appearing before the House and Senate Judiciary Committees to testify about the firings of nine U.S. attorneys.[7] The twin committees are investigating suspected perjury and endeavors to impede a congressional investigation by Attorney General Alberto Gonzales, illegal politicization of the civil service at the Department of Justice, and the firings of the U.S. attorneys to manipulate law enforcement to the advantage of the Republican Party.[8]

The outlandishness of the president's executive privilege claim can be underscored by hearkening back to the spring of 1973 and the transfixing testimony of former White House Counsel John Dean before the Senate Watergate Committee. Dean disclosed numerous incriminating conversations with President Richard M. Nixon in the Oval Office.[9] The two explored the Watergate cover-up—that is, the attempt to conceal the connection between the Committee to Re-elect the President and the burglary of the Democratic National Committee at the Watergate Hotel. President Nixon flirted with paying money to the burglars for their silence, but then, in a memorable exchange with Dean, insincerely insisted that it would be wrong.[10]

Dean's testimony about his presidential conversations occasioned the discovery of the White House tapes and prompted three articles of impeachment voted against President Nixon by the House Judiciary Committee; the Supreme Court's decision in *United States v. Nixon* (1974)[11] ordering the president to produce certain tapes and documents relating to his conversations with aides and advisers; and President Nixon's resignation in disgrace on August 9, 1974.[12] Without Dean's disclosures, Nixon's cover-up would probably have succeeded. The Constitution would have been defiled. The president might have become a virtual king.

To believe that the Constitution would have authorized President Nixon to block Dean's testimony before Congress to conceal presidential crimes would be preposterous. The Constitution frowns on unchecked power; and Dean's testimony enabled Congress and the judiciary to check the president's wrongdoing. The Constitution recognizes a sweeping congressional power to investigate the executive for crimes or maladministration. The Senate Watergate Committee had reasonable suspicion to believe that the White House was implicated in political crimes and had misused its influence with the Central Intelligence Agency.[13]

President Bush's superinflated conception of executive privilege, however, would have justified Nixon's silencing of Dean. That prospect, without more, casts extreme doubt on its validity. The president's privilege claim is even more outlandish because it asserts a power to prevent presidential aides from even appearing before Congress, not simply a power to prohibit answers to congressional questions that would require breaching presidential confidentiality. The Fifth Amendment privilege against compulsory self-incrimination provides an informative analogy. A witness may not decline to appear before a grand jury or Congress because it is thought likely that the Fifth Amendment would justify refusing to answer some, most, or all of the anticipated questions. The privilege must be asserted on a question-by-question basis. G. Gordon Liddy spent 18 months in jail for refusing to testify before a House committee investigating Watergate.[14]

Bush's assertions of the privilege to frustrate congressional oversight of major executive functions are constitutionally frivolous and disturbing to government by the consent of the governed. As David Wise and Thomas B. Ross have written in *The Invisible Government*, "[T]here can be no meaningful consent where those who are governed do not know to what they are consenting."[15]

James Madison wrote, "A popular Government without popular information or the means of acquiring it, is but a Prologue to a Farce or a Tragedy or perhaps both. Knowledge will forever govern ignorance, and a people who mean to be their own Governors, must arm themselves with the power knowledge gives."[16] Citizens and Congress must know what their government is doing so that they can evaluate public officials, and adjust their political loyalties and activities accordingly. That is the core of self-government. Consent means informed consent, not blind consent or consent elicited by lies. Transparency, to be sure, does not mean publicly disclosing troop locations or weapons like the Manhattan Project that could assist the enemy. But it does mean public disclosure of basic policy decisions with sufficient detail to enable an intelligent evaluation of their utility or wisdom.

Secrecy encourages three distinct vices: lies, lawlessness, and ineptitude. It encourages government lies to advance the president's political agenda, to defame his opponents, and to conceal errors. Remember the lies that President Lyndon B. Johnson told about the Gulf of Tonkin and the lies that President Bush told about weapons of mass destruction and Saddam Hussein's collusion with Al Qaeda in Iraq.[17] Throughout its history, the CIA has distorted facts and analysis at the behest of the White House to promote the president's view of the world. And the Defense Department lied about Pat Tillman's friendly fire death to conceal negligence or perhaps worse.[18]

Secrecy also invites lawlessness. The absence of exacting congressional oversight of the FBI, CIA, and NSA occasioned decades of illegal spying, which was later revealed by the Church Committee.[19] Scooter Libby lied and obstructed justice in the investigation of the Valerie Plame leak because he believed that he was above the law.[20] And contemplate what the crime rate would be among private citizens if they knew that their wrongdoing—theft, larceny, embezzlement, assault, or otherwise—would never be revealed. Secrecy spawned the waterboarding crimes of CIA interrogators and their superiors. As soon as the matter surfaced publicly, the practice ceased, and incriminating videotapes were destroyed.

Secrecy encourages indolence and ineptitude. A nontrivial percentage of government officials would be inattentive and lazy if they operated in a public fishbowl. The fear of public embarrassment or punishment is the spur of excellence for the ordinary person.

Secrecy is mentioned only once in the Constitution. Article I, Section 5, Clause 3 provides, "Each House shall keep a Journal of its Proceedings, and from time to time publish the same, excepting such Parts as may in their Judgment require secrecy."[21] Article I, Section 9, Clause 7, however, is an explicit instruction in favor of transparency: "No Money shall be drawn from the Treasury, but in Consequence of Appropriations made by Law; and, a regular Statement and Account of the Receipts and Expenditures of all Public Money shall be published from time to time."[22]

In *United States v. Richardson* (1974),[23] the Supreme Court addressed the constitutionality of the Central Intelligence Agency Act of 1949, which authorized the Agency to account for its expenditures "solely on the certificate of the Director."[24] A 5–4 majority dodged a decision on the merits but hinted that Congress had discretion to choose some secrecy in budget matters necessary to protect intelligence sources or methods.[25] Under that authority, Congress has both published and concealed the CIA's budget, indicating the elusiveness of determining whether a disclosure might damage the national security. In 1997 and 1998, CIA Director George Tenet released the agency's intelligence budgets showing expenditures of $26.6 billion, and $26.7 billion, respectively.[26] The agency's budget then remained concealed, until President Bush signed the 9/11 Act in 2007.[27] As recommended by the 9/11 Commission, the act requires disclosure of the intelligence community budget for fiscal years 2007 and 2008, and thereafter, unless the president convinces Congress that publicity would harm the national security.[28]

It seems farfetched to believe that publicizing the budget of the intelligence community would clue adversaries to anything important. An aggregate budget does not disclose amounts expended for particular operations or components. The aggregate budget is not an intelligence community playbook for the enemy. Indeed, the budget disclosure probably diminishes spying against the United States. Foreign intelligence agencies are notorious, like their U.S. counterpart, for overestimating the intelligence resources of their rivals to bloat their own budgets.

By publicizing the U.S. intelligence budget, foreign intelligence agencies are hindered in frightening their respective governments into spiraling intelligence expenditures. Thus, not a crumb of evidence indicates that disclosing the CIA's budget in 1997 and 1998 created a national security risk.

Skepticism about the national security harm caused by stolen secrets is justified by considering the notorious atomic spy case. Ethel and Julius Rosenberg, among others, were convicted and executed for stealing secrets about the atomic bomb for the Soviet Union.[29] The espionage may have accelerated the Soviet acquisition of the bomb, which came in1949—a few years earlier than American experts had projected.[30] It has been assumed that the acceleration was catastrophic for the United States and justified the Rosenberg executions. But the assumption is questionable. The United States was the sole atomic or nuclear-weapons state from 1945 to 1949. That advantage, however, did not deter Soviet aggression or adventurism. It did not prevent Stalin from flouting the Yalta accords and refusing to hold free and fair elections in Eastern and Central Europe, including Poland.[31] It did not prevent the Iron Curtain. It did not prevent the 1948 Berlin blockade or the Communist coup in Czechoslovakia.[32] The United States did not respond to the Berlin crisis by threatening an atomic strike, but rather by an airlift that avoided a direct confrontation with the Soviet Union.

A retrospective on Soviet espionage to steal atomic secrets suggests that seemingly vital state secrets may occasion little or no actual harm to national security. That observation does not dispute that some information must remain secret—for example, the identities of informants who would be killed if their names were publicized or communicated to the enemy, or the location of troops. But it does warn against a readiness to sacrifice transparency on the altar of alleged national security. Ordinarily, the game is not worth the gamble. Secrecy carries huge costs to a democratic dispensation resting on the rule of law as well as to an informed public.

In contrast to the legislative branch, not a single syllable in the Constitution hints at a privilege to conceal presidential advice or deliberations. However, a qualified privilege may be deduced from the Constitution's separation of powers. Neither Congress nor the judiciary should enjoy a right of access to executive communications or information that would confer on either a overriding influence over an executive function. Moreover, the powers of Congress are limited. It has no authority to expose presidential communications for the sake of political voyeurism or embarrassment. Its powers are confined to gathering information relevant to legislation, oversight, or informing the public.

The first invocation of executive privilege by President George Washington underscores its hyperinflation under President Bush. President Washington had deputed John Jay as his minister to negotiate what proved to be the highly unpopular Jay Treaty of 1795 with Great Britain.[33] As required by the Constitution, the Senate ratified the treaty by a two-thirds majority. The House of Representatives was upset for political reasons and sought a copy of President Washington's instructions to Jay, together with correspondence and other documents relative to the treaty, "excepting such of the said papers as any existing negotiation may render improper to be disclosed."[34]

President Washington responded by first acknowledging an unflagging dedication to disclose any information enjoined by the Constitution and an eagerness to harmonize the executive with its coequal branches.[35] He assumed that in some cases— for example, an impeachment inquiry—Congress could compel presidential disclosures, and that in all cases, the president should seek cooperation rather than confrontation:

> I trust that no part of my conduct has ever indicated a disposition to withhold any information which the Constitution has enjoined upon the President as a duty to give, or which could be required of him by either House of Congress as a right; and with truth I affirm that it has been, as it will continue to be

while I have the honor to preside in the Government, my constant endeavor to harmonize with the other branches thereof so far as the trust delegated to me by the people of the United States and my sense of obligation it imposes to "preserve, protect, and defend the Constitution" will permit.[36]

President Washington explained that disclosure of the requested papers would interfere with the ability of the president to negotiate treaties favorable to the United States. Publicizing the measures, demands, or eventual concessions, which may have been proposed or contemplated, might compromise future negotiations and negotiating flexibility by causing political embarrassment or by revealing negotiating strategy akin to a state secret. President Washington further amplified that the intent of the Constitution's makers to confine the treaty-making power to the president and a small Senate in order to safeguard secrecy would be ruined if the multitudinous House of Representatives enjoyed routine access to negotiation papers that had been shared with the Senate:

> The nature of foreign negotiations requires caution, and their success must often depend on secrecy; and even when brought to a conclusion a full disclosure of all measures, demands, or eventual concessions which may have been proposed or contemplated would be extremely impolitic; for this might have a pernicious influence on future negotiations, or produce immediate inconveniences, perhaps danger and mischief, in relation to other powers. The necessity of such caution and secrecy was one cogent reason for vesting the power of making treaties in the President, with the advise and consent of the Senate, the principle on which that body was formed confining it to a small number of members. To admit, then, a right in the House of Representatives to demand and to have as a matter of course all the papers respecting a negotiation with a foreign power would be to establish a dangerous precedent.[37]

President Washington again summoned the Constitution to elaborate that the House had no need to be informed of negotiating instructions or correspondence to perform its legitimate functions. The president acknowledged, however, that if the House was investigating suspected bribery or other potential impeachable offenses connected with the Jay Treaty, then its right to demand the negotiating papers would be compelling. He also stated that he did not subscribe to secrecy for the sake of secrecy:

> It does not occur that the inspection of the papers asked for can be relative to any purpose under the cognizance of the House of Representatives, except that of an impeachment, which the resolution has not expressed. I repeat that I have no disposition to withhold any information which the duty of my station will permit or the public good shall require to be disclosed; and, in fact, all the papers affecting the negotiation with Great Britain were laid before the Senate when the treaty itself was communicated for their consideration.[38]

President Washington then relied on the original intent of the Constitution to conclude that treaties are complete and legally binding in themselves, without legislative action by the House of Representatives, and that he was declining to disclose the requested negotiating papers to prevent the House from snooping into business that belonged to other government departments:

> The course which the debate has taken on the resolution of the House leads to some observations on the mode of making treaties under the Constitution of the United States.
>
> Having been a member of the General Convention, and knowing the principles on which the Constitution was formed, I have ever entertained but one opinion on this subject; and from the first establishment of the Government to

this moment my conduct has exemplified that opinion that the power of making treaties is exclusively vested in the President, by and with the advise and consent of the Senate, provided two-thirds of the Senators present concur, and that every treaty so made and promulgated thenceforward became the law of the land. It is thus that the treaty-making power has been understood by foreign nations, and in all the treaties made with them we have declared and they have believed that, when ratified by the President, with the advice and consent of the Senate, they become obligatory. In this construction of the Constitution every House of Representatives has heretofore acquiesced, and until the present time not a doubt or suspicion has appeared, to my knowledge, that this construction was not the true one. Nay, they have more than acquiesced; for till now, without controverting the obligation of such treaties, they have made all the requisite provisions for carrying them into effect.

If other proofs than these and the plain letter of the Constitution itself be necessary to ascertain the point under consideration, they may be found in the journals of the General Convention, which I have deposited in the office of the Department of State. In those journals it will appear that a proposition was made "that no treaty should be binding on the United States which was not ratified by law," and that the proposition was explicitly rejected.

As, therefore, it is perfectly clear to my understanding that the assent of the House of Representatives is not necessary to the validity of a treaty; as the treaty with Great Britain exhibits in itself all the objects requiring legislative provision, and on these the papers called for can throw no light, and as it is essential to the due administration of the Government that the boundaries fixed by the Constitution between the different departments should be preserved, a just regard to the Constitution and to the duty of my office, under all the circumstances of this case, forbids a compliance with your request.[39]

President Washington's response established a cluster of rules for congressional oversight and executive privilege that honored the intent of the Constitution's makers. First, the House and Senate were entitled to request documents or testimony pertinent to the discharge of their constitutional powers—for example, the ratification of treaties, the enactment of legislation, impeachment for high crimes and misdemeanors, or detecting lawlessness or maladministration in the executive branch.[40] But Congress was not entitled to survey the executive branch just to satisfy its curiosity.

Second, if Congress could establish relevance to a legitimate function, the president was required to provide the requested information. Thus, President Washington had provided to the Senate all of the negotiating papers requested by the House because of the Senate's need to determine whether to ratify the treaty with Great Britain.[41]

Third, the president could not withhold confidential presidential advice or communications from Congress to encourage candor by presidential communicants, simpliciter. President Washington nowhere hinted in his response to the House of Representatives that he feared a chilling effect on presidential advisers if their communications were shared with Congress. Indeed, he had delivered all of the requested negotiating correspondence to the Senate.[42]

The president and Congress have sparred over executive privilege, with President Washington's response as a guidepost, for more than two centuries without precipitating a decision by the U.S. Supreme Court. The most relevant case concerned an executive-judicial dispute and militates overwhelmingly against President Bush's privilege claims vis-à-vis Congress, regarding its investigation of the firings of nine U.S. attorneys and the secret spying programs of the president, including the TSP.

In *United States v. Nixon*, a federal grand jury returned an indictment charging seven named individuals with, among other things, conspiracy to defraud the United States and to obstruct justice. The seven were John Mitchell, H. R. Haldeman, John Ehrlichman, Charles Colson, Robert Mardian, Kenneth Parkinson, and Gordon Strachan. Each had occupied either a position of responsibility on the White House staff or a position with the Committee for the Re-election of the President.[43]

A subpoena was issued to President Nixon requiring certain tapes, memoranda, papers, transcripts, or other writings relating to precisely identified meetings between the president and others. President Nixon claimed an absolute privilege, unreviewable by the judiciary, to withhold confidential conversations between a president and his close advisers from the Congress, the judiciary, and from the people.[44] In other words, the president was insisting that he should be the judge of his own authority to obstruct the functioning of coequal branches of government and to hide from the people knowledge of what their government was saying and doing. A unanimous Supreme Court rejected that claim based on the Constitution's checks and balances.[45]

Writing for the Court, Chief Justice Warren Burger amplified,

The impediment that an absolute, unqualified privilege would place in the way of the primary constitutional duty of the Judicial Branch to do justice in criminal prosecutions would plainly conflict with the function of courts under Article III. In designing the structure of our Government and dividing and allocating sovereign power among three co-equal branches, the Framers of the Constitution sought to provide a comprehensive system, but the separate powers were not intended to operate with absolute independence. . . . To read the Article II powers of the President as providing an absolute privilege as against a subpoena essential to enforcement of criminal statutes on no more than a generalized claim of public interest in confidentiality of nonmilitary and nondiplomatic discussions would upset the balance of "a workable government" and gravely impair the role of courts under Article III.[46]

Chief Justice Burger, however, recognized a qualified constitutional privilege in the president to withhold presidential communications from Congress or the courts. The chief justice's reasons were characteristically feeble and warred with actual practice. He declared,

> Human experience teaches that those who expect public dissemination of their remarks may well temper candor with a concern for appearances and for their own interests to the detriment of the decision-making process. Whatever the nature of the privilege of confidentiality of Presidential communications in the exercise of Article II powers, the privilege can be said to derive from the supremacy of each branch within its own assigned area of constitutional duties. Certain powers and privileges flow from the nature of enumerated powers; the protection of Presidential communications has similar constitutional underpinnings.[47]

The chief justice stumbled because of his simpleminded understanding of the dynamics of presidential advice.

I have worked in and out of the federal government in all three branches for 38 years. I have never heard any high or low executive-branch official so much as insinuate that presidential advice had been, or might be, skewed or withheld if confidentiality were not guaranteed. The gravity of advising the president overcomes anxieties over possible embarrassment through subsequent publicity. Moreover, *every presidential adviser knows that confidentiality is never ironclad.* Presidents routinely waive executive privilege in jockeying with Congress. President Ronald Reagan, for example, waived the privilege to permit the testimonies of National Security Advisers Admiral John Poindexter and Bud McFarlane, Secretary of Defense Casper Weinberger, and Secretary of State George Shultz in the congressional investigation of covert arms sales to Iran. He did so to dispel the suspicion that he was personally implicated in diverting monies to the Nicaraguan resistance, specifically to Sandanista Daniel Ortega. CIA Director George Tenet writes about the disclosure of his "slam dunk" evidence of weapons of mass destruction in Iraq in *At the Center of the Storm*: "I have a few tips for future CIA directors, and anyone who aspires to participate in government at a similar level. First, you are never off stage. Anything you say can be used down the road to make someone else's point. That's the way Washington has evolved—there are no private conversations, even in the Oval Office."[48]

Additionally, confidentiality is always subservient to a criminal investigation or prosecution under the *Nixon* precedent. Leaks to the media of confidential presidential memos or conversations also overflow like the Nile. Indeed, President Bush has waived the privilege repeatedly in the ongoing congressional investigations of the firings of U.S. attorneys. In addition, White House officials routinely write memoirs after leaving office, which reveal confidential presidential advice—for example, Scott McClellan's *What Happened*.[49] No high-level executive official ever speaks to the president with an expectation of confidentiality.

Ignoring the reality of White House advice and deliberations, Chief Justice Burger maintained,

The expectation of a President to the confidentiality of his conversations and correspondence, like the claim of confidentiality of judicial deliberations, for example, has all the values to which we accord deference for the privacy of all citizens and, added to those values, is the necessity for protection of the public interest in candid, objective, and even blunt or harsh opinions in Presidential decision-making. A President and those who assist him must be free to explore alternatives in the process of shaping policies and making decisions and to do so in a way many would be unwilling to accept except privately. These are the considerations justifying a presumptive privilege for Presidential communications. The privilege is fundamental to the operation of Government and inextricably rooted in the separation of powers under the Constitution.[50]

The chief justice's likening of the executive to the judicial branch was misplaced. Supreme Court Justices are not elected; no democratic interest is advanced by exposing judicial deliberations. The law binding on the nation is the written opinion of the judges, not the preliminary thinking or discourse. In contrast, the executive *is* elected. The people have an interest in knowing what the executive is saying, doing, or thinking to evaluate his character and wisdom, and to adapt their political loyalties and actions accordingly. The people have a legitimate interest in knowing about maladministration in the executive branch in order to force corrective political action or to inflict political retaliation through their votes. Whereas, the remedy for erroneous judging in the federal judiciary is an appeal to a higher court or a legislative or constitutional amendment, not political retaliation against the offending judge, which would undermine an independent judiciary. No public interest would be advanced by transparency of federal judicial deliberations—except perhaps to deter the use of the judicial cloister to plot crimes. Corruption within the federal judiciary, however, has never been a major problem.

Nevertheless, the chief justice subordinated the concocted need of the president for confidentiality to the rule of law and criminal justice. He elaborated,

We have elected to employ an adversary system of criminal justice in which the parties contest issues before a court of law. The need to develop all relevant facts in the adversary system is both fundamental and comprehensive. The ends of criminal justice would be defeated if judgments were to be founded on a partial or speculative presentation of the facts. The very integrity of the judicial system and public confidence in the system depend on full disclosure of all the facts within the framework of the rules of evidence. To ensure that justice is done, it is imperative to the function of courts that compulsory process be available for the production of evidence needed either by the prosecution or by the defense. . . . In this case the President challenges a subpoena served on him as a third party requiring the production of materials for use in a criminal prosecution; he does so on the claim that he has a privilege against disclosure of confidential communications. He does not place his claim of privilege on the ground that they are military or diplomatic secrets. . . .

No case of this Court, however, has extended this high degree of deference to a President's generalized interest in confidentiality. Nowhere in the Constitution . . . is there any explicit reference to a privilege of confidentiality, yet to the extent this interest relates to the effective discharge of a President's powers, it is constitutionally based.

In this case we must weigh the importance of the general privilege of confidentiality of Presidential communications in the performance of the President's responsibilities against the inroads of such a privilege on the fair administration of criminal justice. The interest in preserving confidentiality is weighty indeed and entitled to great respect. However, we cannot conclude that advisers will be moved to temper the candor of their remarks by the infrequent occasions of disclosure because of the possibility that such conversations will be called for in the context of a criminal prosecution. On the other hand, the allowance of the privilege to withhold evidence that is demonstrably relevant in a criminal trial would cut deeply into the guarantees of due process of law and gravely impair the basic function of courts. A President's acknowledged need for confidentiality in the communications of his office is general in nature, whereas the constitutional need for production of relevant evidence in a criminal proceeding is specific and central to the fair adjudication of a particular criminal case in the administration of justice. Without access to specific facts a criminal prosecution may be totally frustrated. The President's broad interest in confidentiality will not be vitiated by disclosure of a limited number of conversations preliminarily shown to have some bearing on the pending criminal cases.[51]

The rationale of *United States v. Nixon* overwhelmingly supports subordinating the president's qualified privilege in confidentiality to the information needs of Congress in overseeing the executive branch for lawlessness or maladministration and for informing the public of what their government is doing and why. In that case, the special prosecutor's need for President Nixon's tapes and similar materials was thin. The presidential communications were relevant to the prosecution and admissible as evidence, but they were not shown to have been indispensable, crucial, or major components of the special prosecutor's proof of guilt. Indeed, the special prosecutor might have proved his case beyond a reasonable doubt without any presidential communications as evidence.

In addition, the special prosecutor held no constitutional right to the president's communications. Nothing guarantees the government access to evidence needed to convict. A criminal defendant, in contrast, might claim a right to obtain presidential communications to enforce his Sixth Amendment rights "to be confronted with the witnesses against him"[52] and "to have compulsory process for obtaining witnesses in his favor."[53] Furthermore, the constitution purposely tilts in favor of the defendant in criminal prosecutions—for example, by establishing a Fifth Amendment privilege against compulsory self-incrimination and saddling the government with the burden of proving guilt beyond a reasonable doubt. In contrast, there is no corresponding constitutional solicitude for the government's winning its prosecution.

Suppose that in *United States v. Nixon* the Court had sustained President Nixon's claim of privilege and the prosecution had failed as a result. The president's privilege would no more have undermined the ends of criminal justice than would a defendant's invocation of the Fifth Amendment. In addition, sustaining Nixon's assertion of privilege would have had an infinitesimal impact on the judicial branch because of the microscopic number of cases in which presidential communications are both relevant and admissible in a criminal prosecution. In sum, the key to understanding *United States v. Nixon* is that the Court forced the president to subordinate his qualified privilege to advance a relatively trivial prosecutorial or judicial interest.

Congressional oversight of the executive branch is vastly more important to the rule of law and democracy than the rare prosecution of crimes in which presidential conversations may be needed as evidence. Without congressional oversight, executive lawlessness, folly, incompetence, and sloth are invited. Moreover, self-government is thwarted because the people need to know what their government is doing in order to adapt their political affiliations and actions, and vote accordingly. The injury to the functioning of the legislative branch occasioned by the president's invocation of executive privilege is enormously greater than the corresponding injury to the judicial branch when the privilege would deny government prosecutors access to relevant evidence. This is all the more reason to reject executive privilege in conjunction with congressional oversight hearings where the presidential communications sought are relevant to detecting lawlessness, abuse, or faulty executive-branch conduct.

On the other hand, congressional oversight hearings are daily occurrences, whereas criminal prosecutions in need of presidential communications are rarities. Thus, there is a greater risk that presidential advisers would "be moved to temper the candor of their remarks"[54] if the privilege were not recognized before Congress, because the frequency of compelled disclosures would be far greater. But as explained previously, the presumed chilling effect on candid presidential advice if executive privilege were not honored has no grounding in either logic or experience.

United States v. Nixon compels the conclusion that executive privilege should have no place in congressional oversight hearings into the firings of the nine U.S. attorneys. The reasons for that conclusion deserve further amplification to demonstrate that President Bush's invocation of the privilege is not a good faith interpretation of his constitutional obligations; it is a crime against the Constitution's checks and balances.

Justice, like Caesar's wife, must be above suspicion.[55] Public confidence in the evenhanded administration of justice and cooperation with law-enforcement authorities will recede if it is generally thought that law enforcement is a partisan tool. Moreover, Congress and the American people are entitled to know about the president's criteria or motivations for hiring or firing U.S. attorneys if they are to evaluate his performance. U.S. attorneys are exceptionally important because little constrains their prosecutorial discretion, which can easily destroy lives or fortunes without due process of law by a simple grand jury investigation or indictment. Approximately 60 years ago, then–Attorney General Robert Jackson worried about that same danger in speaking to U.S. attorneys:

> It would probably be within the range of that exaggeration permitted in Washington to say that assembled in this room is one of the most powerful peace-time forces known to our country. The prosecutor has more control over life, liberty, and reputation than any other person in America. His discretion is tremendous. He can have citizens investigated and, if he is that kind of person, he can have this done to the tune of public statements and veiled or unveiled intimations. Or the prosecutor may choose a more subtle course and simply have a citizen's friends interviewed. The prosecutor can order arrests, present cases to the grand jury in secret session, and on the basis of his one-sided presentation of the facts, can cause the citizen to be indicted and held for trial. He may dismiss the case before trial, in which case the defense never has

a chance to be heard. Or he may go on with a public trial. If he obtains a conviction, the prosecutor can still make recommendations as to sentence, as to whether the prisoner should get probation or a suspended sentence, and after he is put away, as to whether he is a fit subject for parole. While the prosecutor at his best is one of the most beneficent forces in our society, when he acts from malice or other base motives, he is one of the worst.

There is a most important reason why the prosecutor should have, as nearly as possible, a detached and impartial view of all groups in his community. Law enforcement is not automatic. It isn't blind. One of the greatest difficulties of the position of prosecutor is that he must pick his cases, because no prosecutor can even investigate all of the cases in which he receives complaints. If the Department of Justice were to make even a pretense of reaching every probable violation of federal law, ten times its present staff would be inadequate. We know that no local police force can strictly enforce the traffic laws, or it would arrest half the driving population on any given morning. What every prosecutor is practically required to do is to select the cases for prosecution and to select those in which the offense is the most flagrant, the public harm the greatest, and the proof the most certain.

If the prosecutor is obliged to choose his cases, it follows that he can choose his defendants. Therein is the most dangerous power of the prosecutor: that he will pick people that he thinks he should get, rather than pick cases that need to be prosecuted. With the law books filled with a great assortment of crimes, a prosecutor stands a fair chance of finding at least a technical violation of some act on the part of almost anyone. In such a case, it is not a question of discovering the commission of a crime and then looking for the man who has committed it, it is a question of picking the man and then searching the law books, or putting investigators to work, to pin some offense on him. It is in this realm—in which the prosecutor picks some person whom he dislikes or desires to embarrass, or selects some group of unpopular persons and then looks for an offense, that the greatest danger of abuse of prosecuting power lies. It is here that law enforcement becomes personal, and the real crime becomes that of being unpopular with the predominant or governing group, being attached to the wrong political views, or being personally obnoxious to or in the way of the prosecutor himself.[56]

The firings under investigation by Congress were suspicious because they involved President Bush discharging the same Republican U.S. attorneys whom he had previously appointed.[57] In contrast, it has been routine for an incoming administration to fire the U.S. attorneys appointed by the predecessor president. Every White House has a constitutional right to its own law-enforcement team.

The firings were further suspect because they were not based on standardized or even nonstandardized performance ratings, although Attorney General Gonzales at one time insisted otherwise.[58] Indeed, several of the discharged U.S. attorneys had earned Justice Department acclaim—for example, David Iglesias of New Mexico.[59] When placed under oath before Congress, the attorney general was generally unable to recollect why any of the U.S. attorneys had been fired or who had urged their discharges.[60] It *was* known, however, that the impetus for the discharges emanated from the White House, including political adviser Karl Rove.[61] The White House, however, generally knows nothing of the dockets of U.S. attorneys or cares who they are, except to placate a Senator or to reward a friend. Otherwise, the sole interest of the White House in U.S. attorneys is to manipulate their choice of cases for a partisan advantage. Its only interest in the office is to answer a political complaint or to enlist law enforcement in aid of a partisan agenda. Thus, the White House became concerned with Iglesias because New

Mexican Senator Pete Domenici complained about his noncooperation in providing politically sensitive prosecutorial information. The Senate Ethics Committee later officially admonished Senator Domenici for making an improper phone call to Iglesias's home.[62]

That is not what the Constitution expects. The president should and does enjoy the right to insist that U.S. attorneys follow his law-enforcement priorities and policies. President Bush, for example, could have properly instructed his appointees to focus their resources on international terrorism, immigration smuggling, drug trafficking, obscenity prosecutions, public corruption, and voting fraud. He could have directed the Department of Justice to prepare a running scorecard for each U.S. attorney, indicating how many cases were being pursued in each priority category, the success rate of prosecutions, and the manpower involved. It would have been quite proper to have fired U.S. attorneys based on poor scorecards indicating either incompetence or resistance to the president's priorities.

But neither the White House nor the Department of Justice prepared such scorecards. The White House communicated with Attorney General Gonzales regarding gripes about insufficient enthusiasm in particular districts for initiating federal voting-fraud prosecutions. Within political circles, it is generally thought that voting fraud implicates substantially more Democrats than Republicans—even though its incidence as a whole is tiny. It is also thought that a voting-fraud prosecution would frighten substantially more Democrats than Republicans away from the polling booth.

Voting fraud crimes, however, are largely matters of state law. Federal statutes are narrow and the evidence necessary for conviction is demanding. Generally speaking, federal law punishes intimidation or coercion to prevent voting in a federal election, or the offering or receiving something of value in exchange for voting or not voting. Between 2002 and 2005, the Department of

Justice secured only 26 voting-fraud convictions or guilty pleas (8–9 annually). In addition, the White House had no way of knowing whether evidence would support a voting fraud conviction. The U.S. Supreme Court lectured in *Berger v. New York* (1935),[63]

> The United States Attorney is the representative not of an ordinary party to a controversy, but of a sovereignty whose obligation to govern impartially is as compelling as its obligation to govern at all; and whose interest, therefore, in a criminal prosecution is not that it shall win a case, but that justice shall be done. As such, he is in a peculiar and very definite sense the servant of the law, the twofold aim of which is that guilt shall not escape or innocence suffer. He may prosecute with earnestness and vigor—indeed, he should do so. But, while he may strike hard blows, he is not at liberty to strike foul ones. It is as much his duty to refrain from improper methods calculated to produce a wrongful conviction as it is to use every legitimate means to bring about a just one.[64]

Congress and the American people held an overwhelming interest in learning the White House's motivations and involvement in the firings of the U.S. attorneys because they can easily transform law enforcement into an engine of despotism or persecution. Both Congress and the American people have a strong need to know whether U.S. attorneys are selected or removed based on their willingness to compromise their obligation of impartiality as elaborated in *Berger*. Furthermore, President Bush's power to hire and fire U.S. attorneys is not absolute. The Constitution forbids race or religion to be a significant motivating factor.[65] And it would be within the power of Congress under the Necessary and Proper Clause to require U.S. attorneys to satisfy certain experience benchmarks—for example, lead counsel in three federal court trials.

Even assuming that President Bush enjoyed absolute hiring and firing discretion over U.S. attorneys, he would not be entitled to a corollary right to shield his personnel decisions from public scrutiny. A congressional requirement that an executive decision be publicly explained and defended does not crown Congress with an overriding influence over the executive power at issue. President Gerald R. Ford testified before the House Judiciary Committee about his pardon of former President Nixon to dispel public suspicion that the former had promised the latter a pardon as a quid pro quo for Nixon's resignation.[66] The testimony, however, in no way compromised the president's pardon power. Similarly, if President Bush or his subordinates are required to explain before Congress their decisions to fire U.S. attorneys, they might be deterred from corrupt motivations, but the testimony would not compromise the president's power to remove them. Political discomfort or embarrassment goes with the White House territory.

In addition to exploring whether the firings of the nine U.S. attorneys threatened an impartial administration of the law, Congress also needs the testimonies of Harriet Miers, Karl Rove, and Joshua Bolten, as well as White House documents to determine whether Attorney General Gonzales committed perjury or obstructed a congressional investigation with his shifting explanations of how and why the U.S. attorneys were placed on the discharge list.

President Bush errantly claims that Congress must prove that presidential communications are "demonstrably critical"[67] to its oversight functions in order to trump executive privilege, based on a decision by the U.S. Court of Appeals for the District of Columbia Circuit in *Senate Select Committee v. Nixon* (1974).[68] But in that case, one arm of Congress already had in its possession most of the tapes and documents sought by another. Furthermore, the information at issue was sought for purposes of legislation, not oversight, as is the case regarding the firings of the U.S. attorneys. The court of appeals' "demonstrably criti-cal"[69] test was fashioned for legislation, not oversight, because Congress could arguably claim everything in the executive branch might assist its legislative deliberations and snoop into executive affairs for the sake of snooping.

In the *United States v. Nixon* case, however, the Supreme Court did not require the special prosecutor to establish that the presidential tapes and documents at issue were "demonstrably critical"[70] to winning convictions. Relevance was sufficient. The standard for Congress should be no different when criminality or maladministration is under investigation. Evidence must be examined to know whether it is the proverbial smoking gun, akin to Dean's testimony against Nixon. If Congress knew in advance the contents of the information it was seeking, then fur-ther investigation would be superfluous.

President Bush's theory of executive privilege also facilitates distorting the public record to his advantage. It authorizes the president to waive the privilege to publicize facts or opinions that he believes are favorable while invoking the privilege to conceal for facts and opinions that would undercut his political agenda or popularity, for example, evidence discrediting WMD in Iraq. The result is a deception of Congress and the people, who need the whole truth to discharge their constitutional responsibili-ties. In other settings, a partial waiver of an evidentiary privi-lege is forbidden. A witness may not selectively invoke the Fifth Amendment privilege against compulsory self-incrimination. If the witness chooses to testify about one subject, the testimony may not stop in midstream. The witness has a choice of all or nothing.

President Bush has also summoned executive privilege to thwart congressional oversight of the TSP and sister secret-spying programs that have yet to leak to the media. During his con-firmation hearing to be the director of Central Intelligence, General Michael Hayden, for example, invoked the privilege to decline to answer a question by Senator Diane Feinstein as to whether the NSA had ever sought a warrant for a pen register—a device that records telephone numbers dialed.[71] The importance of oversight was underscored by the recent declassification of a legal memorandum authored by then–Deputy Assistant Attorney General for the Office of Legal Counsel John C. Yoo justifying the TSP, later abandoned, and even later made available to Congress. Rhode Island Democratic Senator Sheldon Whitehouse remarked, "I cannot reconcile the plain language of FISA that it is the exclusive procedure for electronic surveillance of Americans with the OLC opinion saying Congress didn't say that. Once again, behind the veil of secrecy, OLC appears to have cooked up extravagant or misguided legal theories which would never survive in the light of day."[72] California Democratic Senator Diane Feinstein added, "The declassified OLC opinion claimed that FISA didn't restrain the president's authorities. The OLC was wrong, and new FISA legislation must have strong exclusivity language to make clear that we cannot have such abuses again in the future."[73]

Impeachment is the only viable remedy for chronic presidential abuses of executive privilege. Although a statute saddles government prosecutors with a "duty"[74] to bring criminal contempt matters "before the grand jury for its action,"[75] the president's constitutional prerogatives over criminal law enforcement trumps the statute.

The U.S. Supreme Court declared in *United States v. Nixon* that, "the Executive Branch has exclusive authority and absolute discretion whether to prosecute a case."[76] In *United States v. Cox* (1965),[77] the U.S. Court of Appeals for the Fifth Circuit overturned a district court order directing the U.S. attorney to file an indictment returned by the grand jury. The court elaborated,

> The discretionary power of the attorney for the United States
> in determining whether a prosecution shall be commenced or
> maintained may well depend upon matters of policy wholly
> apart from any question of probable cause. . . . [I]t is as an

officer of the executive department that he exercises a discretion as to whether or not there shall be a prosecution in a particular case. It follows, as an incident of the constitutional separation of powers, that the courts are not to interfere with the free exercise of the discretionary powers of the attorneys of the United States in their control over criminal prosecutions.[78]

Under the *Nixon* and *Cox* precedents, President Bush also enjoys absolute authority to determine whether to prosecute his subordinates for perjury before Congress or corruptly endeavoring to derail a congressional investigation. And the idea that Bush, whose John Hancock is loyalty to obedient vassals, would ever authorize their prosecution for deceiving Congress is chimerical. Remember Bush's commutation of the sentence of Scooter Libby and his recanting of his pledge to fire anyone in the White House implicated in the Valerie Plame leak in an effort to salvage Karl Rove.

Short of impeachment, Congress could address the alarming problem of executive evasion of congressional oversight through a modified version of the old Independent Counsel Act. It created a special three-judge panel, selected by the chief justice of the United States, entrusted with the appointments of independent counsels.[79] These prosecutors operated independently from the president, and their targets were high-level executive branch or political party officials. Leaving their investigations to the president would have meant letting him investigate his own trusted inner circle—an obvious conflict of interest.

The Supreme Court sustained the constitutionality of independent counsels despite their encroachments on the president's prosecutorial discretion in *Morrison v. Olson* (1988).[80] Writing for an 8–1 majority, Chief Justice William H. Rehnquist explained that independent counsels who were unencumbered with conflicts of interest assisted rather than sabotaged the president's unflagging duty to take care that the laws be faithfully executed.[81]

Armed with *Morrison*, Congress could pass a new Independent Counsel Act,[82] but with a modified universe of crimes and targets within the jurisdiction of independent prosecutors—namely, criminal contempt, perjury, or corruptly endeavoring to obstruct a congressional investigation by current or former executive branch officials appointed by the president.

Criminal prosecutions, however, are too lead-footed to serve as an effective remedy for baseless assertions of executive privilege. The privilege issue would invariably be decided after the withheld information had become politically stale. Furthermore, a prosecution punishes a subordinate for presidential wrongdoing, and the president would probably pardon any of his vassals who were convicted.

Self-government is a farce if the people and Congress are denied knowledge of what the president is doing and why. Thus, the House Judiciary Committee voted an article of impeachment against President Nixon for refusing to supply information needed to evaluate his official conduct. President Bush and his successors should be held to the same exacting disclosure standard. A president's knowledge that he is operating in a fishbowl is the best insurance policy for constitutional rectitude.

EIGHT

State Secrets—
Extraordinary Rendition

The state secrets doctrine was not invented by President George W. Bush. It was summoned into being by a naïve U.S. Supreme Court in *United States v. Reynolds* (1953),[1] and has been employed by the Bush administration to thwart civil suits brought by victims of its constitutional wrongdoing. The *Reynolds* decision empowers the president to task CIA officials, or their proxies, to kidnap and imprison American citizens abroad, and prevent the victim of the constitutional outrage from suing for redress by claiming that proof of the government's wrongdoing would expose intelligence sources. The case will be amplified later in the chapter. President Bush deserves censure for opposing legislation in Congress that would lessen the injustice of the doctrine and its encouragement of lawlessness and government deceit under oath.

The decision by the U.S. Court of Appeals for the Fourth Circuit in *Khalid El-Masri v. United States* (2007)[2] highlights the menace of the state secrets privilege to constitutional rights.

Khaled el-Masri, a German citizen, filed suit seeking damages against former Director of Central Intelligence George Tenet, 10 unnamed CIA employees, and 10 unnamed employees of corporations. The complaint alleged a grim tale of what is known as "extraordinary rendition"[3] in international law. While traveling in Macedonia, el-Masri was detained by Macedonian law-enforcement officials. He was delivered to CIA operatives, who flew him to a CIA-run detention facility in Afghanistan. There he was subjected to cruel, inhumane, and degrading treatment for five months. He was then transported to Albania and dumped in a remote area. El-Masri was never charged with a crime or terrorist activity. No judge ever determined that a scintilla of evidence implicated el-Masri in wrongdoing. He could just as easily have been you or me traveling abroad.

El-Masri's complaint alleged that his detention and interrogation were "carried out pursuant to an unlawful policy and practice devised by former Director Tenet known as 'extraordinary rendition': the clandestine abduction and detention outside the United States of persons suspected of involvement in terrorist activities and their subsequent interrogation using methods impermissible under U.S. and international laws."[4]

The United States intervened and asserted that el-Masri's complaint should be dismissed based on the state secrets doctrine. A sworn affidavit submitted by then-Director of Central Intelligence Porter Goss insisted that a trial of el-Masri's claims would risk disclosures that would be detrimental to national security. The court of appeals agreed that *Reynolds* mandated a dismissal.[5]

In *Reynolds*, an Air Force bomber crashed during testing of secret electronic equipment. Three civilian observers on board were killed. Their widows sued the United States, alleging negligence under the Federal Tort Claims Act.[6] They sought discovery of the Air Force's accident report and companion materials to prove their negligence claim. The Air Force balked. It contended that disclosing the accident information would "seriously hamper . . . national security, flying safety, and the development of highly technical and secret military equipment."[7]

The U.S. Supreme Court sustained the Air Force. The Court reasoned that the common law of evidence recognized a state secrets privilege to protect the president's constitutional responsibilities over the military and foreign affairs. The Court further declared that utmost deference must be given to the president's determination that a disclosure might harm national security because facially innocuous information to a judge could be the missing piece in an intelligence jigsaw puzzle to intelligence experts. If information falls within the state secrets privilege, the plaintiff's case must ordinarily be dismissed without even secret review by a judge to test the truth of the government's national security fears.

Reynolds blinds itself to the government's propensity for national security lies to avert civil or criminal liability or political embarrassment. Decades after *Reynolds* was decided, Judith Loether, the daughter of one of the civilian engineers who died on the plane, discovered the Air Force accident report on the Internet after it had been declassified. Nowhere does it mention secret spying equipment. But too much time had elapsed to permit Ms. Loether to obtain redress for the prevarication under oath according to a decision by the U.S. Court of Appeals for the Third Circuit.[8]

The government's deceit in *Reynolds* was no aberration. In the Pentagon Papers case, President Richard M. Nixon falsely claimed in *New York Times v. United States* (1971)[9] that publication would cripple the diplomacy of the United States. Indeed, virtually no day passes without a burst of media disclosures of leaked classified information, followed by the absence of adverse reverberations. Indeed, an enormous percentage of Ron Suskind's book *The One Percent Doctrine* is based on government leaks of classified information, yet the Bush administration made no attempt to suppress the book or to bring a criminal prosecution. Consider the following snippet from Suskind's book, which highlights a motive for government officials to lie. The exchange is between CIA Director Tenet and a CIA officer (Rolf Mowatt-Larssen) over weapons of mass destruction:

> *Tenet*: "You've got to be wrong—not analytically wrong . . . but just way out front [on WMD]. . . . You see, all our failures are because we failed to anticipate. Intelligence failures follow a failure of anticipation. They come from only following the information you know and not worrying about what you don't know."
>
> He grabbed Rolf's other bicep and squeezed, eye-to-eye. "You need to be passionate—passionate *about what you don't know*."[10]

Suskind also recounts an exchange between Tenet and President Bush in which the president virtually instructs the director of Central Intelligence to discover something that would bolster the importance of an inconsequential Al Qaeda detainee named Zubaydah to avoid embarrassing the president, who had publicly declared him important.[11]

Even if the government did not chronically lie, the state secrets doctrine would still be alarming. Suppose the president instructed the CIA to assassinate Americans residing in NATO (North Atlantic Treaty Organization) countries who criticized his foreign policies. The estates of the assassinated would sue the CIA culprits, alleging an unconstitutional taking of life without due process. The president would file an affidavit insisting that proof of the assassinations would jeopardize U.S. relations with NATO allies. *Reynolds* would dictate dismissal of the suits; proof of the CIA's assassination squads in a public courtroom would cast the United States in an evil light to the international community.

At present, the state secrets doctrine is a tyrant's dream policy. Pending congressional legislation would ameliorate its mischief, but more is needed. Eminent domain should provide the model for new legislation. If the government takes private property for a public purpose, just compensation must be paid. A private cause of action for damages is a type of property. If the government effectively confiscates the property to protect national security for all citizens by invoking the state secrets doctrine, the government should pay the plaintiff the value of his legal claim. It would be determined by a judge based on the plaintiff's proof of harm proximately caused by the government's alleged constitutional wrongdoing. A government obligation to pay for its lawlessness would provide a needed incentive to respect the Constitution.

Extraordinary rendition is an intellectual cousin of the state secrets doctrine. Both endorse government criminality with impunity in the name of national security. The ends justify the means. The enemy will be defeated by aping the enemy. The repugnancy of extraordinary rendition and its dangers for American citizens is demonstrated by the following parable:

An American citizen visited St. Petersburg in 2008 for the aesthetic thrills of the Hermitage. Russian Prime Minister Vladimir Putin ordered the Federal Security Service to kidnap the American for delivery to a Belarus dungeon for daily torture. In his order, the prime minister explained that Russia is engulfed in a perpetual war with Chechen terrorists, who have threatened to kill Russians everywhere. Thus, the entire world is a battlefield where military force and tactics are acceptable. Prime Minister Putin added that the American provided material support for Chechen terrorists by broadcasting editorials assailing crimes against Chechens perpetrated by the Russian military and educating them about international law.

After Putin's order was executed, the American ambassador to Moscow protested. The ambassador argued that the kidnapping, imprisonment, and torture of the American were crimes under international law and must be repudiated. The ambassador lectured that the world would degenerate to a hobbesian state of nature if governments could unilaterally disappear foreigners into dungeons forever with no legal recourse and no more justification than an executive directive.

Prime Minister Putin remonstrated that he had simply followed the example of the American ambassador's boss— President George W. Bush. President Bush had dispatched a team of CIA operatives to Milan, Italy, to kidnap an Egyptian cleric, Abu Omar. The cleric was transported to Egypt, where he was predictably tortured. The CIA operatives were charged with crimes by an Italian prosecutor, but President Bush had balked at extradition. President Bush explained that when he orders kidnappings or torture in the name of defeating terrorism, it is legal.[12]

Putin also adverted to the case of Khaled el-Masri, the German citizen of Lebanese descent discussed earlier in this chapter. President Bush had also ordered his kidnapping and maltreatment in an Afghan prison with no proof of his complicity in criminality or terrorism. A German prosecutor has charged 13 CIA operatives with criminal wrongdoing, but President Bush is resisting their prosecution.[13]

The ambassador disputed Putin's logic. He sermonized that only President Bush was infallible on issues of national security or terrorism. The ambassador also clucked that while all nations are equal, the United States is more equal than the others. He chastised Putin for failing to comprehend that it is not worth being the planet's sole superpower if you cannot have double standards.

The prime minister was unpersuaded by the ambassador's tutorial. The kidnapped American died of ill health after spending five years in the Belarus dungeon. In the afterlife, the American met Afghan Abdul Razzak Hekmati, who had died of cancer in Guantanamo Bay prison on December 30, 2007, after five years of detention without accusation or trial.[14] They both concurred on the indispensability of the rule of law to civilization.

Although President Bush protests that he does not learn by reading, he might attempt two exceptions. First, these lines from *Macbeth*, Act 1, Scene 7:

if the assassination
Could trammel up the consequence, and catch
With his surcease success; that but this blow
Might be the be-all and the end-all here,
But here, upon this bank and shoal of time,
We'ld jump the life to come. But in these cases
We still have judgment here; that we but teach
Bloody instructions, which, being taught, return
To plague the inventor: this even-handed justice
Commends the ingredients of our poison'd chalice
To our own lips.[15]

President Bush's contempt for the rule of law is making the American people less safe. He is generating popular resentment against the United States everywhere in the world by insisting that the United States be permitted to pursue its perceived national security interests by fair means or foul, but that the actions of other nations abide by Queensbury rules. According to Jane Mayer in *The Dark Side*, expert FBI interrogators boycotted CIA questioning of terroist detainees to avoid complicity in war crimes.[16] President Bush errantly believes that his actions are divinely blessed and that America is above sinning. He might be disabused of his error by reading Edmund Burke on the British Empire: "I dread our own power and our own ambition. I dread our being too much dreaded. It is ridiculous to say that we are not men, and that, as men, we shall never wish to aggrandize ourselves."[17]

NINE

Military Commissions—
Tyranny for the Sake of Tyranny

In the aftermath of 9/11, President George W. Bush issued an executive order creating military commissions for the trial of alleged war crimes. The commissions combined the functions of judge, jury, and prosecutor and placed them in the hands of the executive branch—an action that the Founding Fathers condemned in Federalist No. 47: "The accumulation of all powers, legislative, executive and judiciary in the same hands . . . may justly be pronounced the very definition of tyranny."[1] The commissions were denuded of additional procedural safeguards recognized in every system of civilized justice as indispensable to preventing erroneous convictions—for example, the right of the accused to confront and seek to discredit all incriminating evidence.

In *Hamdan v. Rumsfeld* (2006),[2] the U.S. Supreme Court held that the president's executive order was unauthorized by the Uniform Code of Military Justice and offended the Geneva Conventions.[3] The president then turned to Congress and received its blessing for military commissions in the Military Commissions Act of 2006.[4] Congress, however, was presented with no evidence that military commissions were needed to prosecute war crimes. Indeed, in testimony before the Senate Judiciary Committee on November 28, 2001, then–Assistant Attorney General for the Criminal Division Michael Chertoff (later secretary of Homeland Security) boasted, "[O]ur [regular] legal system is terrific and can handle these [terrorism] cases. . . . [It is clear] that the history of this government in prosecuting terrorists in domestic courts has been one of unmitigated success and one in which the judges have done a superb job of managing the courtroom and not compromising our concerns about security and our concerns about classified information."[5]

A selected list of successful prosecutions of international terrorists in federal courts would include the following:

1. Ramzi Yousef and Sheikh Omar Abdel-Rahman—convicted of crimes connected with the 1993 bombing of the World Trade Center.
2. Mohamed Rashed Daoud al-'Owhali, Khalfan Khamis Mohammed, Wadih el-Hage, and Mohamed Sadeek Odeh—convicted of conspiring to murder Americans in conjunction with the 1998 bombings of the U.S. embassies in Kenya and Tanzania.
3. Zacarias Moussaoui—convicted of conspiring to kill Americans in the 9/11 attacks.
4. John Walker Lindh—pled guilty to providing material assistance to a terrorist organization.
5. José Padilla—convicted of conspiring to provide material assistance to a terrorist organization.

President Bush's military commissions and their resurrection by Congress flirted with tyranny for the sake of partisan political advantage. The commissions were embraced not because federal civilian courts were ill suited for the trials of international terrorism cases, but because the Bush–Cheney presidency craved the appearance of being tough on terrorism. In an interview with Tim Russert on *Meet the Press* on September 16, 2001, Vice President Cheney declared that in confronting Al Qaeda, the president needed to "work through, sort of, the dark side. . . . That's the world these folks operate in. And so it's going to be vital for us to use any means at our disposal, basically, to achieve our objective." What could be more reassuring to the American people than promising to mimic the "dark side" of Al Qaeda?[6]

Bush and Cheney did not care that the commissions were irrelevant to defeating terrorism. During the seven years that have elapsed since September 11, 2001, there has been but one commission prosecution: Australian David Hicks pled guilty to training in a terrorist camp—that is, "providing material support for terrorism"[7]—and he received a prison term of nine months, which he served in Australia. As of this writing, a second trial in underway against Salim Ahmed Hamdan, who is not accused of killing a single American.

There are pending commission charges against approximately 18 Al Qaeda detainees for alleged complicity in the 9/11 abominations—the same crime prosecuted against Moussaoui in a federal civilian court. The "high value" detainees include Khalid Shaikh Mohammad, Abu Zubaydah, and Ramzi bin al-Shibh. These cases will probably shipwreck before a commission trial. Among other things, evidence obtained from torture or coercion has probably tainted the prosecutions. Moroever, the Supreme Court's decision in *Boumediene v. Bush* (June 12, 2008)[8] cast a dark constitutional cloud over the commissions by tacitly rejecting the idea that Al Qaeda raises a war-like danger to the American people.

Military commissions needlessly risk convicting the innocent and creating poster children for Al Qaeda. They are unworthy of a civilized people who care about justice. And they create a precedent that justifies kangaroo courts against American civilians or military personnel by either state or nonstate actors. This is a steep price to pay to enable the Bush–Cheney administration to enjoy a bogus appearance of implacably fighting terrorism.

In a federal civilian trial, the accused is entitled to be present at all stages of the prosecution and to be informed of all the evidence against him in order to marshal a defense. In contrast, under Bush's executive order, in a trial before a military commission, the accused and his civilian counsel could have been excluded from and precluded from knowing from others what evidence was presented during any part of the proceeding that either the appointing authority or the presiding officer determined to "close."[9] Closure would have been justified to protect "information classified or classifiable . . . ; information protected by law or rule from unauthorized disclosure; the physical safety of participants in Commission proceedings, including prospective witnesses; intelligence and law enforcement sources, methods, or activities; and, other national security interests."[10]

Secret trials and secret evidence authorized by President Bush, however, are instruments of state despotism and terror. These same practices were celebrated by Spanish Grand Inquisitor Thomas de Torqemada. They are commonplace in China or Russia. In testifying before Congress, Brigadier General James C. Walker, the chief uniformed lawyer for the marines, urged without result that the United States should not "become the first"[11] civilized country to deny a defendant access to the prosecutor's case. Think of how helpless and furious you would feel as the accused, not knowing what was said against you, or by whom, when your life and liberty were at stake.

Supreme Court Justice William O. Douglas wrote about closely analogous circumstances in *Joint Anti-Fascist Refugee Committee v. McGrath* (1951)[12]:

> The Loyalty Board convicts on evidence which it cannot even appraise. The critical evidence may be the word of an unknown witness who is "a paragon of veracity, a knave, or the village idiot."[13] His name, his reputation, his prejudices,

his animosities, his trustworthiness are unknown both to the judge and to the accused. The accused has no opportunity to show that the witness lied or was prejudiced or venal. Without knowing who her accusers are, she has no way of defending. She has nothing to offer except her own word and the character testimony of her friends.[14]

In addition to secret evidence, President Bush's military commissions were authorized to admit any evidence that, in the opinion of the presiding officer, "would have probative value to a reasonable person."[15] Testimonial hearsay and evidence extracted by torture or coercion was admissible, as was unsworn oral or written testimony. In sum, before a military commission, the accused would be denied the right to cross-examine incriminating evidence—the greatest vehicle ever invented for the discovery of truth, according to evidence maven Professor John Henry Wigmore.

Hamdan corroborates that military commissions are not needed to prosecute war crimes allegedly perpetrated by international terrorists. He had been captured by militia forces in Afghanistan and turned over to the United States. On July 13, 2005, the U.S. military issued a charging document alleging that Salim Ahmed Hamdan had conspired to kill Americans. There was no allegation that the accused had any command responsibilities, had enjoyed a leadership role, or had participated in the planning of any terrorist activity. To further the conspiracy, it was said that Hamdan acted as Osama bin Laden's driver and bodyguard; transported weapons for Al Qaeda; drove bin Laden to press conferences; and received weapons training in Al Qaeda camps.

Why could Hamdan not have been tried in a civilian court like many other alleged Al Qaeda or other international terrorists, such as Moussaoui? Intelligence sources and methods could have been protected under the Classified Information Procedures Act of 1980,[16] as Secretary Chertoff confirmed. Hamdan was not being held in a theater of war. The alleged conspiratorial acts aiming to kill Americans did not present special difficulties of proof. There was no hurry to try the case. Prosecution witnesses from Afghanistan could have been transported to the United States without disrupting the war effort there. President Bush apparently decided to try Hamdan before a military commission, with all its grim trappings of war, to inflate public fear of international terrorists, which would lead to public acceptance of permanent war. And Bush hoped that public fear would be further magnified by a guilty verdict before a biased and procedurally deficient military commission, which would have been impossible in a federal civilian court. Guilty verdicts are also necessary to convince the American people that they are confronting an external danger tantamount to war.

Congress responded to *Hamdan* like sheep. It raced to enact the Military Commissions Act of 2006 to authorize what Bush had previously done by executive order: establish military commissions for the trial of war crimes allegedly committed by alien unlawful enemy combatants. The latter are defined to include not only persons who have engaged in hostilities against the United States but also those who have "purposefully and materially supported hostilities against the United States."[17] The loose definition would include an Iraqi civilian who authored a newspaper column or delivered a speech denouncing the U.S. occupation as immoral. It might be said that the expression strengthened the resolve of Iraqis seeking to expel the United States by force.

The act generally repeated the glaring procedural deficiencies in Bush's executive order. Statements obtained by coercion are admissible. Hearsay is admissible. The accused can be excluded from his own trial and is denied the right to confront all of his accusers. The proceedings can be closed to the public to protect classified information. The prosecution's case may include secret evidence. In marshaling a defense, the defense counsel is limited to "a reasonable opportunity to obtain witnesses and other evidence as provided in regulations prescribed by the Secretary of Defense."[18] Finally, military commissions continued to combine the functions of judge, jury, and prosecutor in a single branch—a virtual guarantee of guilty verdicts. Why would the military acquit an accused person whom the military had chosen to prosecute based on a belief of guilt? Defendants summoned before the congressionally authorized commissions are challenging their constitutionality based on the *Boumediene* rationale.

A war crime can be committed only if there is a state of war. Military commissions to try war crimes are nonsensical unless the nation is at war. But as Chapter [X] elaborated, the nation is not at war with international terrorism in the constitutional sense. International terrorists should be treated, captured, tried, and punished as reprehensible criminals, not as warriors.

At the time of this writing, no terrorist plots targeting the United States since September 11, 2001, have come close to success. Embryonic plans or conspiracies have been detected and prosecuted in civilian courts. Take the so-called Lackawanna Six—a group of men from Lackawanna, New York, who trained for weeks at an Al Qaeda camp in Afghanistan in the summer of 2001. The Federal Bureau of Investigation learned of the training and kept up surveillance when they returned. Time passed with no evidence that they intended to graduate from training to actual violence or criminality. But the government viewed them as dangerous in light of their past training. All were charged in federal civilian court with providing material assistance to a foreign terrorist organization, and ultimately they entered guilty pleas.

Only three citizens or resident aliens have been detained as unlawful enemy combatants. One was deported to Saudi Arabia. Another was reclassified as a criminal defendant and prosecuted for conspiring to provide material assistance to a foreign terrorist organization. A third is challenging his detention in federal courts.

No American shies from domestic travel or shopping for fear of an international terrorist attack. Americans were more frightened during the 23 days of fear in October 2002 that were generated by the Washington, DC, snipers, John Allen Muhammed and John Lee Malvo, than they are of international terrorism.

Approximately three thousand people died from the criminal 9/11 abominations. But approximately sixteen to seventeen thousand people are murdered annually in the United States. Since September 11, 2001, there have been zero terrorist deaths compared to approximately 107,000 murders. Yet the nation is not on a war footing against murderers.

The Israeli Supreme Court in *The Public Committee against Torture in Israel v. The Government of Israel* (December 11, 2006),[19] confronted the issue of whether Israel was in a state of "armed conflict"[20] with terrorism. Answering in the affirmative, the Court recounted a chronicle of horrors that are conspicuously absent in the United States:

> In February 2000, the second *intifada* began. A massive assault of terrorism was directed against the State of Israel, and against Israelis, merely because they are Israelis. This assault of terrorism differentiates neither between combatants and civilians, nor between men, women, and children. The terrorist attacks take place both in the territory of Judea, Samaria, and the Gaza Strip, and within the borders of the State of Israel. They are directed against civilian centers, shopping centers and markets, coffee houses and restaurants. Over the past five years, thousands of acts of terrorism have been committed against Israel. In the attacks, more than one thousand Israeli civilians have been killed. Thousands of Israeli citizens have been wounded. . . . In these terrorist attacks, the terrorist organizations use military means *par excellence*, whereas the common denominator of them all is their lethality and cruelty. Among those means are shooting attacks, suicide bombings, mortar fire, rocket fire, car bombs, *et cetera.*[21]

An argument that the United States would be as beset with terrorism as is Israel without the Bush–Cheney post-9/11 usurpations or abuses would be absurd. Military commissions have slept. When the Protect America Act lapsed, no intelligence lapses caused any American harm. Habeas corpus has never released a single terrorist. Torture has never stopped a terrorist conspiracy. Congress should pass a bill declaring that the United States is not at war with international terrorism and that international terrorists should be treated as criminals for law-enforcement purposes and otherwise. The declaration would make the American people safer by encouraging cooperation from foreign countries in pursuing suspected criminals who would be provided due process and by avoiding U.S. precedents that could be employed by foreign nations against American citizens. It would deny the president authority to use military force and impose military law throughout the United States in seeking to kill or capture suspected terrorists. And it would honor the intent of the Founding Fathers that war should be reserved for dangers of the highest order.

Coda

No person with active cerebral faculties can be optimistic about the survival of a Republican form of government and checks and balances in the United States. I testified before the House Judiciary Committee on July 25, 2008, regarding an impeachment inquiry. All pejorative references to President Bush or Vice President Cheney insinuating deceit or impeachable high crimes and misdemeanors were censored under a House rule derived from the British Parliament's prohibition on voicing "irreverence" toward the king!

The Constitution and democracy invariably come to mean whatever the American people want them to mean irrespective of the text or external forms. Chief Justice Tawny interpreted the Constitution to mean that blacks were nonpersons in *Dred Scott v. Sanford*, but he was trumped by the Civil War and the Civil War amendments. Proponents of racial equality under the law enshrined their objective in the Fourteenth and Fifteenth Amendments, but they were trumped for a century by the ascendancy of racial bigots. The Supreme Court, frightened by the specter of socialism or communism, declared a federal income tax invalid in *Pollock v. Farmers' Loan & Trust Co.* (1895). But the court was defeated by the federal income tax amendment.

At present, I do not believe the American people will exert themselves through free speech, the vote, or running for office to make the Constitution's checks and balances and protections against government abuses mean what the Founding Fathers intended them to mean. The vast majority are agnostic between self-government and vassalage to a supreme leader in the White House.

The Founding Fathers protested the Stamp Act. The American people today in those circumstances would have been too preoccupied with dieting and clothes. They would not have found King George III's despotism cause for rebellion— especially if he thwarted Native American raiding parties.

In *Concord Hymn*, Ralph Waldo Emerson's first stanza versified,

> By the rude bridge that arched the flood,
> Their flag to April's breeze unfurled;
> Here once the embattled farmers stood;
> And fired the shot heard round the world.

A commanding of contemporary Americans would not have joined the Minutemen. Their example heard round the world is lawlessness, double standards, and duplicity in the name of national security.

The expansion of equality under the Constitution and in society has been impressive and laudatory. Discriminatory barriers have tumbled for racial or ethnic minorities and women. But the decisive triumph of equality over liberty has yielded a mass culture that drives everything toward a lowest common denominator. True excellence and leadership have taken a vertical plunge. America's ascendant culture could never produce a Beethoven, Mozart, Shakespeare, Michelangelo, Rembrandt, or Homer. And as regards political leadership and wisdom, no American president since Abraham Lincoln has been able to hold a candle to the first six: George Washington, John Adams, Thomas Jefferson, James Madison, James Monroe, and John Quincy Adams.

A nation without true leaders is like an acephalous church— it will drift and decay.

It might be asked, if the overwhelming majority of Americans are vastly more thrilled by sporting events and creature comforts than they are by the moral challenges and burdens of self-government, then why struggle against this inexorable tide? The answer is twofold. Anything else would be dishonorable. And you might leave footprints in the sands of time to inspire someone yet to be born to champion freedom in more propitious circumstances.

Conclusion

Grenada's Maurice Bishop, leader of the Marxist-Leninist New Jewel Movement,[1] explained in a 1982 address to his true believers how he made and enforced the law:

> Just consider, comrades, how laws are made in this country. Laws are made in this country when the Cabinet agrees and when I sign a document on behalf of the Cabinet. And then that is what everybody in the country—like it or don't like it—has to follow. Or consider how people get detained in this country. We don't go and call for no votes. You get detained when I sign an order after discussing it with the National Security Committee of the party, or with a higher party body. Once I sign it—like it or don't like it—it's up the hill for them.[2]

Two decades later in the aftermath of 9/11, President George W. Bush commenced indefinite detentions at Guantanamo Bay of persons he decreed were enemy combatants based on his signature "gut instincts." Secretary of Defense Donald H. Rumsfeld characterized the detainees as the "worst of the worst," like a mixture of Satan and Mephistopheles.[3] As the number approached six hundred in 2002, a Central Intelligence Agency analyst warned the Bush administration that approximately one-third "had no connection with terrorism whatsoever,"[4] according to Jane Mayer's new book *The Dark Side*.[5] They had been whisked away in dragnet captures or delivered to the United

States by bounty hunters. Mayer further reports that the top military commander at Guantanamo at the time, General Michael Dunlavey, believed up to 50 percent of the detainees were false positives.

But the spirit of Maurice Bishop silenced the doubters. According to Mayer, Vice President Cheney's counsel David Addington sneered at the idea of questioning President Bush's infallibility: "There will be no review. The president has determined that they are ALL enemy combatants. We are not going to revisit it."[6] (Of the more than 770 people who have been detained at Guantanamo Bay, approximately 500 were later released, according to a study by McClatchy Newspapers posted on June 15, 2008.)[7]

There may be philosophical distinctions between Marxist-Leninist Maurice Bishop and President George W. Bush, but if there are, they do not readily come to mind.

Notes

PREFACE

1. Eccles. 1:2 (KJV).
2. Alexander Pope, *Essay on Man*, epistle III:VI, 303–4 (1734).
3. Shakespeare, *Hamlet*, act 4, scene 4.
4. 2 Cor. 3:6 (KJV).
5. Edward Gibbon, *Epitaph for the People of Ancient Athens* (attributed).
6. 1 Sam. 8 (KJV).
7. Alexis De Tocqueville, *Democracy in America* (New York: The Colonial Press, 1900), 1:241.
8. Judge Learned Hand, "The Spirit of Liberty" (speech at an "I Am an American Day" ceremony, Central Park, New York, NY, May 21, 1944).
9. Edward Gibbon, *The History of the Decline and Fall of the Roman Empire* (London: T. Cadell, Strand, 1837), 25–27, 483–85.
10. Archibald H. Grimke, *William Lloyd Garrison: The Abolitionist* (New York: Funk & Wagnalls, 1891), 120–31, 387.
11. National American Woman Suffrage Association, *The History of Woman Suffrage*, ed. Ida Husted Harper (New York: J. J. Little & Ives, 1922).
12. John F. Kennedy, *Profiles in Courage* (New York: Harper & Brothers, 1956), 139.
13. Senator Edmund G. Ross, "Historic Moments: The Impeachment Trial," *Scribner's Magazine* XI (Apr. 1892): 519–24.
14. Kennedy, *Profiles in Courage*, 126.
15. Susan Ferrechio, "Pelosi: Bush Impeachment 'Off the Table,'" *New York Times*, November 8, 2006.

CHAPTER I

1. S.J.R. 23, H.J.R. 64, 107th Cong., 1st sess., *Congressional Record* 147, nos. 107–40 (September 18, 2001).
2. An unlawful enemy combatant wears no distinctive insignia, does not bear arms openly, does not respond to a hierarchy of command, or does not adhere to the laws of war.
3. President George W. Bush, Executive Order, "Blocking of Certain Persons Who Threaten Stabilization Efforts in Iraq, Executive Order 13438." *Federal Register* 72, no. 138 (July 19, 2007).
4. James Madison, Federalist No. 48, in Henry Cabot Lodge, ed., *The Federalist Papers: A Commentary on the Constitution of the United States* (New York: G. P. Putnam's Sons, 1892), 308, 311.
5. President Bush, Military Order, "Detention, Treatment, and Trial of Certain Non-Citizens in the War Against Terrorism," *Federal Register* 66, no. 57833 (November 13, 2001); President Bush, Executive Order, "Further Implementation of the Presidential Records Act, Executive Order 13233," 3 *Code Federal Regulations* 815 (November 1, 2001); Charlie Savage, "Bush Challenges Hundreds of Laws: President Cites Powers of His Office," *Boston Globe*, April 30, 2006, 3rd ed., sec. national/foreign, p. A1; *Rasul v. Bush*, 542 US 466, 480–85 (2004); President Bush, Executive Order, "Trial of Unlawful Enemy Combatants by Military Commissions, Executive Order 13425," *Federal Register* 72, no. 7737 (February 14, 2007).
6. James Risen and Eric Lichtblau, "Bush Lets U.S. Spy on Callers without Courts," *New York Times*, December 16, 2005, late ed., sec. A, col. 1, p. 1; Craig Whitlock, "Europeans Investigate CIA Role in Abductions; Suspects Possibly Taken to Nations that Torture," *Washington Post*, March 13, 2005, final ed., sec. A, p. 1; Joel Brinkley, "Rice Is Challenged in Europe over Secret Prisons," *New York Times*, December 7, 2005, late ed., sec. A, col. 2, p. 1; President, Executive Order, "Interpretation of the Geneva Conventions Common Article 3 as Applied to a Program of Detention and Interrogation Operated by the Central Intelligence Agency, Executive Order 13440," 3 *Code Federal Regulations* 815 (July 20, 2007).
7. George Tenet, *At the Center of the Storm* (New York: Harper Collins, 2007), 116.
8. U.S. Constitution, Art. I, Sec. 3.
9. *Myers v. United States* 272 US 52 (1926).
10. James Boswell, *The Life of Samuel Johnson, LLD*, ed. William Wallace (Edinburg: William P. Nimmo, 1873), 338.
11. Duties in American Colonies Act 1765, "American Stamp Act," *Parliamentary Archives*, 5 Geo. III, c. 12.
12. Declaratory Act of 1766, "American Stamp Act," *Parliamentary Archives*, 6 Geo. III, c. 12.

13. Ibid.
14. Worthington C. Ford et al., eds., *Journals of the Continental Congress, 1774–1789* (Washington, DC: 1904–1937), 2:133.
15. Customs Act of 1766 and Duties on Tea (American Plantations) Act, "The Townshend Acts," *Parliamentary Archives*, 7 Geo. III, c. 41 and c. 46.
16. "1775 Declaration of the Causes and Necessity for Taking Up Arms," in *Journals of the Continental Congress, 1774–1789*, ed. Worthington C. Ford et al. (Washington, DC: 1904–1937) 2:140–57.
17. Ibid., 146.
16. *Sherman Antitrust Act*, 51st Cong., 1st sess., July 2, 1890, *U.S. Code*, vol. 15 secs. 1–7.
17. *Padilla v. Hanft*, 389 F. Supp. 2d 678 (2005).
18. Ford et al., eds., *Journals of the Continental Congress, 1774–178*, 1:140–57.
19. Alexander Hamilton, Federalist No. 70, in Henry Cabot Lodge, ed., *The Federalist Papers: A Commentary on the Constitution of the United States* (New York: G. P. Putnam's Sons, 1892), 436, 441.
20. Hamilton, Federalist No. 69, in Henry Cabot Lodge, ed., *The Federalist Papers: A Commentary on the Constitution of the United States* (New York: G. P. Putnam's Sons, 1892), 428, 430–31.
21. Hamilton, Federalist No. 75, in Henry Cabot Lodge, ed., *The Federalist Papers: A Commentary on the Constitution of the United States* (New York: G. P. Putnam's Sons, 1892), 465, 467–68.
22. Hamilton, Federalist No. 37, in Henry Cabot Lodge, ed., *The Federalist Papers: A Commentary on the Constitution of the United States* (New York: G. P. Putnam's Sons, 1892), 215, 219.
23. Madison to Thomas Jefferson, October 24, 1787, in *The Writings of James Madison*, ed. Gaillard Hunt (New York: G. P. Putnam's Sons, 1900) 5:26.
24. Hamilton, Federalist No. 75, in Henry Cabot Lodge, ed., *The Federalist Papers: A Commentary on the Constitution of the United States* (New York: G. P. Putnam's Sons, 1892), 465, 466–67.
25. *Chevron USA Inc. v. Natural Resource's Defense Council, Inc.*, 467 US 837 (1984).
26. *Civil Rights Act*, 42 US Code sec. 21 (1964).
27. *Contractors Association of Eastern Pa. v. Secretary of Labor*, 442 F.2d 159 (3d Cir 1969).
28. *Sibbach v. Wilson & Co.*, 312 US 1 (1941).
29. *Morrison v. Olson*, 487 US 654 (1988).
30. *Humphrey's Executor v. US*, 295 US 602 (1935).
31. U.S. Constitution, Art. I, Sec. 5, Cl. 1.
32. Administrative Procedures Act, 5 U.S. Code ch. 5 secs. 511–99.
33. U.S. Constitution, Art. I, Sec. 8, Cl. 12.
34. Carroll Kilpatrick, "Concern for National Security Limited Watergate Investigation, Nixon Says," *Washington Post*, May 23, 1973, p. A1.

35. *Roe v. Wade*, 410 US 113 (1973).
36. *Lawrence v. Texas*, 539 US 558 (2003).
37. *Civil Rights Act*, 42 U.S. Code sec. 21 (1964); *National Voting Rights Act*, 42 U.S. Code sec. 1973 (1965).
38. "Liuzzo Death Described by FBI 'Plant' in Klan," *Washington Post*, May 5, 1965, p. A3. Gary Thomas Rowe Jr., an FBI informant, played spectator to the murder.
39. Adam Smith, *Inquiry into the Nature and Causes of the Wealth of Nations*, 2 vols. (New York: Penguin, 1999).
40. *Dred Scott v. Sanford*, 60 US 393 (1857).
41. *Lochner v. New York*, 198 US 45 (1905).
42. *National Labor Relations Board v. Jones & Laughlin*, 331 US 416 (1937).
43. President, Executive Order, "Providing for the Stabilization of Prices, Rents, Wages and Salaries, Executive Order 11615." 3 *Code Federal Regulations* 1971–1975 Comp. 602–5 (August 15, 1971); President, Executive Order, "Providing for the Orderly Termination of Economic Stabilization Activities, Executive Order 11788" 3 *Code of Federal Regulations* 1971–1975 Comp. 877–81 (June 18, 1974), 877–81.
44. *National Labor Relations Board v. Jones & Laughlin*, 331 US 416 (1937).
45. Ibid., 247.
46. *Congressional Record*, 73rd Cong., 2nd sess., 1934, 78, pt. 2: 1920–1921.
47. Ford et al., eds., *Journals of the Continental Congress, 1774–178*, 2:510–15.
48. Madison, Federalist No. 58, in Henry Cabot Lodge, ed., *The Federalist Papers: A Commentary on the Constitution of the United States* (New York: G. P. Putnam's Sons, 1892), 326, 365.
49. *Military Commissions Act of 2006*, H.R. 6054, 109th Cong., 2nd sess.; *U.S. Code*, vol. 10, secs. 948a–950j.
50. *The Protect America Act of 2007*, S. 2011, 109th Cong., 1st sess.; *U.S. Code*, vol. 50, secs. 1801–5c.
51. *John Warner National Defense Authorization Act of 2007*, H.R. 5122; Public Law 364, 109th Cong., 1st sess., October 17, 2006.
52. *Senate Legislative Information System*, 109th Cong., 2nd sess., June 22, 2006, 00186.
53. H.R. 5122; Public Law 364, 109th Cong., 1st sess., October 17, 2006; *U.S. Code*, vol. 10, sec. 333.

CHAPTER 2

1. President George W. Bush, transcript, Address to a Joint Session of Congress and the American People, September 20, 2001.
2. *Boumediene v. Bush*, 553 US ____ (2008).
3. James Risen and Eric Lichtblau, "Bush Lets U.S. Spy on Callers without Courts," *New York Times*, December 16, 2005, late ed., sec. A, col. 1, p. 1.

4. Lichtblau, "F.B.I. Gets Mixed Review in Report on Interrogation," *New York Times*, May 17, 2008, late ed., sec. A, col. 0, p. 10.

5. Thomas Jefferson, *The Writings of Thomas Jefferson* (New York: G. P. Putnam's Sons, 1893), 2:42–58.

6. Alexander Hamilton, Federalist No. 65, in *The Federalist Papers: A Commentary on the Constitution of the United States*, ed. Henry Cabot Lodge (New York: G. P. Putnam's Sons, 1892), 407.

7. Natan Sharansky, *Fear No Evil: The Classic Memoir of One Man's Triumph Over a Police State* (New York: Public Affairs, 1998); Vladimir Bukovsky, "Vladimir's Voice," *Time*, January 3, 1977; Aleksandr Solzhenitsyn, *The Gulag Archipelago 1918–1956* (New York: Westview Press, 1997).

8. U.S. Constitution, Art. I, Sec. 2; Art. II, Sec. 1; Art. II, Sec. 4.

9. Niles Lathem, "Bush Hits Iraq Bottom: Among Least-Popular Presidents of All Time As War Takes Toll in Poll," *New York Post*, January 29, 2007, p. 9.

10. "18%? Just How Low Is," *Washington Post*, March 5, 2006, outlook, p. B03.

11. Howard Schneider, "Radical States Assail Act; Allies Muted," *Washington Post*, August 22, 1998, sec. A, pg. A22.

12. *Clinton v. Jones*, 520 US 681 (1997).

13. President Gerald Ford, Executive Order, "United States Foreign Intelligence Activities, Executive Order 11905," *Federal Register* 41 (February 19, 1976).

14. U.S. Senate Select Committee to Study Governmental Operations, "Alleged Assassination Plots Involving Foreign Leaders," *Interim Report of the Select Committee to Study Governmental Operations with Respect to Intelligence Activities*, 94th Cong., 1st sess., November 20, 1975, Rept. 94-465.

15. U.S. Senate Select Committee to Study Governmental Operations, "Intelligence Activities Senate Resolution 21," *Report of the Senate Select Committee to Study Governmental Operations with Respect to Intelligence Activities*, 94th Cong., 1st–2nd sess., 1975–76.

16. US Constitution, Art. I, Sec. 5, Cl. 7; House Rules clause 2(k), rule XI; Senate Rule XXIX.

17. "The CIA's Secret Funding and the Constitution," *Yale Law Journal* 84, no. 3 (January 1975): 608.

18. Brad Wright, "Most Leaks Come from Executive Branch, CIA Director Says," *Cable News Network*, http://www.cnn.com/ALLPOLITICS/stories/1999/07/22/leaks/ (accessed February 23, 2008).

19. U.S. Senate Select Committee to Study Governmental Operations, "The Investigation of the Assassination of John F. Kennedy: Performance of the Intelligence Agencies" *Final Report of the Senate Select Committee to Study Governmental Operations with Respect to Intelligence Activities*, Book V, 94th Cong., 1st–2nd sess., April 23, 1976, Rept. 94-755.

20. President Gerald Ford, Executive Order, "United States Foreign Intelligence Activities, Executive Order 11905," *Federal Register* 41 (February 19, 1976).

21. 1974 Hughes-Ryan Act, Foreign Assistance Act of 1974, Section 662 (a), Pub. No. 93-559.

22. *FBI Statutory Charter*: Hearings Before the Senate Committee on the Judiciary, 95th Cong. pt. 1, 20–26 (1978) and in *FBI Oversight*: Hearings Before the Subcommittee on Civil and Constitutional Rights of the House Judiciary Committee on the Judiciary, 95th Cong. 181–87 (1978).

23. "FBI Hired Chicago Spies," *Washington Post*, January 21, 1978, A1.

24. House Judiciary Committee, "Constitutional Limitations on Domestic Surveillance," Hearing before the Subcommittee on the Constitution, Civil Rights, and Civil Liberties, June 7, 2007, no. 110-45.

25. Alberto Gonzales, Letter to Patrick Leahy and Arlen Specter, reprinted in *New York Times*, 17 January 2007.

26. *The Protect America Act of 2007*, 109th Cong., 1st sess., S. 2011.

27. Dana Priest, "Justice Dept. Memo Says Torture 'May be Justified'" *Washington Post* June 13, 2004, sec. A, p.A01; Bybee memo of January 22, 2002, "Re: Application for Treaties and Laws to al Qaeda and Taliban Detainees."

28. William Blackstone, George Sharswood, and Barron Field, *Commentaries on the Laws of England: In Four Books* (Philadelphia: J. B. Lippincott, 1908), 46.

29. Paul Kane, "Rove, Bolten Found in Contempt of Congress; Senate Committee Cites Top Bush Advisers in Prove of U.S. Attorney Firings" *Washington Post*, December 14, 2007, sec. A, p.08; Robert Barnes and Dan Eggen, "Hill Panel Initiates Contempt Charges Against Miers; Executive Privilege Battle May Hit Courts," *Washington Post*, July 13, 2007, sec. A, p. 03.

30. *Committee on the Judiciary v. Harriet Miers and Joshua Bolten*, Case 1:08-cv-00409, March 10, 2008.

31. *McGrain v. Daugherty*, 273 US 135 (1927).

32. House Committee on the Judiciary, Articles of Impeachment Adopted by the Committee on the Judiciary, 93rd Cong., 2nd sess., 1974.

33. Shakespeare, *The Tragedy of Julius Ceasar*, ed. Lawrence Mason (New Haven, CT: Yale University Press, 1919), act 3, scene 2.

34. *Korematsu v. United States*, 323 US 214 (1944).

35. Hannis Taylor and Mary Lillie Taylor Hunt, *Cicero, A Sketch of His Life and Works* (Chicago: A. C. McClurg, 1916), 582.

36. William Glaberson, "Judge's Guantanamo Ruling Bodes Ill for System," *New York Times*, May 11, 2008, sec. A, col. 0, p. 26.

37. Patrick Healy, "Clinton Clearly Outduels Obama in Pennsylvania," *New York Times*, April 23, 2008, late ed., sec. A, col. 0, p. 1.

38. Arthur M. Schlesinger Jr., *The Imperial Presidency* (New York: Mariner Books, 2004), 331.

39. George Santayana, "Reason in Common Sense," in *Life of Reason*, by Santayana (New York: Scribner's, 1905), 284.

40. Susan Ferrechio. "Pelosi: Bush Impeachment 'Off the Table,'" *New York Times*, November 8, 2006.

41. Edmund Burke, *Reflections on the Revolution in France* (attributed).

42. William Strabala and Michael Palecek, *Prophets Without Honor: A Requiem for Moral Patriotism* (New York: Algora Publishing, 2002), 352.

43. Alla Shahine, "Interview: Egyptian cleric to sue Italy over CIA abduction," *Reuters*, May 13, 2008; Dennis R. O'Connor et al., "Report of the Events Relating to Maher Arar: Factual Background," Volume I, September 2006; *El-Masri v. United States*, 479 F3d 296 (4th Cir. 2007); *Boumediene v. Bush*, 553 U.S. ____ (2008).

44. Ben Fox and Alfred de Montesquiou, "Al-Jazeera Cameraman still at Guantanamo," *Washington Post*, February 23, 2007.

45. Carlotta Gall and Andy Worthington, "Time Runs Out for an Afghan Held by the U.S.," *New York Times*, February 5, 2008, sec. A, p. 1.

46. *Hirayabashi v. United States*, 320 US 81 (1943); *Korematsu v. United States*, 323 US 214 (1944).

47. Andrea Stone, "Most think founders wanted Christian USA," *USA Today*, September 12, 2007, p. 10A.

48. Stephen Labaton, "McCain Casts Muslim as Less Fit to Lead," *New York Times*, September 30, 2007, late ed., sec. 1, col. 0, p. 22.

49. U.S. Constitution, Preamble: "We the people of the United States, in order to form a more perfect union, establish justice, insure domestic tranquility, provide for the common defense, promote the general welfare, and secure the blessings of liberty to ourselves and our posterity, do ordain and establish this Constitution for the United States of America."

50. *The Works of Benjamin Franklin: Including the Private as well as Official and Scientific Correspondence*, ed. John Bigelow (New York: G. P. Putnam's Sons, 1904), 11:376–78.

51. Edwin Paxton Hood, *Oliver Cromwell: His Life, Times, Battlefields, and Contemporaries*, 2nd ed. (London: Hodder and Stoughton, 1884), 398.

52. U.S. Congress., Hon. Henry S. Reuss quoting Niemoller, *Congressional Record*, 90th Cong., 2nd sess., 1968, vol. 114, pt. 24:31636.

53. Dan Eggen, "NSA Spying Part of Broader Effort: Intelligence Chief Says Bush Authorized Secret Activities under One Order," *Washington Post*, August 1, 2007, sec. A, p. 1; James Risen and Eric Lichtblau, "Bush Lets U.S. Spy on Callers without Courts," *New York Times*, December 16, 2005, late ed., sec. A, col. 1, p. 1.

54. "Lawyers Group Criticizes Surveillance Program," *Washington Post*, February 14, 2006, sec. A, p. A06; *ACLU v. NSA*, 438 F. Supp. 2d 754

(declared TSP unconstitutional); *ACLU v. NSA*, 493 F. 3d 644 (ruled ACLU had no standing).

55. Gail Gibson, "NSA says it's too secret to be sued; State secrets doctrine almost always wins," *Baltimore Sun*, July 11, 2006, telegraph, p. 1A.

56. The Protect America Act of 2007, 109th Cong., 1st sess., S. 2011.

57. Ibid., sec. 105B.

58. Ibid., sec. 105C(b).

59. John Adams, *The Works of John Adams, Second President of the United States: With a Life of the Author, Notes and Illustrations*, ed. Charles Francis Adams (Boston: Charles C. Little and James Brown, 1850), 2:317.

60. *Hamdan v. Rumsfeld*, 548 US 557 (2006).

61. Dan Eggen and Brooke A. Masters, "U.S. Won't Seek Death for Walker; Fighter Charged with Conspiracy," *Washington Post*, January 16, 2002, sec. A, p. A01; William Glaberson, "Plea of Guilty from Detainee in Guantanamo," *New York Times*, March 27, 2007, late ed., sec. A, col. 6, p. 1.

62. *Padilla v. Hanft*, 389 F. Supp. 2d 678 (2005); 476 F 3d 1181 (2007).

63. Maureen O'Hagan, "A terrorism case that went awry," *The Seattle Times*, 22 November 2004, 4th edition, p. A1.

64. *Rasul v. Bush*, 542 U.S. 466, 480–85 (2004).

65. Military Commissions Act of 2006, H.R. 6054, 109th Cong., 2nd sess.; U.S. Code, Vol. 10, secs. 948a–950j.

66. Neil A. Lewis, "Freed from Guantanamo but Stranded Far From Home," *New York Times*, August 15, 2006, sec. A, col. 1, p. 15.

67. *Boumediene v. Bush*, 553 US ____ (2008).

68. *Ex Parte Quirin*, 317 US 1 (1942); Third Geneva Convention, Part I: General Provisions, Article IV.

69. U.S. Constitution, Art. IV, Sec. 3.

70. Glenn Greenwald, "CNN, the Pentagon's 'military analyst program' and Gitmo," *Salon*, May 9, 2008.

71. Senate Committee on Armed Services, *Nominations: Confirmation Hearing on Charles E. Wilson to be Secretary of Defense*, 83rd Cong., 1st Sess., January 15, 1953, vol. 99, pt. 1:26.

72. "Archibald Cox, 92, Is Dead; Helped Prosecute Watergate," *New York Times*, May 30, 2004.

73. U.S. Government Printing Office, Grover Cleveland's First Inaugural Address, in *Inaugural Addresses of the Presidents of the United States: From George Washington 1789 to George Bush 1989* (Washington, DC: U.S. Government Printing Office, 1989), 171.

74. Edward Gibbon, *The History of the Decline and Fall of the Roman Empire* (London: T. Cadell, Strand, 1837), 38.

CHAPTER 3

1. Henry Cabot Lodge, *American Statesmen: George Washington*, ed. John T. Morse (Boston: Houghton Mifflin, 1917), 2:31.
2. *National Treasury Workers Union v. Nixon*, 521 F. 2d 317 (DC Cir. 1975).
3. Vincent Buranelli, *Louis XIV* (New York: Twayne, 1966), 31.
4. Richard M. Nixon, audio and transcript, Address to the Nation about Watergate Investigations, April 30, 1973 (Charlottesville, VA: Miller Center of Public Affairs).
5. *Nixon v. Sirica*, 487 F. 2d 700 (DC Cir. 1973).
6. Department of Justice, Attorney General Order No. 551-73, Federal Register 38, no. 30738, as amended, Order No. 554-73, Federal Register 38, no. 32805 (1973) reprinted in *Special Prosecutor: Hearings Before the Senate Comm. on the Judiciary*, 93rd Cong., 1st sess. (1973), pp. 261–63.
7. Gerald S. Greenberg, *Historical Encyclopedia of U.S. Independent Counsel Investigations* (London: Greenwood Press, 2000), 76, 163, 109.
8. *Dyer v. Calderon*, 151 F3d 970, 984 (1998).
9. *Nixon v. Sirica*, 487 F. 2d 700 (DC Cir. 1973).
10. *Ex Parte Milligan*, 71 US 2 (1866).
11. Ibid., 76.
12. Bruce Fein, "Power of the purse purloined?" *The Washington Times*, 5 February 2008, commentary, p. A17.
13. David Frost, "Excerpts from Interview with Nixon about Domestic Effects of Indochina War," *New York Times*, May 20, 1977, p. A16.
14. Earl Warren, *A Republic, If You Can Keep It* (New York: Quadrangle Books, 1972).
15. Thomas Jefferson, *The Writings of Thomas Jefferson* (New York: G. P. Putnam's Sons, 1893), 2:43.
16. James Madison, "Political Observations: April 20, 1795," in *Letters and Other Writings of James Madison* (Philadelphia: J. B. Lippincott & Co., 1865), 4:491–92.
17. James Madison, Letter to Thomas Jefferson, May 13, 1798, in *Letters and Other Writings of James Madison* (Philadelphia: J. B. Lippincott & Co., 1865), 2:141.
18. Robert J. Hanyok, "Skunks, Bogies, Silent Hounds, and the Flying Fish: The Gulf of Tonkin Mystery, August 2–4, 1964," *Cryptology Quarterly* (1998): 1–55.
19. Gulf of Tonkin Resolution, H.J.R. 1145, 88th Cong., 2nd sess., *Congressional Record*, 147, nos. 88–408 (January 7, 1964).
20. *The Macmillan Book of Proverbs, Maxims, and Famous Phrases*, ed. Burton Stevenson (New York: Macmillan, 1948), 2445.
21. Samuel Johnson, "The Idler No. 30," *London Universal Chronicle*, November 11, 1758.
22. *New York Times v. United States*, 403 US 713 (1971).

23. Report by Winston Churchill to War Cabinet, August 19, 1941, CAB 65/19, WM 84(41), British Public Record Office (PRO), Kew, UK.

24. Ibid.

25. Abraham Lincoln, *Collected Works: The Abraham Lincoln Association*, ed. Roy P. Basler (New Brunswick, NJ: Rutgers University Press, 1953–1955), 5:421.

26. Ibid., 439.

27. James Madison, Letter to Thomas Jefferson, April 2, 1798, in *The Writings of James Madison*, ed. Gaillard Hunt (New York: G. P. Putnam's Sons, 1900), 6:312–13.

28. John Bach McMaster and Frederick D. Stone, eds., *Pennsylvania and the Federal Constitution, 1787–1788* (Lancaster: Historical Society of Pennsylvania, 1888), 414–18.

29. Scott McClellan, *What Happened Inside the Bush White House and Washington's Culture of Deception* (New York: Public Affairs, 2008), 131.

30. Harriett Beecher Stowe, *A Key to Uncle Tom's Cabin: Presenting the Original Facts and Documents upon Which the Story Is Founded* (Boston: John P. Jewett & Co., 1858).

31. *Dred Scott v. Sanford*, 60 U.S. 393 (1857).

32. C. Vann Woodward, *The Strange Career of Jim Crow* (New York: Oxford University Press, 1966).

33. L. H. Butterfield, ed., *Adams Family Correspondence* (Cambridge, MA: Belknap Press, 1963), 1:369.

34. *Bradwell v. People of State of Illinois*, 83 US 130 (1873).

35. Ibid., 141.

36. *Minor v. Happersett*, 88 US 162 (1874).

37. *Reed v. Reed*, 404 US 71 (1971).

38. Paul Andrew Hutton, *Phil Sheridan & His Army* (Lincoln, NE: University of Oklahoma Press, 1985), 180.

39. *Korematsu v. United States*, 323 US 214, 235-6 (1944).

40. *Hirayabashi v. United States*, 320 US 81 (1943).

41. *Korematsu v. United States*, 323 US 214 (1944).

42. Alexis de Tocqueville, *Democracy in America*, trans. Henry Reeve (New York: D. Appleton & Co., 1904), 1:290.

43. William MacDonald, *Select Documents Illustrative of the History of the United States 1776–1861* (New York: Macmillan, 1901), 146.

44. Francis S. Betten, S.J., *The Roman Index of Forbidden Books*, 5th ed. (St. Louis, MO: B. Herder, 1917), 24–27.

45. Leonard A. Cole, *Politics and the Restraint of Science* (Totowa, NJ: Roman & Allanheld, 1983), 4–5, 13, 16–19.

46. Ibid., 91–94.

47. Ibid., 19–22.

48. Ibid., 21–22.

49. Hugh Tredennick and Harold Tarrant, *The Last Days of Socrates* (Harmondsworth, UK: Penguin, 1993), 63, 67.
50. Ibid.
51. *Abrams v. United States*, 250 US 616 (1919).
52. Ibid., 630.
53. *Whitney v. California*, 274 US 357 (1927).
54. Ibid., 375.
55. Jefferson, Letter to Colonel Edward Carrington: January 16, 1787, in *The Writings of Thomas Jefferson*, ed. Andrew A. Lipscomb and Albert Ellery Bergh (Washington, DC: Thomas Jefferson Memorial Association, 1905), 6:57.
56. *Miller v. United States*, 357 US 301, 307 (1958).
57. Jacqueline E. Ross, "The Place of Covert Surveillance in Democratic Societies: A Comparative Study of the United States and Germany," *The American Journal of Comparative Law* 55 (2007): 493–579.
58. *Journals of the Continental Congress, 1774–1789*, ed. Worthington C. Ford (Washington, DC: 1904–1937), 5:512.
59. Lawrence Meyers, "How Watergate Still Haunts Those Who Lived It," *Washington Post*, June 13, 1982, sec. SM, p. 10–19.
60. Ibid.
61. John Henry Wigmore, *A Treatise on the System of Evidence in Trials at Common Law* (Boston: Little, Brown, & Co., 1904), 4:2963, 3077–79, 3094.
62. Madison, Federalist No. 62, in *The Federalist Papers: A Commentary on the Constitution of the United States*, ed. Henry Cabot Lodge (New York: G. P. Putnam's Sons, 1892), 384, 390.
63. Benjamin Franklin, *The Writings of Benjamin Franklin*, ed. Albert Henry Smith (New York: Macmillan, 1907), 10:297.
64. Alexander Hamilton, Federalist No. 15, in *The Federalist Papers: A Commentary on the Constitution of the United States*, ed. Henry Cabot Lodge (New York: G. P. Putnam's Sons, 1892), 76, 84.
65. Hadley Cantril, *The Human Dimension: Experiences in Policy Research* (New Brunswick, NJ: Rutgers University Press, 1967), 5.
66. Jefferson, Resolutions Relative to the Alien and Sedition Acts: November 10, 1798, in *The Writings of Thomas Jefferson*, eds. Andrew A. Lipscomb and Albert Ellery Bergh (Washington, DC: Thomas Jefferson Memorial Association, 1905), 17:389.
67. Albert P. Blaustein, "The Influence of the United States Constitution Abroad," *Oklahoma City University Law Review* 12 (1987): 435–36.
68. Irving Brant, *Impeachment: Trials and Errors* (New York: Alfred A. Knopf, 1972), 4.
69. Edward Gibbon, *The History of the Decline and Fall of the Roman Empire* (London: T. Cadell, Strand, 1837).

70. Thomas Paine, "The American Crisis No. 1 December 23, 1776," in *The Complete Writings of Thomas Paine*, ed. Philip S. Foner (New York: Citadel Press, 1945), 1:49.

71. U.S. Constitution, Art. II, Sec. 4.

72. House Committee on the Judiciary, Articles of Impeachment Adopted by the Committee on the Judiciary, 93rd Cong., 2nd sess., 1974.

73. Ibid.

74. Ibid.

75. *United States v. Nixon*, 418 US 683 (1974).

76. John Dean, transcript, President Richard M. Nixon Watergate Tapes "Cancer on the Presidency" with John Dean and H.R. Haldeman, Washington, DC, 1973.

77. George Washington, Address to Congress, in *The Debates and Proceedings of the United States Congress*, ed. Joseph Gales (Washington, DC: Gales and Seaton, 1834), 934.

78. U.S. Constitution, Art. II, Sec. 1.

79. *Jones v. Clinton*, 36 F Supp 2d 1118, 1134 (E.D. Ark. 1999).

80. Kenneth Starr, Referral to the United States House of Representatives. pursuant to Title 28, United States Code, § 595(c) Submitted by The Office of Independent Counsel, 105th Cong., 2nd sess., pp. 70, 133.

81. *Olmstead v. United States*, 277 US 438 (1928).

82. Ibid., 485.

83. *ABF Freight System, Inc v. NLRB*, 510 US 317 (1994).

84. Ibid., 323.

85. Impeaching William Jefferson Clinton, President of the United States, for High Crimes and Misdemeanors, 105th Cong., 2nd sess., H.R. 611.

86. Ibid.

87. Robert Bolt, *A Man for All Seasons*, act 1.

CHAPTER 4

1. Peter Baker and Jim VandeHei, "Clash Is Latest Chapter in Bush Effort to Widen Executive Power," *Washington Post*, December 21, 2005, final ed., sec. A, p. 1.

2. William Taft, *Taft Papers on League of Nations*, ed. Theodore Marburg and Horace E. Flack (New York: Macmillan, 1920).

3. John N. Petrie, *American Neutrality in the 20th Century: The Impossible Dream* (Washington, DC: Institute for National Strategic Studies, 1995), 40.

4. War Powers Resolution, H.J.R. 542, 93rd Cong., 1st sess., *Congressional Record* 147, nos. 93–148 (November 7, 1973), enacted in U.S. Code, Vol. 50, ch. 33.

5. Ibid., sec. 2(c).

6. Ibid., sec. 8(d)(1).
7. *Goldwater v. Carter*, 444 US 996 (1979).
8. *Dames & Moore v. Regan*, 453 US 654 (1981).
9. Ibid., 662–62.
10. *Snepp v. United States*, 444 US 507 (1980).
11. Arms Export Control Act of 1976. U.S. Code, Vol. 22, sec. 2778.
12. Intelligence Authorization Act for Fiscal Year 1984, Public Law 98-215, 98th Cong., 1st sess. (December 9, 1983).
13. *Immigration and Naturalization Service v. Chadha*, 462 US 919 (1983).
14. Thomas L. Friedman, "Fighting in Panama: Reaction; Congress Generally Supports Attack, but Many Fear Consequences" *New York Times*, December 21, 1989, sec. A, col. 3, p. 21; Authorization for Use of Military Force, S.J.R. 23, H.J.R. 64, 107th Cong., 1st sess., *Congressional Record* 147, nos. 107–40 (September 18, 2001); Art Pine and Janet Hook, "Crisis in Yugoslavia," *Los Angeles Times*, April 14, 1999, sec. A, p. 15.
15. Foreign Intelligence Surveillance Act of 1978, U.S. Code, Vol. 50, secs. 1801–71.
16. *United States v. Alvarez-Machain*, 504 US 655 (1992).
17. *United States v. Verdugo-Urquidez*, 494 US 259 (1990).
18. *Nixon v. Fitzgerald*, 457 US 731 (1982).
19. Ibid., 749; Independent Counsel Act, U.S. Code, Vol. 28, secs. 591–99.
20. *United States v. Moussaoui*, 382 F 3d 453 (2005); 365 F 3d 292 (2004); 336 F 3d 279 (2003).
21. *United States v. Ramzi Ahmed Yousef*, 327 F 3d 56 (2003).
22. *Padilla v. Hanft*, 389 F. Supp. 2d 678 (2005); 476 F 3d 1181 (2007).
23. *United States v. McVeigh*, 153 F 3d 1166 (1999).
24. Colum Lynch, "N.Y. Trial Opens for Alleged Terrorists; Prosecutor Vows to Reveal Role of Four in Embassy Bombings in Africa," *Washington Post*, February 6, 2001, final ed., sec. A, p. 2.
25. John Ritter, "Dec. 7 and Sept. 11: Generations Apart, Forever Linked," *USA Today*, December 7, 2001, final ed., sec. news, p. 1A; "U.S. Deaths in Iraq, War on Terror Surpass 9/11 Toll," *Cable News Network*, September 3, 2006; Glenn Kutler, "U.S. Military Fatalities in Iraq: A Perspective on Year 5," *iCasualties.org*, Summer 2008.
26. Department of Justice, Bureau of Justice Statistics, "Homicide Trends in the U.S.," in *Federal Bureau of Investigation Uniform Crime Reports 1950–2005*.
27. U.S. Constitution, Art. 1, Sec. 4, Cl. 2.
28. President George W. Bush, Military Order, "Detention, Treatment, and Trial of Certain Non-Citizens in the War against Terrorism." *Federal Register* 66, no. 222 (November 16, 2001): 57831–36.
29. *Boumediene v. Bush*, 553 U.S. ____ (2008).

30. President George W. Bush, Executive Order, "Blocking of Certain Persons Who Threaten Stabilization Efforts in Iraq, Executive Order 13438," *Federal Register* 72, no. 138 (July 19, 2007).
31. The Classified Information Procedures Act of 1980, Public Law 96-456, 96th Cong., 2nd sess.
32. Bret Stephens, "Who Needs Jacques Bauer? The Napoleonic Code is more conducive to counterterrorism than the U.S. Constitution," *Wall Street Journal*, February 25, 2007.
33. President George W. Bush, Executive Order, "Executive Order on Terrorist Financing: Blocking Property and Prohibiting Transactions With Persons Who Commit, or Support Terrorism, Executive Order 13224." *Federal Register* 66, no. 186 (September 23, 2001).
34. Tom Weiner, *Legacy of Ashes* (New York: Doubleday, 2007), 275–77.
35. *Journals of the Continental Congress, 1774–1789*, ed. Worthington C. Ford et al. (Washington, DC: 1904–1937), 5:510.
36. Jack Goldsmith, "Global Convergence on Terror," *American Enterprise Institute for Public Policy Research*, August 1, 2007, AEI Print Index No. 22034.
37. Aleksandr Solzhenitsyn, *The Gulag Archipelago* (New York: Harper Perennial Modern Classics, 2002).
38. *Padilla v. Hanft*, 476 F 3d 1181, 1184-89 (2005).
39. Richard A. Serrano, "Last 'Lackawanna Six' Defendant Pleads Guilty," *Los Angeles Times*, May 20, 2003.
40. *Al-Marri v. Wright*, 487 F 3d 160, 179, 197 (4th Cir. 2007); Josh White, "Australian's Guilty Plea Is First at Guantanamo," *Washington Post*, March 27, 2007, met 2 ed., sec. A, p. 1.
41. Abraham Lincoln, Address to Congress, July 4, 1861, in *Abraham Lincoln Papers at the Library of Congress: Series 1. General Correspondence. 1833–1916* (Washington, DC: American Memory Project, 2000–2002).
42. Ernesto Londoño and Amit R. Paley, "In Iraq, a Surge in U.S. Airstrikes," *Washington Post*, May 23, 2008, sec. A, p. 10.

CHAPTER 5

1. Loch K. Johnson, *America's Secret Power: The CIA in a Democratic Society* (New York: Oxford University Press, 1991), 144.
2. Egil Krogh, "The Break-In that History Forgot," *International Herald Tribune*, June 30, 2007, late ed., sec. A.
3. Senate Select Committee to Study Governmental Operations with Respect to Intelligence Activities, *Book II: Intelligence Activities and the Rights of Americans*, S. Rep. No. 94-755 (Washington, DC: U.S. Government Printing Office, 1976), 290.
4. Ibid., 289.

5. Foreign Intelligence Surveillance Act (FISA), U.S. Code, vol. 50, secs.1821–29.
6. Dan Eggen, "NSA Spying Part of Broader Effort: Intelligence Chief Says Bush Authorized Secret Activities under One Order," *Washington Post*, August 1, 2007, sec. A, p. 1.
7. James Risen and Eric Lichtblau, "Bush Lets U.S. Spy on Callers without Courts," *New York Times*, December 16, 2005, late ed., sec. A, col. 1, p. 1.
8. Mark M. Lowenthal, "The Real Intelligence Failure? Spineless Spies," *Washington Post*, May 25, 2008, sec. B, p. 1.
9. Alberto Gonzales, Letter to Patrick Leahy and Arlen Specter, repr. in *New York Times*, January 17, 2007.
10. Senate Committee on the Judiciary, Amendment of the Foreign Intelligence Surveillance Act of 1978 to Allow Surveillance of Non-United States Persons Who Engage in or Prepare for International Terrorism without Affiliation with a Foreign Government or International Terrorist Group, 108th Cong. 1st, sess., April 29, 2003; S. Rpt. 108-40; USA PATRIOT Act "Uniting and Strengthening America by Providing Appropriate Tools Required to Intercept and Obstruct Terrorism Act of 2001," H.R. 3162, 107th Cong., 1st sess., January 3, 2001.
11. Dan Eggen and Walter Pincus, "Campaign to Justify Spying Intensifies: NSA Effort Called Legal and Necessary," *Washington Post*, January 24, 2006, sec. A, p. 4.
12. Jack Goldsmith, *The Terror Presidency: Law and Judgment Inside the Bush Administration* (New York: W. W. Norton & Co., 2007), 181.
13. Abraham Lincoln, Address before the Young Men's Lyceum of Springfield, Illinois, January 27, 1838, in *The Writings of Abraham Lincoln* (New York: G. P. Putnam's Sons, 1906), 148–60.
14. *United States v. Nixon*, 418 US 683 (1974).
15. Eric Lichtblau, *Bush's Law: The Remaking of American Justice* (New York: Pantheon, 2008), 151–52, 199–200.
16. *Gravel v. United States*, 408 US 606 (1972).
17. Edmund Burke, *Reflections on the Revolution in France* (attributed).
18. Senate Select Committee to Study Governmental Operations with Respect to Intelligence Activities, *Book II: Intelligence Activities and the Rights of Americans*, S. Rep. No. 94-755 (Washington, DC: U.S. Government Printing Office, 1976), 290.
19. Barton Gellman and Dafna Linzer, "A 'Concerted Effort' to Discredit Bush Critic: Prosecutor Describes Cheney, Libby as Key Voices Pitching Iraq-Niger Story," *Washington Post*, April 9, 2006, sec. A, p. 1.
20. George Orwell, *1984* (New York: Everyman's Library, 1992); Stephen Bates, "Odd Clothes and Unorthodox Views—Why MI5 Spied on Orwell for a Decade," *Guardian* (UK), September 4, 2007, Top Stories, p. 3.

21. David K. Watson, *The Constitution of the United States: Its History Application and Construction* (Chicago: Callaghan & Co., 1910), 1414–30.
22. James Otis, "On the Writs of Assistance," February 1761, in *Early American Orations: 1760–1824*, ed. Louie Regina Heller (New York: Macmillan, 1902), 4.
23. Ibid., 5.
24. John T. Morse Jr., *John Adams* (Boston: Houghton Mifflin, 1912), 25.
25. *Boyd v. United States*, 116, US 616, 626 (1886).
26. *Entick v. Carrington*, 19 How. St. Tr. 1029, 1063; 95 Eng. Rep. 807 (1765).
27. U.S. Constitution, Amend IV.
28. Foreign Intelligence Surveillance Act, sec. 1809.
29. Senate Committee on the Judiciary, Hearing on Wartime Executive Power and the NSA's Surveillance Authority, 109th Cong., 2nd sess., February 6 and 28, and March 28, 2006; S. Hrg. 109-59, pp. 25–26.
30. U.S. Constitution, Art. 1, Sec. 5, Cl. 3.
31. James Risen and Eric Lichtblau, "Bush Lets U.S. Spy on Callers without Courts," *New York Times*, December 16, 2005, late ed., sec. A, col. 1, p. 1; Eric Lichtblau, "Bush Defends Spy Program and Denies Misleading Public," *New York Times*, January 2, 2006, sec. A, p. 11.
32. *United States v. Verdugo-Urquidez*, 494 US 259 (1990).
33. Leslie Cauley, "NSA Has Massive Database of Americans' Phone Calls," *USA Today*, May 11, 2006, news, p. 1A.
34. Patrick Leahy to Arlen Specter, "The FISA Program" in *Congressional Record* (Senate), January 17, 2007, pp. S646–S647.
35. President George W. Bush, transcript, President's Radio Address (Washington, DC: Roosevelt Room), December 17, 2005.
36. President George W. Bush, transcript, Information Sharing, Patriot Act Vital to Homeland Security (Buffalo, NY: Kleinshans Music Hall), April 20, 2004.
37. President George W. Bush, transcript, Remarks in Waukesha, Wisconsin (Waukesha, WI: Waukesha County Exposition Center), July 14, 2004.
38. President George W. Bush, transcript, Discusses Patriot Act (Columbus, OH: Ohio State Highway Patrol Academy), June 9, 2005.
39. William Safire, "On Language; Alone With 'Alone,' or What 'Is' Is," *New York Times*, magazine, sec. 6, col. 2, p. 22.
40. "Previous Statements by the President" *Special to the New York Times*, April 18, 1973, p. 16.
41. President George W. Bush, transcript, President's Radio Address (Washington, DC: Roosevelt Room), December 17, 2005.
42. Senate Judiciary Committee, "Preserving Prosecutorial Independence: Is the Department of Justice Politicizing the Hiring and Firing of U.S.

Attorneys?–Part IV" *Congressional Quarterly*, 110th Cong., 2nd sess., May 15, 2007, pp. 11–12,

43. Ibid. 19–22.
44. Attorney General Alberto Gonzales and General Michael Hayden, transcript, Press Briefing (Washington, DC: James S. Brady Briefing Room) December 19, 2005.
45. Ibid.
46. Ibid.
47. President George W. Bush, transcript, President's Radio Address (Washington, DC), May 13, 2006.
48. Ibid.
49. President George W. Bush, transcript, President Bush Discusses NSA Surveillance Program (Washington, DC: Diplomatic Reception Room) May 11, 2006.
50. President George W. Bush, transcript, President Bush Signs Military Commissions Act of 2006 (Washington, DC: East Room) October 17, 2006.
51. Leslie Cauley, "NSA has massive database of Americans' phone calls," *USA Today*, 11 May 2006, news, p. 1A.
52. Patrick Leahy to Arlen Specter, "The FISA Program," *Congressional Record* (Senate), January 17, 2007, pp. S646–S647.
53. Ibid.
54. Tom Weiner, *Legacy of Ashes* (New York: Doubleday, 2007), 353.
55. Senate Select Committee to Study Governmental Operations with Respect to Intelligence Activities, The National Security Agency and Fourth Amendment Rights: Hearings on S.R. 21, 94th Cong., 1st sess., November 6, 1975, pp. 66–67.
56. Ibid., 67.
57. Ibid., 68.
58. Ibid.
59. Ibid., 69.
60. Ibid.
61. Seymour M. Hersh, "Huge C.I.A. Operation Reported in U.S. against Antiwar Forces, Other Dissidents in Nixon Years," *New York Times*, December 22, 1974, p. 1.
62. Ibid.
63. James R. Schlesinger, Memorandum to all Central Intelligence Agency employees, May 9, 1973, in *The CIA's Family Jewels* (Washington, DC: The National Security Archive, 1995–2008).
64. Ibid.
65. Ibid.
66. Karen DeYoung and Walter Pincus, "CIA to Air Decades of Dirty Laundry: Assassination Attempts among Abuses Detailed," *Washington Post*, June 22, 2007, sec. A, p. 1.

67. The CIA's Family Jewels, *National Security Archive Electronic Briefing Book No. 222*, ed. Thomas Blanton, June 21, 2007, p. 522.
68. Ibid., 466.
69. Ibid., 27.
70. Ibid.
71. James A. Wilderotter, Associate Deputy General, Memorandum "CIA Matters," January 3, 1975, declassified May 24, 2000, p. 2.
72. Ibid., 3.
73. Ibid.
74. Senate Select Committee to Study Governmental Operations with Respect to Intelligence Activities, Mail Opening: Hearings on S.R. 21, 94th Cong., 1st sess., October 21, 1975, p. 1.
75. Ibid., 6.
76. James A. Wilderotter, Associate Deputy General, Memorandum "CIA Matters," January 3, 1975, declassified May 24, 2000, 5.
77. William E. Colby, "Memorandum of Conversation: Allegations of CIA Domestic Activities" (Washington, DC: Oval Office) January 3, 1975, 1.
78. Senate Select Committee to Study Governmental Operations with Respect to Intelligence Activities, The National Security Agency and Fourth Amendment Rights: Hearings on S.R. 21, vol. 4, 94th Cong., 1st sess., October 21, 1975, p. 1.
79. Ibid., 6.
80. Senate Select Committee to Study Governmental Operations with Respect to Intelligence Activities, The National Security Agency and Fourth Amendment Rights: Hearings on S.R. 21, vol. 5, 94th Cong., 1st sess., October 29, 1975, pp. 10–11.
81. Ibid., 1.
82. Ibid., 60.
83. Ibid., 62.
84. House Permanent Select Committee Report, H.R. Rep No. 95-1283(I), 21.
85. Foreign Intelligence Surveillance Act, S. Rep. 95-701, 95th Cong., 2nd sess. (1978), 72.
86. Ibid., 71.

CHAPTER 6

1. Senate Committee on the Judiciary, Confirmation Hearing on the Nomination of Alberto R. Gonzales to be Attorney General of the United States, 109th Cong., 1st sess., February 6, 2005, S. Hrg. 109-4, referring to Bybee memo of January 22, 2002, "Re: Application for Treaties and Laws to al Qaeda and Taliban Detainees.
2. Foreign Intelligence Surveillance Act of 1978, U.S. Code, Vol. 50, ch. 36.

3. Robert Barnes, "Sentence in Memo Discounted FISA," *Washington Post*, May 23, 2008, sec. A, p. A15.

4. Foreign Intelligence Surveillance Act of 1978, U.S. Code, Vol. 50, ch.36, secs. 1811.

5. Ibid.

6. Ibid., sec. 1801(e).

7. Brian A. Benczkowski to Diane Feinstein and Sheldon Whitehouse, May 13, 2008, *Congressional Record*, Washington, DC, 2008, pp. S5355–S5357.

8. U.S. Constitution, Art. I, Sec. 8, Cl. 18.

9. U.S. Constitution, Art. II, Sec. 2, Cl. 2.

10. Ibid.

11. U.S. Constitution, Art. II, Sec. 8.

12. *McCulloch v. Maryland*, 17 US 316 (1819).

13. Ibid., 407, 415–16, 421.

14. George C. Chalou, *The Secret War: The Office of Strategic Services in World War II* (Washington, DC: National Archives and Records Administration, 1995), 358; emphasis added.

15. *Katz v. United States*, 389 US 347 (1967).

16. *Olmstead v. United States*, 277 US 438 (1928).

17. Ibid., 457.

18. Richard A. Posner, *Not a Suicide Pact: The Constitution in a Time of National Emergency* (Oxford: Oxford University Press, 2006), 149.

19. Ibid., 145.

20. Ibid., 144.

21. Eric Lichtblau, *Bush's Law: The Remaking of American Justice* (New York: Pantheon, 2008).

22. Curt Gentry, *J. Edgar Hoover: The Man and the Secrets* (New York: W. W. Norton & Co., 1991), 632.

23. Ibid., 637.

24. Senate Committee on the Judiciary, Wartime Executive Power and the National Security Agency's Surveillance Authority: Hearings before the Senate Committee on the Judiciary, 109th Cong., 2nd sess., February 28, 2006, pp. 431–32.

25. James Madison, Federalist No. 47, in *The Federalist Papers: A Commentary on the Constitution of the United States*, ed. Henry Cabot Lodge (New York: G. P. Putnam's Sons, 1892), 299, 331.

26. James Madison, Federalist No. 48, in *The Federalist Papers: A Commentary on the Constitution of the United States*, ed. Henry Cabot Lodge (New York: G. P. Putnam's Sons, 1892), 338–39.

27. The Debates and Proceedings in the Congress of the United States, *The Congressional Globe*, 4th Cong., 1st Sess., March 1796 (Washington, DC: Gales and Seaton, 1849), 449.

28. House Committee on the Judiciary, *Legislative Proposals to Update the Foreign Intelligence Surveillance Act (FISA): Hearings before the House Sub-Committee on Crime, Terrorism, and Homeland Security,* 109th Cong., 2nd sess., September 6, 2006, p. 20.

29. Senate Select Committee on Intelligence, Prepared Statement of James Baker, *Amendments to the Foreign Intelligence Surveillance Act: Hearings on S. 2586 and S. 2659,* 107th Cong., 2nd sess., July 31, 2002, S. Hrg. 107–1013.

30. Ibid.

31. James Risen, "Obama Voters Protest His Switch on Telecom Immunity," *New York Times,* July 2, 2008, sec. A, col. 0, p. 14.

32. *Continuing Appropriations Resolution for Fiscal Year 1974,* Public Law 93-52, 93rd Cong., 2nd sess., June 30, 1973.

33. *Department of Defense Appropriations Act for Fiscal Year 1995,* Public Law 103-335, 103rd Cong., 2nd sess., September 30, 1994.

34. Ibid.

35. John Yoo, *War by Other Means: An Insider's Account of the War on Terror* (New York: Atlantic Monthly Press, 2006), 125.

36. *Youngstown Sheet & Tube Co. v. Sawyer,* 343 US 579 (1952).

37. *Crimes and Criminal Procedure,* U.S. Code, Vol. 18, sec. 2511(2)(f).

38. U.S. Department of Justice, "Legal Authorities Supporting the Activities of the National Security Agency Described by the President," Washington, DC, January 19, 2006.

39. *Authorization for Use of Military Force Act,* Public Law 107-40, 107th Cong., 1st sess., September 18, 2001, sec. 2(a).

40. Ibid.

41. *Foreign Intelligence Surveillance Act,* sec. 1811.

42. Ibid., sec. 1809(a).

43. *Foreign Intelligence Surveillance Act,* H.R. 6304 sec. 201(b); enacted sec. 1801(b).

44. President George W. Bush, transcript, Address to a Joint Session of Congress and the American People, September 20, 2001.

45. *United States v. Robel,* 389 US 258 (1967).

46. Ibid., 264.

47. George Tenet, *At the Center of the Storm* (New York: HarperCollins, 2007), 264.

CHAPTER 7

1. John Adams, *The Works of John Adams, Second President of the United States,* ed. Charles Francis Adams (Boston: Little, Brown, & Co., 1865), 438.

2. Ibid., 456.

3. Senate, Summary of Findings and Recommendations in Report of the Senate Commission on Protecting and Reducing Government Secrecy, 103rd Cong., 2nd sess., March 3, 1997, S. Doc 105-2,

4. Ibid., xxi.

5. Ibid., xxii.

6. George W. Bush and John Kerry, *The Second Bush-Kerry Debate* (St. Louis: Commission on Presidential Debates, October 8, 2004).

7. Paul Kane, "Rove, Bolten Found in Contempt of Congress; Senate Committee Cites Top Bush Advisers in Probe of U.S. Attorney Firings," *Washington Post*, December 14, 2007, sec. A, p. 8.

8. Kathy Kiely and David Jackson, "Conflict Builds as Gonzales Targeted; Senate Dems Subpoena Rove," *USA Today*, p. 1A.

9. George Lardner Jr. and Walter Pincus, "Nixon Ordered Tapes Destroyed," *Washington Post*, October 30, 1997, sec. A, p. 1.

10. Ibid.

11. *United States v. Nixon*, 418 US 683, 707 (1974).

12. Carroll Kilpatrick, "Nixon Resigns," *Washington Post*, August 9, 1974, sec. A, p. 1.

13. Senate Select Committee on Presidential Campaign Activities, 93rd Cong.; Judiciary Committee Impeachment Hearings, 93rd Cong., *Book I, Events Prior to the Watergate Break-in* (Washington, DC: U.S. Government Printing Office, 1974).

14. Todd S. Purdum, "Questions on Accepted Legal Practice," *New York Times*, October 2, 1997, sec. A, p. 1.

15. David Wise and Thomas B. Ross, *The Invisible Government* (New York: Random House, 1964), 1858.

16. James Madison, Letter to W. T. Barry, August 4, 1822, in *Letters and Other Writings of James Madison* (Philadelphia: J. B. Lippincott & Co., 1865), 4:276.

17. William Strabala, *WMD, Nukes, and Nuns* (New York: Algora, 2006), 123.

18. Robert Scheer, "A Cover-Up as Shameful as Tillman's Death," *The Nation*, May 31, 2005, http://www.thenation.com/doc/20050613/scheer0531 (accessed May 4, 2008).

19. Senate Select Committee to Study Governmental Operations with Respect to Intelligence Activities, *Book II: Intelligence Activities and the Rights of Americans*, S. Rep. No. 94-755 (Washington, DC: U.S. Government Printing Office, 1976), 290.

20. Barton Gellman and Dafna Linzer, "A 'Concerted Effort' to Discredit Bush Critic: Prosecutor Describes Cheney, Libby as Key Voices Pitching Iraq-Niger Story," *Washington Post*, April 9, 2006, sec. A, p. 1.

21. U.S. Constitution, Art. 1, Sec. 5, Cl. 3.

22. Ibid., Art. 1, Sec. 9, Cl. 7.

23. *United States v. Richardson*, 418 US 166 (1974).
24. Ibid., 169.
25. Ibid.
26. Congressional Research Service, Intelligence Spending: Public Disclosure Issues, 110th Cong., 1st sess., pp. 41–42.
27. Implementing Recommendations of the 9/11 Commission Act of 2007, Public Law 110-53, 110th Cong., 1st sess.
28. Ibid.
29. William J. Broad, "How a Soviet Secret Was Finally Pierced," *New York Times*, June 26, 1984, sec. C, p. 1.
30. Serge Schmemann, "Soviet A-Bomb Built from U.S. Data, Russia Says," *New York Times*, January 14, 1993, sec. A, p. 12.
31. Frederick H. Hartmann, *The Relations of Nations* (New York: Macmillan, 1957), 474.
32. Ibid.
33. Charles Henry Butler, *The Treaty-Making Power of the United States* (New York: Banks Law, 1902), 1:423.
34. The Debates and Proceedings in the Congress of the United States, *The Congressional Globe*, 11th Cong., 1st and 2nd Sess., January 1810 (Washington, DC: Gales and Seaton, 1853), 1053.
35. George Washington, Address to the House of Representatives, March 30, 1796, in *A Compilation of the Messages and Papers of the Presidents 1789–1897*, eds. James D. Richardson and George Raywood Devitt (Washington, DC: U.S. Government Printing Office, 1897), 1:194–96.
36. Ibid., 194.
37. Ibid.
38. Ibid., 195.
39. Ibid., 195–96.
40. U.S. Constitution, Art. 1, Sec. 1 (legislative powers); Sec. 3 (impeachment powers), Cl. 3; Art. II, Sec. 2 (treaty ratification power).
41. George Washington, Address to the House of Representatives, March 30, 1796, in *A Compilation of the Messages and Papers of the Presidents 1789–1897*, eds. James D. Richardson and George Raywood Devitt (Washington, DC: U.S. Government Printing Office, 1897), 1:195.
42. Ibid.
43. *United States v. Nixon*, 418 US 683, 687 (1974).
44. Ibid., 703.
45. Ibid., 715–16.
46. Ibid., 707.
47. Ibid., 705.
48. George Tenet, *At the Center of the Storm* (New York: HarperCollins, 2007), 363.
49. Scott McClellan, *What Happened Inside the Bush White House and Washington's Culture of Deception* (New York: Public Affairs, 2008).

50. *United States v. Nixon*, 418 US at 708.
51. Ibid., 709–13.
52. U.S. Constitution, Amend. VI.
53. Ibid.
54. *United States v. Nixon*, 418 US at 712.
55. . George Bernard Shaw, *The Man of Destiny* (New York: Brentano's, 1907), 62.
56. Robert H. Jackson, "The Federal Prosecutor," *Journal of the American Judicature Society* 24, no. 18 (1940): 18.
57. Senate Committee on the Judiciary, "Preserving Prosecutorial Independence: Is the Department of Justice Politicizing the Hiring and Firing of U.S. Attorneys?" 110th Cong., 1st sess., February 6, 2007, S. Hrg. 110-61.
58. Sheryl Gay Stolberg and Jeff Zeleny, "'Mistakes' Made on Prosecutores, Gonzales Admits" *New York Times*, March 13, 2007, late ed., sec. A, col. 6, p. 1.
59. Amy Goldstein, "Justice Department Recognized Prosecutor's Work on Election Fraud Before His Firing," *Washington Post*, March 19, 2007, sec. A, p. 4.
60. Senate Committee on the Judiciary, "Preserving Prosecutorial Independence: Is the Department of Justice Politicizing the Hiring and Firing of U.S. Attorneys?" 110th Cong., 1st sess., February 6, 2007, S. Hrg. 110–61, p. 9.
61. David Kirkpatrick and Jim Rutenberg, "E-Mail Shows Rove's Role in Fate of Prosecutors," *New York Times*, March 29, 2007, sec. A, col. 1, p. 20.
62. David M. Herszenhorn, "Ethics Panel Admonishes Domenici," *New York Times*, late ed., sec. A, col. 0, p. 25.
63. *Berger v. New York*, 295 US 78 (1935).
64. Ibid., 88.
65. U.S. Constitution, Amend. I and XV.
66. Seymour Hersh, "The Pardon," *Atlantic Monthly*, August 1983.
67. *Senate Select Committee v. Nixon*, 498 F2d 725 (DC Cir. 1974).
68. Ibid., 731.
69. *United States v. Nixon*, 418 US 683, 700 (1974).
70. Ibid.
71. Senate Select Committee on Intelligence, Hearing on the Nomination of Lt. Gen. Michael Hayden, USAF to be Principal Deputy Director of the CIA, 109th Cong., 2nd sess., April 14, 2005, pp. 68–70.
72. Robert Barnes, "Sentence in Memo Discounted FISA," *Washington Post*, May 23, 2008, sec. A, p. 15.
73. Ibid.
74. Independent Counsel Act, U.S. Code. vol. 28, secs. 593.
75. Ibid., 594.
76. *United States v. Nixon*, 418 US 683, 693 (1974).

77. *United States v. Cox*, 342 F2d 167, 168 (5th Cir. 1965).
78. Ibid., 171.
79. Independent Counsel Act, U.S. Code. vol. 28, secs. 591–99 (1978).
80. *Morrison v. Olson*, 487 US 654 (1988).
81. Ibid., 659.
82. Independent Counsel Act, U.S. Code. vol. 28, secs. 591–99 (1978).

CHAPTER 8

1. *United States v. Reynolds*, 345 US 1 (1953). This will be explored further later on in the chapter.
2. *El-Masri v. United States*, 479 F3d 296 (4th Cir. 2007).
3. Ibid., 4–5.
4. Ibid.
5. Ibid., 28–41.
6. *United States v. Reynolds* at 2.
7. Ibid., 6.
8. *Herring v. United States of America*, 424 F. 3d 384, 390-91 (2005).
9. *New York Times Co. v. United States*, 403 US 713 (1971).
10. Don Suskind, *The One Percent Doctrine: Deep Inside America's Pursuit of Its Enemies since 9/11* (New York: Simon & Schuster, 2006), 51.
11. Ibid. at 152.
12. Craig Whitlock, "CIA Ruse is Said to Have Damaged Probe in Milan," *Washington Post*, December 6, 2005, sec. A p. 01.
13. Craig Whitlock, "Germans Drop Bid for Extraditions in CIA Case; 13 Agency Operatives Charged in Kidnapping," *Washington Post*, September 24, 2007, sec. foreign, p. A9.
14. Carlotta Gall and Andy Worthington, "Time Runs Out for an Afghan Held by the U.S.," *New York Times*, February 5, 2008, sec. A, p.1.
15. Shakespeare, *Macbeth*, ed. James M. Garrnett (Boston: Leach, Shewell, & Sanborn, 1897), act 1, scene 7.
16. Jane Mayer, *The Dark Side: The Inside Story of How the War on Terror Turned into a Way on American ideals* (New York: Doubleday, 2008), 157.
17. Edmund Burke, *The Works of Edmund Burke with a Memoir* (New York: Harper & Bros., 1849), 2:132.

CHAPTER 9

1. James Madison, Federalist No. 47, in *The Federalist Papers: A Commentary on the Constitution of the United States*, ed. Henry Cabot Lodge (New York: G. P. Putnam's Sons, 1892), 299, 300.
2. *Hamdan v. Rumsfeld*, 548 U.S. 557 (2006).

3. Ibid., 557.
4. Military Commissions Act of 2006, H.R. 6054, 109th Cong., 2nd sess.; U.S. Code, Vol. 10, secs. 948a–950j.
5. Senate Committee on the Judiciary, Department of Justice Oversight: Preserving Our Freedoms While Defending Against Terrorism, statement of Michael Chertoff, Asst. Attorney Gen. for Criminal Division, 107th Cong., 1st sess., November 28, 2001, pp. 40, 48, 107–704.
6. Dick Cheney on Meet the Press with Tim Russert, transcript, Camp David, MD, September 16, 2001. http://www.whitehouse.gov/vicepresident/news-speeches/speeches/vp20010916.html (accessed June 5, 2008).
7. William Glaberson, "Plea of Guilty from Detainee in Guantanamo," New York Times, March 27, 2007, late ed., sec. A, col. 6, p. 1.
8. *Boumediene v. Bush*, 553 U.S. ____ (2008).
9. Military Commissions Act of 2006, H.R. 6054, 109th Cong., 2nd sess.; U.S. Code, Vol. 10, secs. 949d and 949j.
10. Ibid., 949d(d).
11. House Committee on Armed Services, Standards of Military Commissions and Tribunals, 109th Cong., 2nd sess., September 7, 2006, pp. 17, 109–20.
12. *Joint Anti-Fascist Refugee Committee v. McGrath*, 341 U.S. 123 (1951).
13. Ibid., 180.
14. Ibid.
15. Military Commissions Act of 2006, H.R. 6054, 109th Cong., 2nd sess.; U.S. Code, Vol. 10, secs. 949b(2)(A).
16. Classified Information Procedures Act of 1980, "A bill to procide certain pretrial, trial, and appellate procedures for criminal cases involving classified information." S. 1482, 96th Cong., 1st sess.; Pub. L. 96-456; U.S. Code, Vol. 28 sec. 17.17.
17. Military Commissions Act of 2006, H.R. 6054, 109th Cong., 2nd sess.; U.S. Code, Vol. 10, secs. 948a.
18. Ibid., 949j(a).
19. *The Public Committee against Torture in Israel v. The Government of Israel*, 46 I.L.M. 375, 391 (Isr. S. Ct. 2007); HCJ 769/02, 16 (December 12, 2006).
20. Ibid.
21. Ibid.

CONCLUSION

1. Maurice Bishop, "Line of March" speech, September 15, 1982 in *The Grenada Papers: The Inside Story of the Grenadian Revolution and the Making of a Totalitarian State—As Told in Captured Documents*, ed. Paul Seabury

and Walter A. McDougall (San Francisco: Institute for Contemporary Studies, 1984), 71.

2. Ibid.

3. Nat Hentoff, "Gitmo: The Worst of the Worst?" *Village Voice*, February 28, 2006, p. 24.

4. Jane Mayer, *The Dark Side: The Inside Story of How The War on Terror Turned into a War on American Ideals* (New York: Doubleday, 2008), 183.

5. Ibid.

6. Ibid., 186.

7. Tom Lasseter, "Prison camp snared the lowly, unlucky" *McClatchy Newspapers: The News & Observer*, June 15, 2008, p. A1.

Index

9/11 Commission, 31, 90, 93, 102–4, 112, 156

A

ABF Freight System, Inc v. NLRB (1994), 83
Abrams v. United States (1919), 66
Abu Ghraib, 37
Adams, John, 47, 53, 65, 107, 151
Addington, David, 37, 104, 200
Administrative Procedures Act, 18
Al Qaeda
    9/11 and, 191, 193
    attacks by, 91–95, 191, 193
    Cheney, Richard (Dick) on, 149, 191
    domestic spying and, 103, 109–10, 112, 114–16, 124
    FISA and, 143
    Lackawanna Six and, 195
    war on terror and, 2, 8, 18, 29, 31, 133, 184
Alito, Samuel, 20
Allen, Lew, 125
Allen, Robert, 123
Amendments, Constitutional
    Fifteenth, 62
    Fifth, 154, 168–69, 176
    First, 26, 34, 36, 119, 136–37
    Fourteenth, 20, 22, 62
    Fourth, 36, 46, 67, 90, 106, 108, 110–11, 121, 128, 136–37, 140, 149
    Nineteenth, 64
    Sixth, 168
    Thirteenth, 24, 62
American Indians, 62, 64
Anderson, Jack, 123
Anthony, Susan B., 64
appropriations, 144, 156
Articles of Confederation, 49, 69
Ashcroft, John, 48, 114
At the Center of the Storm (Tenet), 5, 165
Authorization of the Use of Military Force (AUMF), 1–3, 131, 145–47

B

Baker, James A., 141–42
Batista, Fulgencio, 70
Bay of Pigs, 35, 70
Berger v. New York, 174
bin Laden, Osama, 49, 193
Bishop, Maurice, 199–200
Boland Amendment, 89
Bolten, Joshua, 38, 50, 152, 175
Bork, Robert, 20, 54, 56
Boumediene v. Bush (2008), 30, 49, 92, 191, 195
Boyd v. United States (1886), 107
Bradley, Joseph, 63–64
Bradwell v. Illinois (1873), 63–64
Brandeis, Louis, 53, 66, 83
Bukovsky, Vladimir, 33
Bureau of Narcotics and Dangerous Drugs (BNDD), 126
Burger, Warren, 163

Bush, George H.W., 89
Bush, George W.
    9/11 and, 101–6, 199–200
    AUMF and, 1–4
    Constitution and, 25–26
    election, 85
    extraordinary rendition and,
        181–84, 186–87
    FISA crimes, 101–6, 108–17,
        124–25, 131–49
    impeachable offenses, 29–52, 73
    Libby, Lewis (Scooter) and, 83
    McClellan, Scott and, 61–62
    military commissions and,
        189–91, 193–94, 196
    presidential power, 87–93
    secret government and, 151–52,
        154–56, 158, 162, 165, 170,
        172–76, 178–79
    unitary executive theory and,
        7–9, 12, 14, 18–20
Bush's Law (Lichtblau), 138

C

Cambodia, 60, 68, 139, 144
Cantril, Hadley, 70
Carter, Jimmy, 88
Castro, Fidel, 34–35, 70
Chechnya, 32, 185
Cheney, Richard (Dick)
    AUMF and, 3–4
    Constitution and, 25–26
    FISA crimes, 104–5, 137, 149
    impeachable offenses, 32–34,
        39–41, 45
    military commissions and, 191,
        196
    "one percent" risk standard, 149
    presidential power and, 87, 89
    unitary executive theory and, 7,
        9, 12, 18–20, 200
Chertoff, Michael, 190, 193

Chevron USA Inc. v. NRDC (1984),
    16
Church, Frank, 34, 121
Church Committee, 34–36, 44, 101,
    106, 118, 121–22, 124–25,
    127, 136, 155
Churchill, Winston, 60–61, 79
Civil Rights Act (1964), 16, 20
Clark, Jim, 62
Clark, Tom C., 119
Clark Amendment, 89
Classified Information Procedures
    Act (1980), 93, 193
Cleveland, Grover, 51
Clifford, Clark, 139
Clinton, Hillary, 6, 40, 82
Clinton, William Jefferson (Bill),
    4–6, 20, 33–34, 40, 81–85,
    89–90, 113, 140
Clinton v. Jones (1997), 34
Colby, William, 122, 124
Colson, Charles, 163
Comey, James, 114
confidentiality, 138, 154, 162–68
Connor, Bull, 62
Contractors Association of Eastern
    Pennsylvania v. Secretary of
    Labor (1969), 16
Conyers, John, 41
Coolidge, Calvin, 55
Cox, Archibald, 50, 54–56, 73
Cromwell, Oliver, 43

D

Dames & Moore v. Regan (1981), 88
Dark Side, The (Mayer), 199
Davis, David, 56–57
Dean, John, 54, 80, 113, 153–54,
    176
Declaration of Independence, 24,
    32, 49, 52, 58, 68, 72, 94

Declaration of the Causes and
    Necessity for Taking Up Arms
    (1775), 8
Declaratory Act (1766), 8–9
Deitz, Robert L., 140–41
Democracy in America
    (Tocqueville), 64
DeWine, Mike, 142
Domenici, Pete, 173
Douglas, William O., 192–93
Dred Scott v. Sanford (1857), 22, 62
Dunlavey, Michael, 200

E

Edens, Timothy J., 97
Ehrlichman, John, 54, 80, 108, 163
Ellsberg, Daniel, 43, 68, 100–101, 108
Endangered Species Act (1973), 33
enemy combatants, 2, 7, 30, 33, 45,
    48–49, 90, 92–94, 96, 194–95,
    199–200
English Bill of Rights, 48–49
Entick v. Carrington (1765), 107–8
Ex parte Merryman (1861), 134
Ex parte Milligan (1866), 56–57
Executive Order 11905, 35
executive privilege
    Bush–Cheney administration
        and, 4, 30, 34, 37–38, 40,
        44–45
    Nixon, Richard M. and, 78–79, 105
    secret government and, 151–54,
        158, 162, 164, 169–70,
        175–77, 179
    TSP and, 109
extraordinary rendition, 181–87

F

Fadhil, Zahara, 97
Federal Bureau of Investigations
    (FBI), 31, 34, 36, 46, 51, 54,
        94, 100, 120, 124–25, 137–39,
        155
Federal Communications
    Commission (FCC), 17
Federal Tort Claims Act, 182
Federal Trade Commission (FTC),
    17
Federalist Papers, 43, 49, 52, 152
    No. 15, 69
    No. 37, 14
    No. 47, 140, 189
    No. 48, 3, 140
    No. 58, 25
    No. 62, 69
    No. 65, 32
    No. 69, 12–13
    No. 70, 10–11
    No. 75, 13, 14–15
Feinstein, Diane, 133, 176–77
Felt, Mark, 138
Fielding, Lewis, 43, 60, 77,
    100–101
FISA. *see* Foreign Intelligence
    Surveillance Act of 1978
Ford, Gerald R., 4, 34–35, 50, 80,
    124, 175
Foreign Intelligence Surveillance
    Act of 1978 (FISA), 4, 7, 25,
        30, 33–37, 44, 89, 101–6,
        108–18, 124, 129, 131–49, 177
Franklin, Benjamin, 43, 57, 60, 69
Free, Lloyd A., 70
freedom of speech, 19, 24, 65–66
Frick, William, 23
Frost, David, 57

G

Geneva Conventions, 189
Getler, Mike, 123
Gettysburg Address, 49, 52
Gibbon, Edward, 52, 72
Gilbert, G.M., 23

Gladstone, William Ewart, 71
Goering, Herman, 23–24
Goldsmith, Jack, 95
Goldwater, Barry, 79, 88
Goldwater v. Carter (1979), 88
Gonzales, Alberto, 30, 37–38, 44,
    51, 103, 108, 114, 116, 131,
    145, 153, 172–73, 175
Gore, Al, 4, 81, 85
Grant, Ulysses S., 55
Guantanamo Bay prison, 2, 30, 42,
    48, 92, 186, 199–200
Gulf of Tonkin Resolution, 59, 155

H

habeas corpus, 4, 9, 29, 38, 45, 48,
    61, 90–91, 103, 133, 197
Hage, Wadih el-, 190
Haldeman, H.R., 54, 163
Hamdan v. Rumsfeld (2006), 47,
    189, 193–94
Hamilton, Alexander, 10, 12–14,
    32, 53, 69
Hanyok, Robert J., 59
Harmon, Jane, 106
Hart, Gary, 128
Hartman, Thomas W., 40
Hayden, Michael, 122, 176
Hekmati, Abdul Razzak, 42, 186
Hersh, Seymour, 121–22
Hicks, David, 47, 191
Hirabayashi v. United States (1943),
    64
*History of the Decline and Fall of the
    Roman Empire, The* (Gibbon),
    72
Holmes, Oliver Wendell, 53, 66
Homeland Security, Department of,
    16, 30, 190
Hoover, Herbert, 136
Hoover, J. Edgar, 100, 120, 137
Hughes-Ryan Act (1974), 35

Hume, Brit, 123
Humphrey's Executor v. United States
    (1936), 17
Hunt, E. Howard, 100, 122
Hurricane Katrina, 49
Hussayn, Sami Omar al-, 48
Hussein, Saddam, 89, 152
Huston Plan, 68, 99–101

I

Iglesias, David, 172–73
*Immigration and Naturalization
    Service v. Chadha* (1983), 89
Impoundment Act (1974), 33
independent counsels, 17, 90, 178
Intelligence Oversight Act (1980),
    35
International Emergency Economic
    Powers Act (IEEPA), 88
Invisible Government, The (Wise and
    Ross), 154
Iran, 12, 18, 20, 40, 88–89, 104,
    111, 164
Iran-Contra Affair, 89
Iraq, 2–3, 12, 26, 31, 37, 62, 87,
    89, 91, 96–97, 106, 152, 155,
    165, 194

J

Jackson, Robert, 39, 145, 170
Jackson State University, 99
Jaworski, Leon, 73
Jefferson, Thomas, 8, 14, 32, 53,
    65, 67, 70
John Warner National Defense
    Authorization Act (2006), 26
Johnson, Andrew, 5, 7, 71
Johnson, Hiram, 60
Johnson, Lyndon B., 16, 40, 59–60,
    123, 155
Johnson, Samuel, 7

Joint Anti-Fascist Refugee Committee v. McGrath (1951), 192–93
Jones v. Clinton (E.D. Ark. 1999), 82
Julius Caesar, 5, 39

K

Katz v. United States (1967), 136
Kempthorne, Dirk, 48
Kennedy, John F., 16, 35, 70, 126
Kennedy, Robert, 35
Kent State University, 99
Kerry, John, 152
Khalid El-Masri v. United States (2007), 181–82
Kissinger, Henry, 6, 139
Korematsu v. United States (1943), 39, 64
Krogh, Egil, 100–101

L

Lackawanna Six, 95
Lawrence v. Texas (2003), 20
Leahy, Patrick, 116
Lee, Bill Lann, 81
Lee, Wen Ho, 138
Levi, Edward, 36, 50, 118–21
Libby, Lewis (Scooter), 83, 137–38, 155, 178
Lichtblau, Eric, 138
Lincoln, Abraham, 52, 53, 61, 96, 103–4, 133–34
Liuzzo, Viola, 20
Lochner v. New York (1905), 22
Locke, John, 133
Lowenthal, Mark M., 101
Lumumba, Patrice, 34
Lysenko, Trofim, 65–66

M

Macbeth (Shakespeare), 186–87
Madison, James, 3, 11, 14, 25, 53, 58–59, 61, 69, 140, 154
Magna Carta, 9, 48–49
Malvo, John Lee, 195
Manhattan Project, 35, 155
Mardian, Robert, 163
Masri, Khaled el-, 181–82, 186
Mayer, Jane, 199–200
McCain, John, 40, 42–43, 45
McClellan, Scott, 61, 165
McCord, James, 122
McCulloch v. Maryland (1819), 135–36
McFarlane, Bud, 164
McGrain v. Daugherty (1927), 38
McNamara, Robert, 59
McVeigh, Timothy, 90–91
Miers, Harriet, 20, 38, 50–51, 152, 175
military commissions, 4, 26, 29, 33, 40, 45, 47–48, 90, 96, 115, 138, 189–97, 200
Military Commissions Act (2006), 26, 48–49, 115, 138, 190, 194
Miller, Ed, 138
Milosevic, Slobodan, 89
Minor v. Happersett (1875), 64
Mitchell, John, 100, 163
Mohammad, Khalid Shaikh, 191
Mohammed, Khalfan Khamis, 190
More, Thomas, 85
Morrison v. Olson (1988), 16–17, 178
Moussaoui, Zacarias, 90, 190–91, 193
Mowatt-Larssen, Rolf, 184
Moynihan Commission, 151–52
Mueller, Robert S., 31, 138
Muhammed, John Allen, 195
Mukasey, Michael B., 30–31
Myers v. United States (1926), 7

N

Nadler, Jerald, 41
National Labor Relations Board v.
Jones & Laughlin Steel Co.
(1937), 22
National Security Agency (NSA)
Church Committee and, 125–28
Congress and, 145, 155
executive privilege and, 176
FISA and, 109–10, 133, 140–41
Gulf of Tonkin incident and, 59
PAA and, 46
SHAMROCK and, 127–28
TSP and, 44, 102, 105, 112, 114, 116
National Treasury Workers Union v.
Nixon (1973), 53
Necessary and Proper Clause,
134–36, 139, 174
New York Times v. United States
(1971), 60, 183
Niemoller, Martin, 43
Nixon, Richard M.
Bush's FISA crimes compared to,
104–5, 111, 113
CIA and, 122–23, 126
Constitution and, 65, 68
Dean, John and, 153–54
executive privilege and, 19–20,
108, 175–79
Huston Plan and, 99–101
impeachment charges and, 33,
39–41, 43, 71–76, 78–81,
83–85
national security and, 33
New York Times v. United States
and, 183
Nixon v. Fitzgerald (1982), 90
public opinion and, 51
resignation, 4–6
rule of law and, 22
United States v. Nixon (1974),
162–63, 165, 168–70
Vietnam War and, 60, 139, 144
Watergate and, 53–57
Nixon v. Fitzgerald (1982), 90
Nixon v. Sirica (1973), 56, 73
Noriega, Manuel, 89

O

Obama, Barack, 8, 40, 45, 142
Odeh, Mohamed Sadeek, 190
Olmstead v. United States (1928),
83, 136
Omar, Abu, 32, 42, 186
One Percent Doctrine, The
(Suskind), 183
Ortega, Daniel, 89, 165
Orwell, George, 106
Otis, James, 107
'Owhali, Mohamed Rashed Daoud
al-, 190

P

Padilla, Jose, 9, 47, 90, 95, 190
Parkinson, Kenneth, 163
Pelosi, Nancy, 4, 41, 106
Pentagon Papers, 60, 100, 183
Pitt, William, 67–68
Plame, Valerie, 106, 137–38, 155,
178
Poindexter, John, 164
Polk, James K., 61
Posner, Richard, 137–38
presidential pardons, 5, 17, 80, 138,
175, 179
Protect America Act (2007), 26, 37,
45–47, 109, 196–97
Public Committee against Torture
in Israel v. The Government of
Israel (2006), 196
Putin, Vladimir, 32, 185–86

R

Rasul v. Bush (2005), 48
Reagan, Ronald, 20, 81, 89, 138, 164
Reed v. Reed (1971), 64
Rehnquist, William H., 20, 178
Richardson, Elliot, 54, 56, 73, 156
Ridge, Tom, 30
Roberts, John, 20
Roe v. Wade (1973), 20
Roosevelt, Franklin D., 60–61, 118–19
Rosenberg, Ethel and Julius, 157
Ross, Thomas B., 154
Rove, Karl, 137, 152, 172, 175, 178
Ruckelshaus, William, 54, 56
rule of law, 21, 22–24, 27, 45, 62, 70, 72, 77, 80–84, 99, 104, 108, 157, 166, 169, 186–87
Rumsfeld, Donald, 47, 189, 199
Russert, Tim, 191

S

Santayana, George, 41
Saturday Night Massacre, 51, 54, 56
Schlesinger, Arthur, 45
Schlesinger, James, 122
Scopes Trial, 65, 67
Scott, Paul, 123
Securities and Exchange Commission (SEC), 17
Sedition Act (1798), 59, 65
Senate Select Committee v. Nixon (1974), 175
September 11, 2001, 1–2, 85, 90–91, 103–4, 114, 138, 143, 191, 195–96
SHAMROCK, 127–29
Sharansky, Anatoly, 33
Shelby, Richard, 35
Sheridan, Philip Henry, 64
Sherman Antitrust Act, 9

Shibh, Ramzi bin al-, 191
Shultz, George, 164
Sibbach v. Wilson & Co. (1941), 16
Simes, Dimitri K., 6
Smith, Adam, 20
Snepp v. United States (1980), 89
Solzhenitsyn, Aleksandr, 33, 95
special prosecutors, 51, 54–56, 73, 79, 160, 176
Stamp Act (1766), 8, 49
Stennis, John C., 56
Stimson, Henry L., 136
Stowe, Harriet Beecher, 62
Strachan, Gordon, 163
subpoenas, 38, 49–50, 55, 78–79, 84, 163, 167
Supplemental Foreign Assistance Appropriations Act (1970), 144
Suskind, Ron, 183–84

T

Taney, Roger B., 62, 134
Teapot Dome scandal, 55
Tenet, George, 5, 35, 156, 165, 182, 184
Terrorist Surveillance Program (TSP)
  abandoning of, 124, 143
  AUMF and, 131, 147–48
  Congress and, 106
  executive privilege and, 162, 176–77
  FISA and, 102–3, 109–17, 143
  legality of, 44, 134, 145, 151
Tillman, Pat, 155
Tocqueville, Alexis de, 52, 64
Townsend Acts (1767), 8
Truman, Harry, 55, 119, 128

U

Uncle Tom's Cabin (Stowe), 62
unitary executive theory, 8–9, 12,
    14, 18–19, 134, 148
United States v. Alvarez Machain
    (1992), 90
United States v. Cox (1965), 177–78
United States v. Nixon (1974), 79,
    105, 153, 162–63, 168–70,
    176–77
United States v. Reynolds (1953),
    181–84
United States v. Richardson (1974),
    148
United States v. Robel (1967), 148
United States v. Verdugo Urdiquez
    (1990), 90, 110

V

Vietnam War, 34, 59–60, 65, 99,
    123, 139, 144, 148
voting fraud, 173–74
Voting Rights Act (1965), 20

W

Walker, James C., 192
Walton, Reggie, 83
war on terror, 29, 141
War Powers Resolution (1973), 87
Warren Report, 126. *see also*
    Kennedy, John F.
Washington, George, 14, 50, 52, 53,
    80, 158–62
waterboarding, 30, 37, 155
Watergate. *see also* Nixon, Richard
    M.; Saturday Night Massacre

Bush's FISA crimes compared to,
    104, 111, 113
CIA and, 122
Congress' investigation of, 33,
    80
executive privilege and, 153–54
impeachment charges and, 75,
    78, 83
Nixon, Richard M. and, 5, 19, 43
Saturday Night Massacre, 51, 56
special prosecutor and, 54
Wealth of Nations (Smith), 20–21
Weinberger, Casper, 164
Weiner, Tim, 117–18
What Happened (McClellan), 62,
    165
Whiskey Ring, 55
White, Theodore, 100
Whitehouse, Sheldon, 133, 177
Whitney v. California (66-7), 66
Whitten, Les, 123
Wigmore, John Henry, 193
Wilson, Charles, 50
Wilson, James, 61
Wilson, Joseph, 106, 137
Wilson, Woodrow, 136
Wise, David, 154
Wright, Susan Webster, 82

Y

Yom Kippur War, 33
Yoo, John, 37, 131–33, 145, 177
Youngstown Sheet & Tube v. Sawyer
    (1952), 145
Yousef, Ramzi, 90–91, 190

Z

Zubaydah, Abu, 184, 191